Routledge Library Editions

RICARDO AND THE THEORY
OF VALUE DISTRIBUTION
AND GROWTH

ECONOMICS

HISTORY OF ECONOMIC THOUGHT
In 23 Volumes

RICARDO AND THE THEORY OF VALUE DISTRIBUTION AND GROWTH

GIOVANNI A CARAVALE AND
DOMENICO A TOSATO

Routledge
Taylor & Francis Group

LONDON AND NEW YORK

First published in 1980

Reprinted in 2003 by
Routledge
2 Park Square, Milton Park, Abingdon, Oxon OX14 4RN

Transferred to Digital Printing 2007

Routledge is an imprint of the Taylor & Francis Group

British Library Cataloguing in Publication Data
A CIP catalogue record for this book
is available from the British Library

Ricardo and the Theory of Value Distribution and Growth
ISBN 0-415-31325-2
ISBN 0-415-31320-1

Miniset: History of Economic Thought

Series: Routledge Library Editions – Economics

Giovanni A. Caravale and
Domenico A. Tosato

Ricardo and the theory of value distribution and growth

Routledge
Taylor & Francis Group

LONDON AND NEW YORK

First published in 1980
by Routledge
2 Park Square, Milton Park, Abingdon,
Oxon, OX14 4RN
Set in IBM Press Roman by
Hope Services, Abingdon, Oxfordshire
Italian edition Un modello ricardiano di sviluppo economico
© Editore Boringhieri 1974
New revised edition © Giovanni A. Caravale and
Domenico A. Tosato 1980
English version © Routledge 1980

British Library Cataloguing in Publication Data

Caravale, Giovanni A

Ricardo and the theory of value distribution
and growth.
1. Ricardo, David
2. Economics
I. Title   II. Tosato, Domenico
330.15'3   HB103.R5   80-40249

ISBN 0 7100 0508 3

Contents

To Lucia, Giorgio, and Benedetta
G.A.C.

To Isabella, Stefano, and Giorgio
D.A.T.

Preface and acknowledgments

It was during the discussions of a workshop on topics of growth theories and disequilibrium dynamics – initiated in the early seventies with the financial support of CNR – Consiglio Nazionale delle Ricerche (Rome, Italy) – that we were impressed by what appeared to be the lack of a consistent analytical framework within which to fit the main component parts of Ricardo's theory of distribution and growth.

Our book *Un modello ricardiano di sviluppo economico* originated in the effort to fill this gap and was meant to contribute to the analysis of a dynamic model incorporating the key Ricardian assumptions of diminishing returns and reinvestment of profits. Although some attention was devoted to problems of value, its emphasis was thus on the growth aspect of the Ricardian investigation. The imbalance implicit in this treatment quickly encouraged us to look deeper into the Ricardian theory of value and to plunge into the current revival of classical theory arising from Sraffa's work.

Our main results, which dealt with the problem of a comparison between the Ricardian and the Sraffian approach, and in particular with the possibility of a significant use of Sraffa's standard commodity in the Ricardian framework of analysis, were published in a long paper in *Rivista di Politica Economica* (January 1978). The emphasis here was obviously on value and distribution. The aim of the present book is to integrate the latter results and the previous research into a consistent whole, thus supplying an analytical reconstruction of the Ricardian system, more balanced (and complete) than that contained in our 1974 work.

Integration has been pursued by means of an interpretative approach centred on the concept of natural equilibrium, in which – contrary to what is often maintained – there is no room for a separation between Ricardo's theory of value and his theory of growth. In other words, the notion of natural equilibrium, which was only implicit in the 1974 book, is here explicitly made the cornerstone of the analysis both of prices (definition of the rate of profit, given the technology and the natural wage) and of the growth process (determination of the time path of the economy in face of a changing technology and with a given natural wage). In this perspective, even Ricardo's reflections on apparently autonomous topics of research such as the 'invariable measure of value' − an issue which we had not tackled in either the 1974 or the 1978 publication − are shown to be parts of the same line of investigation.

The analysis of Ricardo's thought on value and distribution (presented in the first part of this book) is thus almost entirely new with respect to our 1974 publication, while the argument relating to growth (now contained in the second part) has been extensively rewritten for the purpose of a more balanced presentation of the whole subject matter.

In the various stages of the research we have benefited from useful suggestions and constructive criticism on the part of many friends and colleagues. We wish to thank the members of the above-mentioned CNR workshop, as well as those of a similar research group on related topics, with whom we have discussed at length several parts of our work. In particular, we wish to acknowledge the help of Luciano Piccioni for stimulating comments on issues relating to Sraffa's contribution; of Annalisa Rosselli and Enzo Rossi for the mathematical proofs contained in the appendices; and of Memmo Di Bartolomeo for the computer work on which the graphical results presented in Chapters 5–7 are based.

Luigi Pasinetti, Luigi Spaventa and Alessandro Roncaglia have read a first draft of the work, or of parts of it. We are greatly indebted to them for their friendly comments and criticism, which have prompted further reflection on several points of our investigation.

We also wish to thank David Godwin for the knowledgeable and careful editing of the text and Daniela Giacometti and Mirella Garofali for their efficient and conscientious typing of the very tortuous final manuscript.

As already mentioned, our research enjoyed the financial support of CNR, which is here gratefully acknowledged.

We finally wish to express very special thanks to our respective wives, Lucia and Isabella, whose understanding and intelligent presence has been of invaluable help during the long gestation period of this work.

Rome, June 1980   G.A.C.

D.A.T.

Part I
Value and distribution

1 Scope and method of the work

1.1 The renewed interest in Ricardo's theory

Recent years have witnessed a renewed interest in the theoretical work of David Ricardo. On the analytical plane, this circumstance may be attributed both to critical developments in the field of the theory of value and to significant advances in the field of growth theory.

As to the first aspect, it may be recalled that the 'crisis' of the marginal theory of value and distribution is intimately related to the contribution of Piero Sraffa (86), who explicitly points out the connection of his work with the theories of the old classical economists (in particular, of David Ricardo). For Sraffa's suggested reconstruction of the theory of value is based on a logical scheme which rejects the neoclassical supply-and-demand approach and is centred instead upon the notion of 'prices of production', strictly linked to the Ricardian concept of 'natural prices'. As to the second aspect, it may be said that Ricardo can be rightly considered to be a forerunner of modern growth theory, in that he built a simple but impressive macroeconomic model in which the relation between growth and income distribution plays a key role.[1]

On a different plane, an additional reason pointing back to Ricardo may be mentioned – the growing awareness of the relevance of environmental constraints on economic expansion. From this point of view, Ricardo's model with diminishing returns may be viewed as directly pertinent for the problems of a world economy with limited natural resources.

The renewed interest for the analytical issues tackled by Ricardo, and for the crucial assumptions on which his reasoning rests, has led to a passionate revival of study and debate – for which the publication of Ricardo's complete *Works and Correspondence* (84) has represented

3

a significant point of reference. The approach of some of the works on the Ricardian theory is predominantly critical in nature,[2] and tends to concentrate on the ambiguities originating in the objective difficulty of the text, in the use, at times inconsistent, of terms and concepts, and in the incomplete specification of the assumptions.

As opposed to this type of analysis, a 'more constructive' approach[3] tends to state 'explicitly the assumptions needed to eliminate the ambiguities' (Pasinetti (64), p. 78) and to reconstruct Ricardo's analytical propositions – generously interpreting obscure or controversial passages of his writings, as Marshall ((54), p. 670) and Barone ((4), p. 435) have suggested we should do. The present work is to be viewed in this latter perspective.

1.2 Scope of the work

Ricardo's thesis of the long-run tendency of the economy towards a stationary-state situation is based on a set of crucial assumptions – diminishing returns in agriculture, reinvestment of profits and a theory of distribution in which the income of the capitalist class represents a residual. This set of assumptions implies a strict connection between the rate of profit and the rate of capital accumulation. It is thus necessary, for a theory which aims at proving the validity of that thesis, to solve the problem of the unambiguous determination of the profit rate and to show how diminishing returns affect its behaviour through time.

These problems found a straightforward solution within Ricardo's primitive agricultural model of the *Essay on Profits* (67). It was in the attempt to escape the limitations of this model that Ricardo felt, in the *Principles* (68), the need for a 'developed theory of value' (Dobb (21), p. 73), to which – we will maintain – the role was attributed of making it possible to draw in the general case the same type of conclusions, as to the relation between diminishing returns and the rate of growth, that had been reached within the more restricted analytical framework of the *Essay on Profits*. In the Ricardian theoretical construction the theory of value thus performs, in our view, a substantially instrumental role.

It is clear that the thesis, occasionally emerging in the literature, according to which the theory of value represents for Ricardo a field of investigation logically autonomous from the rest of his inquiry, does not fit into this approach.

This does not mean that specific attention should not be devoted to Ricardo's long and troubled reflection on the topic of value, but rather that this problem should be treated with the purpose of emphasizing the strict connection between value and growth in the Ricardian framework of analysis. We shall try to show that this aim can be achieved when the whole of Ricardo's theoretical research is viewed as centred on the rate of profit, as the true key variable of the system.

In this perspective the present work is divided in two parts. Part I deals with the problems of value and distribution, while Part II deals with the issues of distribution and growth.

The scope of Part I is that of exploring the possibility of defining an unambiguous relation between diminishing returns in agriculture and the general rate of profit, and of analysing the way in which Ricardo tackled this problem and tried to solve it. In particular, Chapter 2 aims at defining a general (i.e. free of the limitations of the labour theory of value) framework of analysis for the study of the problems of income distribution arising from diminishing returns in agriculture. The distributive antagonism among social classes, stemming from the limited availability of fertile land, is viewed as an essentially dynamic problem; the difference with Sraffa's approach in *Production of Commodities* (86) is accordingly underlined. It is shown that, in the framework of analysis referred to, the issue of the distributive antagonism cannot find a solution when it is posed in terms of the determination of the impact on the aggregate amount (or, what is the same, on the share) of profits. It is further shown that the solution can be arrived at if the problem is posed instead in terms of the determination of the effects of diminishing returns on the rate of profit. The solution is expressed both as a relation between money wages and the profit rate ('wage equation') and as a relation between the level of the labour input in agriculture and the rate of profit ('profit equation'). The implications of the results obtained are briefly commented on, both with reference to Adam Smith's theory of prices and with respect to more general issues relevant for the Ricardian scheme of analysis.

Chapter 3 brings into the picture Ricardo's search for an invariable measure of value and tries to show how this search is to be interpreted as an attempt to find a general solution to the problem of the determination of the rate of profit along a different logical approach. In other words, the effort is made to clarify how this line of research, so tenaciously and admittedly in vain pursued by Ricardo till the end of his life, is addressed precisely to the solution of his central problem

– the relation between diminishing returns and the rate of profit. The subject of the invariable standard of value has been recently resumed, though in a different framework of analysis, by Sraffa with his construction of the standard commodity. A comparison between the requisites of Ricardo's invariable measure of value and the properties of Sraffa's *numéraire* is then made for the purpose of assessing the possibility of a significant use of the standard commodity in the Ricardian context. The analysis carried out seems to indicate that a negative answer should be given to this question.

Part II is devoted to the study of growth in some simplified versions of the Ricardian dynamic model. While the analysis of Part I belongs to the realm of comparative statics in the sense that only the direction of movement of the rate of profit is shown, the method adopted in Part II is truly dynamic – the time path of the rate of profit *qua* rate of capital accumulation as well as that of the other variables being fully specified.

The point of departure of our analysis (Chapter 4) is represented by an examination of Pasinetti's brilliant mathematical formulation of the Ricardian system (64), which appears to be particularly relevant for our purpose on account of its analytical rigour and close adherence to the fundamental traits of Ricardo's theory. Pasinetti's analysis, centred as it is on the definition of individual natural equilibrium positions of the economy and on the proof that only the stationary-state equilibrium is stable, does not, however, represent a truly dynamic study of the Ricardian system in that his model does not include, as an essential part, the interaction between the population adjustment mechanism and that of capital accumulation.

The effort is then made in the following chapters to present a dynamic Ricardian model characterized by the joint consideration of these two mechanisms. On the basis of this model, it becomes possible to determine the time paths of the variables and to describe the transition of the economy from a 'progressive' situation (with growing population and net capital accumulation) to a stationary situation (in which these events cease to occur), due to the working of diminishing returns in agriculture.

Chapter 5, in particular, studies the connection between growth and distribution with reference to a one-sector (agricultural) Ricardian model. In Chapter 6, the same kind of analysis is extended to a two-sector (agriculture and industry) model; some steps in the direction of further extension to a three-sector model (agriculture, industry and machines) are taken in the appendix to Chapter 6. Chapter 7, finally, examines problems – of 'traverse', in Hicksian terminology (see Hicks (35), ch. 16) – arising from changes in the saving behaviour of social classes.

The time paths of the variables defined in the various models considered are classified in the two categories of *equilibrium* and *disequilibrium paths*. The problems connected with this distinction will be discussed in the following section.

1.3 The concept of natural equilibrium in the Ricardian context

The concept of 'natural equilibrium' is central to Ricardo's theory of value and distribution. This circumstance does not prevent him from recognizing that the working of demand and supply may bring about situations of market equilibrium different from those of natural equilibrium – the basis of the distinction having been laid down by Adam Smith with his definition of 'natural' and 'market' prices. In line with Smith, Ricardo believes that market prices represent only transitory departures from natural prices, which are conceived of as a centre towards which 'the prices of all commodities are continually gravitating' (Smith (80), p. 51). Making direct reference to Smith's *Wealth of Nations*, Ricardo concludes, in effect, the chapter 'On natural and market price' stressing his fundamental theoretical interest for the study of natural values (Ricardo (68), pp. 91-2, italics added):

> Having fully acknowledged the temporary effects which, in particular employments of capital, may be produced on the prices of commodities, as well as on the wages of labour, and the profits of stock, by accidental causes, without influencing the general price of commodities, wages, or profits, since these effects are equally operative in all stages of society, we will leave them entirely out of our consideration, whilst we are treating of *the laws which regulate natural prices, natural wages, and natural profits, effects totally independent of these accidental causes.*

The argument for 'leaving entirely out of consideration' the deviations of market from natural values ultimately rests, as Garegnani aptly points out, 'on the "temporary" nature of these deviations, in contrast with Ricardo's concern with *lasting changes*' ((28), p. 28, italics added). As these lasting changes cannot be conceived of but as a consequence of changes in the difficulty of production owing to diminishing returns, it is clear that when Ricardo speaks of the laws which regulate natural values he has in mind a theory about the behaviour of these values over time. The first part of the present work reflects Ricardo's approach to the problem: the attention is, in fact, concentrated on the behaviour of natural values, to the complete disregard of market prices.

The close connection between Ricardo's theory of value and his theory of growth implies, on the logical plane, that the issues of growth must also be analysed in terms of the concept of natural equilibrium, i.e. as a sequence of positions describing what we shall call a *natural equilibrium path*. The use of this concept in the Ricardian context requires that direct reference be made to the tools of modern growth theory — growth rates and conditions for equilibrium growth. What follows — in the spirit of the 'constructive approach' of the present work — aims at defining a consistent framework of analysis in which Ricardo's remarks about the 'actual' behaviour of the economy may be interpreted as referring to departures from the natural equilibrium path. This may therefore be said to represent — also from a strictly dynamic point of view — the centre of attraction for the movement of the economy through time. The absence of an accepted interpretation of Ricardo along these lines calls for a preliminary consideration of the matter.

With fitting intuition Baumol (5) has associated under the heading of 'magnificent dynamics' Ricardo's 'model' with Harrod's work (33) in growth theory, the common feature being represented by the attempt to describe the process of long-term growth with reference to a very limited number of key variables: 'The method employed has . . . involved simple deduction from fairly broad generalizations . . . in the nature of alleged psychological or technological laws' (Baumol (5), p. 8), with the 'ambitious' aim of explaining the development of the whole economy over long periods of time.

The attempt is here made to carry a step further the logic of the connection suggested by Baumol, applying the tools of modern growth theory to the analysis of the time path of the economic system described by Ricardo's fundamental assumptions. It may be said that the results arrived at appear of more general interest, beyond the scope of the present work, for the study of the issues of growth in all cases characterized by diminishing returns in a key sector of the economy.

The central analytical concept of modern growth theory is represented by the equilibrium path which, in the absence of technical progress, is defined by the equality between the rate of growth of population (and employment) and the rate of capital accumulation (which in the Ricardian context coincides with, or is proportional to, the rate of profit). When the effort is made to apply this approach to the analysis of the Ricardian long-term theory, a relevant difference emerges as to the role of population growth.

In modern theory the rate of growth of population is generally taken as an exogenous variable; consequently, the existence of an equilibrium path requires that the burden of adjustment be carried entirely by the rate of capital accumulation. If the same type of hypothesis about the exogenous nature of population growth were to be made in the Ricardian context, difficulties would clearly arise for the definition of the equilibrium path; for when diminishing returns play a crucial role in the model, the rate of profit·inevitably tends to fall. In this case, then, with a constant wage rate it would be impossible to define an equilibrium path, since the coincidence between the rate of profit and the rate of population growth would obtain only at a single instant of time, after which unemployment would appear and thereafter increase indefinitely. As reference to the simple definition of the 'wages-fund' theory shows, full employment could be maintained through time only at the cost of a continuous reduction of the wage rate such as to compensate fully for the fall in the rate of profit which would otherwise occur as a consequence of diminishing returns. It is highly dubious, however, that a situation of this type could be labelled as one of 'equilibrium' growth.

It may be said, therefore, that in a model with diminishing returns the assumption of an exogenously given population growth is incompatible with the definition of an equilibrium path.

It might be thought that a way out of this difficulty could be represented by the so-called 'bastard golden age' models. In connection with Ricardo's analysis, a model of this type has been proposed by Hicks with his 'fixwage theory' ((38), ch. 5), where the attention is focused on the endogenously determined rate of growth of employment, with an unlimited supply of labour at the given wage rate. The growth path of the economy would then be defined by the progressively falling rate of capital accumulation, to which the rate of growth of employment would automatically adjust. The hypotheses on which these models are based are, however, unacceptable: the effect of unemployment on the prevailing wage rate is disregarded; the reserve army should at least be such as to satisfy the requirements of the economic expansion until the stationary state is reached; and, finally, the supply of potential labour should be thought of, in Joan Robinson's words ((74), p. 40), as 'living on nuts in the jungles, ready to take employment when the standard real wage is offered'.

It is clear, therefore, that in the classical (Ricardian) framework of analysis the definition of an equilibrium growth path requires that the rate of increase of population be considered as an endogenous variable. In effect, this idea, as Solow ((82), p. 12) remarks, is deeply rooted in the classical approach[4] in which the Malthusian adjustment mechanism is one of the building blocks. It can be thus said that the extension of the modern concept of equilibrium growth to the Ricardian model requires that, *at a constant (natural* or *subsistence) wage*, the rate of growth of population fully adjusts to the rate of capital accumulation (profit rate).

It will be maintained in the present work that the fulfilment of this condition defines the *natural equilibrium path* of the Ricardian growth model, or what may be called the Ricardian golden age path. All other possible paths — originating from inappropriate initial conditions or from changes in behavioural parameters — imply a varying wage rate, different from the natural level, and describe a sequence of *market positions*. Inasmuch as the latter represent a departure from a 'norm' — the natural equilibrium path — they will be called *disequilibrium paths.*[5]

The definition of the natural equilibrium path given above involves a departure from the letter — though not, we believe, from the spirit — of Ricardo's text. In the *Principles* ((68), p. 93) Ricardo adopts the following definition: 'The natural price of labour is that price which is necessary to enable the labourers, one with another, to subsist and to perpetuate their race, without either increase or diminution.'

Hicks and Hollander (39) — strictly sticking to this definition and thus departing for this aspect from previous work by Hicks ((35), pp. 42-7; and (38), pp. 48-9) — build a model aiming at supplying a consistent explanation of a Ricardian growth process characterized by a wage rate permanently diverging from its natural level.[6] We believe that the growth paths generated by this model can be better fitted into the overall Ricardian framework of analysis if they are viewed, with reference to our terminology, as belonging to the disequilibrium type;[7] for it is clear that with the definition of the natural price of labour given in the *Principles* the only natural equilibrium position would be that of the stationary state. It may be noted incidentally that this would imply attributing to Ricardo a radical split between the methodological approach adopted in the analysis of value and that followed in the analysis of growth. The relevance of the concept of natural equilibrium in Ricardo's growth theory — and thus the implicit denial of such a split — is openly recognized (though in a different perspective) by Pasinetti ((64), pp. 87-8):

> Most of his [Ricardo's] analysis is carried on *as if* the demographic mechanism has already fully worked through [i.e. the *natural* wage rate has been permanently achieved], while the capital accumulation process has not yet been completed. In other words, he concentrates on describing the changing characteristics of his system in terms of *natural* behaviour of the variables in a process of capital accumulation.

Our definition of the natural equilibrium path goes back, instead, to Ricardo's conception of the *Essay on Profits* ((67), p. 12), where he writes, for example:

> We will, however, suppose that no improvements take place in agriculture, and that *capital and population advance in the proper proportion, so that the real wages of labour continue uniformly the same.* (Italics added)

It is clear that the hypotheses mentioned in this passage are precisely those which define what we have called above the natural equilibrium path of the Ricardian growth model.

The study of the disequilibrium paths is based on the assumption that the economic agents fully perceive the existence of possible divergences from the equilibrium path and react accordingly in the attempt to eliminate them. This requires that the behaviour hypotheses of the model be formulated in a more general way, so as to include both the equilibrium component (describing the behaviour along the natural growth path) and an error-adjustment mechanism (describing how the equilibrium behaviour is modified by the existence of disequilibrium situations). In the Ricardian framework, disequilibrium dynamics centres essentially on two types of adjustment mechanisms, both of which are deeply rooted in classical theory: the reaction of population to divergences between market and natural wage rates, and the reaction of capitalists to differences in sectoral rates of profit. The study of the problems of 'traverse', which belong to disequilibrium dynamics, is obviously based on the same methodological approach.

Notwithstanding the fact that no claim of generality can be made for any specification of the error-adjustment mechanisms, models systematically considering such mechanisms appear to be preferable to models which disregard them altogether and consequently examine the problems of convergence to the equilibrium path on the basis of the same hypotheses that describe the behaviour of the economic agents along that path. From this point of view, the analysis of the present work may appear to be of more general interest.

2 Diminishing returns and the rate of profit in Ricardo's analysis

2.1 Ricardo's theoretical analysis and the problems of his time

The analysis of the effects of income distribution on the process of economic growth represents the core of Ricardo's theoretical contribution.

The choice of this problem as the central theme of economic theory clearly shows Ricardo's keen awareness of, and deep concern for, the most controversial policy issue of his time – the corn laws.[1] As is well known, on this issue a clash of interests broke out – at a time when workers' trade unions were not strong enough to play a decisive role in policy-making – between landowners and the emerging bourgeois capitalist class. In Dobb's words ((21), pp. 72-3):

> these duties [on corn] inevitably raised rents by raising the demand for, and the cost and the price of, home-produced corn; at the same time they had the further inevitable consequence of lowering profit (in the face of a given level of corn wages). Conversely, a repeal of these duties, to allow entry of low-priced foreign corn, would raise profit and thereby promote capital accumulation. The obstacle to so advantageous a course was the landowners' interest in maintaining rents.

This should not be taken to mean that Ricardo did not perceive the possibility of a conflict between capitalists and workers as a consequence of substitution between machines and labour in the face of an increase in real wages. The position taken by Ricardo on this point in the first two editions of the *Principles* significantly changed in the third and final edition, where Ricardo explicitly envisaged the possibility of such a conflict of interest. An increase in the ratio between fixed and circulating capital may in fact – he thought – bring about a permanent reduction in the level of employment.[2] This issue, however, does not belong to the central body of Ricardo's theoretical investigation on distribution and growth and receives only what may be considered minor attention on the part of Ricardo.

Ricardo's theoretical investigation can be interpreted as an attempt to build a rigorous analytical framework for a discussion of the problems arising from the corn laws. The outcome of this investigation was a comprehensive explanation of the process of economic growth with a direct bearing on the policy debate of his time. It seems highly significant in this respect that, as Sraffa points out in his 'Introduction' ((85), p. xiii), Ricardo's publication of the *Principles* is the result of a process originating in the intention 'to produce an enlarged version of the *Essay*', which appeared in February 1815 as one of the pamphlets in the hot debate on the issue of the corn laws. From this point of view, it is plausible to draw, with Hicks ((34), p. 151) an analogy between Ricardo's impact on the repeal of the corn laws and Keynes's contribution to the problem of full employment.[3]

Ricardo's stand in favour of free trade – the most telling arguments for which are to be found in his analytical framework[4] – reveals his clear perception of the fundamental part played by the accumulation of capital in the new economic situation brought about by the industrial revolution. The thought is not to be excluded that Ricardo's opinion on the negative role of landowners in the process of growth might have been in the background of his dispute with Malthus about the possibility of a general overproduction of commodities and of his rejection of Malthus's argument in defence of rentiers' 'unproductive' consumption.

Ricardo's theoretical framework cannot, however, be viewed solely as a tool aiming at clarifying a specific policy issue. His contribution transcends the particular problem originating his investigation and attains validity as a theory of distribution and growth. It is in this respect that Ricardo's 'model' has left a lasting mark on economic analysis.

As already mentioned, the study in Part II of the dynamic properties of some 'stylized' formulation of this model contains a definition of prices based on a theory of value whose premises are, in that context, taken for granted. With the exception of the appendix to Chapter 6, this theory is the labour theory of value. The more general problems connected with the word 'price' (Sraffa (85), p. xxxiv) are considered in the present and in the following chapter. Reference is here made exclusively to situations of natural equilibrium, and particular attention is dedicated to the difficulties faced by Ricardo in connection with the existence of different 'organic compositions' of capital in the various sectors of the economy.

What follows goes in the direction of a tentative reconstruction of the *logical* – rather than the purely exegetical – sequence of the analytical difficulties met by Ricardo. It is obvious that, because of the highly controversial nature of the arguments involved, such an attempt runs a risk of overrationalization.

2.2 Changes in real and money wages in Ricardo: the distributive antagonism as a dynamic problem

As we have just mentioned, the distributive antagonism on which Ricardo's theory is centred is that between the class of landowners and the class of capitalists: the rival shares in net revenue are thus rent and profits.[5] The way in which this antagonism is presented is, however, 'indirect', since Ricardo chooses to develop his argument in terms of a 'conflict' between *money wages* and profits. Changes in money wages reflect changes in the price of wage goods, caused in turn by diminishing returns in agriculture, and are therefore associated with an increase of rent (Ricardo (68), p. 119): 'profits depend on high or low wages, wages on the price of necessaries, and the price of necessaries chiefly on the price of food, because all other requisites may be increased almost without limit.'

While in Ricardo's model money wages (which are functionally dependent on the working of the economic system) are variable, *real (subsistence) wages* are assumed to be fixed. It is in fact crucial to stress that Ricardo's theory of distribution is based on the idea that the real wage is given in terms of a fixed bundle of commodities.[6] Ricardo explicitly admits that this bundle of goods may vary 'at different times and in different countries' (Ricardo (68), pp. 96-7); but for the purpose of his analysis of the interaction between distribution and growth the real wage is taken as given from outside, as a socio-historical datum.

It is obvious that this approach applies only to the situation of natural equilibrium of the system and not to situations of market equilibrium, in which the operation of demand and supply may cause a departure of the market real wage from the natural real wage. As we have pointed out in Chapter 1 with reference to a more general context, the latter is, however, in Ricardo's analytical framework

14

a sort of centre of gravity towards which the former ultimately tends through the working of the Malthusian population adjustment mechanism.[7] The concept of a given natural real wage is therefore central for Ricardo's theory of value and distribution.

In Ricardo's theory, changes in wages thus reflect solely changes in the prices of wage goods, the quantity of the various commodities in the real wage being fixed. Movements in these prices depend in turn on the increase in the quantity of labour required to produce successive units of wage goods, i.e. on the working of the law of diminishing returns in agriculture: 'the only *adequate and permanent* cause for the rise of wages is the increasing difficulty of providing food and necessaries for the increasing number of workmen' (Ricardo (68), p. 296, italics added).

It is then clear that the fundamental distributive antagonism between rent and profits is an intrinsically dynamic issue and cannot be conceived of in static terms. It is, in fact, the direct consequence of the working of the law of diminishing returns, i.e. of a phenomenon which in Ricardo can be thought of only as taking place through time, under the pressure of population growth. The resulting 'conflict' between money wages and profits is therefore an equally dynamic issue.

This interpretative approach appears to diverge significantly from a line of analysis of Ricardo's thought which, in connection with his reflections on the invariable measure of value, tends to identify in Ricardo a logically autonomous problem of distributive alternatives in a static context. Even at the cost of partially anticipating the argument developed in detail in Chapter 3, some points need to be stressed here.

As we shall try to show, in Ricardo's framework of analysis 'a perfect measure of value' ought to make it possible to evaluate without ambiguities – i.e. without disturbances originating from changes in distribution – the effect of changes that might occur in the difficulty of production of commodities. For this purpose, the standard commodity (i) should be invariant with respect to changes in its *own* method of production (i.e. 'the same quantity of labour should at all times be required' for its production), and (ii) should be such as to exclude 'relative variations from a rise or fall of wages'.

On the basis of Sraffa's famous 'Introduction', some authors[8] have maintained the existence in Ricardo of a clear-cut distinction (reflecting the two requisites indicated above for a perfect measure of value) between *two* separate analytical problems: (i) the question of alternative distributive set-ups for a *given* state of technology; and (ii) the issue of the consequences on the distribution of income (as well as on all the other variables of the system) arising from *changes* in the method of production (technology) of wage-goods. The implication of such a distinction is that, while the first type of problem belongs to the realm of economic statics, the second refers to the sphere of economic dynamics.

The preceding discussion on real and money wages in Ricardo aims at showing that such a distinction is not legitimate: changes in income distribution and changes in methods of production (of wage-goods) are in Ricardo's theory one and the same problem. A neoclassical-type problem of hypothetical changes in distribution finds no room in Ricardo's analytical framework.

For such a neoclassical-type problem to be conceived of in the Ricardian theory, one should be entitled to take into consideration, in the presence of unchanged methods of production for *all* commodities, either alternative levels of real wages *or* alternative levels of the prices of wage goods.

The former type of analysis, however, is precisely what the assumption of fixed real wages excludes. In the context of the natural equilibrium analysis which constitutes the main point of reference of Ricardo's theory, the 'rise or fall of wages' of which Ricardo speaks (after assuming that 'the same quantity of labour should at all times be required' in the production of the commodity used as a measure of value) clearly refers to money wages.

It could be argued on the other hand that, given the real wage, alternative values of money wages could be envisaged as 'originating' from hypothetical changes in the prices of wage-goods. These hypothetical changes must, however, be equally ruled out when technology is taken as given, since − as will be shown − a unique price vector is associated with each state of technology.

In conclusion, even in the very peculiar context of the search for an invariable standard of value, nothing warrants the interpretation of the concept of the 'rise or fall of wages' as referring to real wages; nothing, moreover, suggests that alternative levels of money wages can be conceived of independently of changes in the methods of production. In fact, Ricardo's assumption that 'the same quantity of labour should at all times be required' for the production of the commodity to be used as an invariable measure of value does not in any way imply the constancy of the methods of production of the other commodities (particularly wage-goods) on which movements in money wages depend.

A static neoclassical-type problem of distributive alternatives cannot therefore be envisaged in Ricardo's natural equilibrium analysis, i.e. in what certainly is the major line of his investigation on value and distribution.

In order to avoid a possible source of confusion, it is useful to specify the notion of the money wage used in the model considered in this chapter and in the following ones. Let:

$\bar{x}_i$ = the physical quantity of commodity i ($i = 1, 2, \ldots, m$) in the wage basket (some of these quantities may be nil, as in the case of machines)

p_i = the price of commodity i

w = the money wage rate

The *real* wage is defined as the vector of the physical quantities $\bar{x}_i$, while the *money* wage is defined as the *value* of the same basket of commodities:

$$w = \sum_{i=1}^{m} p_i \bar{x}_i \tag{1}$$

As it stands, this definition of w does not specify in what units value is expressed. It may be measured in terms of *paper money*, i.e. a medium of exchange not included among the m commodities produced in the system of the physical quantities but issued from outside this system, for example by the monetary authorities – a financial instrument, not a commodity. Alternatively, it may be expressed in terms of a 'commodity' money, i.e. a standard chosen among the m goods produced in the economy. As is well known, the latter is the type of choice made by Ricardo, who frequently referred to the commodity gold as the unit of value in his analysis of the problems of value and distribution.[9]

It is obvious that, in this case, the money wage is represented by that quantity of *the commodity* chosen as a measure of value which makes it possible to buy the particular bundle of goods constituting the real wage. This fact should not generate, therefore, any confusion between the two notions of money wage and of real wage – the first being represented by a *value*, the second by a *given basket of different commodities*.

It is the concept of *money wage* just defined that occupies a central position in the Ricardian theory of distribution, inasmuch as it provides a basis for the analysis of the dependence of the profit rate on the difficulties of production of one of the wage-goods (corn).

2.3 Effects on profits of changes in wages: two possible interpretations

The idea that a rise in money wages determines a fall in profits is central to Ricardo's theory ((68), pp. 110-11):

> suppose corn to rise in price because more labour is necessary to produce it; that cause will not raise the price of manufactured goods in the production of which no additional quantity of labour is required. If, then, wages continue the same, the profits of manufacturers would remain the same; but if, as is absolutely certain, wages would rise with the rise of corn, then their profits would necessarily fall.[10]

An analytical proof of this proposition, never fully achieved by Ricardo, can be searched for along two different lines of interpretation. According to a first interpretative approach – which appears to be particularly significant for the comprehension of Ricardo's theoretical research on value – the issue can be analysed in terms of the effects on the *share* of profits. The alternative approach – which Ricardo failed to sort out in general terms from the analytical model he had constructed in the *Principles* – consists of the examination of the effects on the *rate* of profit.

Some passages of Sraffa's 'Introduction' may perhaps be interpreted as suggesting that Ricardo looked for the solution of his problem in terms of the determination of the effects on the share of profits (Sraffa (85), p. xlviii):

> The 'principal problem in Political Economy' was in his [Ricardo's] view the division of the national product between classes and in the course of that investigation he was troubled by the fact that the size of this product appears to change when the division changes. Even though nothing has occurred to change the magnitude of the aggregate there may be apparent changes due solely to change in measurement, owing to the fact that measurement is in terms of value and relative values have been altered as a result of a change in the division between wages and profits.

In other words, if the measurement of the national product functionally depends on the distributive variables (wage rate and profit rate), the shares allotted to the different social classes would obviously depend on the values assigned to the wage rate and to the profit rate when the 'size of the product' to be distributed is determined. The assumptions made for the measurement of income would thus influence the results obtained with regard to distributive shares.

The problem can be immediately perceived if reference is made to the national accounting identity between the value of the total product on the one hand, and the income shares distributed to the social classes on the other, both being measured for convenience in terms of the commodity produced by the first sector. Let us assume that there are m sectors, each producing a single commodity; that agricultural products (symbolized by corn)[11] are the output of sector 1; that the luxury good gold is produced in sector 2; that other non-agricultural commodities (which can in principle be purchased by all the social classes) are produced in sectors $3 - (m - 1)$; and that machines are produced in sector m. Let us further assume constant returns in the production of all commodities with the exception of corn, the production of which is subject to diminishing returns. Let us finally suppose that no intermediate goods are required for current production and that no wear and tear of machines occurs; in this context net and gross quantities turn out to coincide. Indicating with:

X_i = physical output of sector i
W = wages fund in terms of corn
P = total profits in value terms
R = rent in terms of corn

the national income accounting identity can be written as

$$\sum_{i=1}^{m} \frac{p_i}{p_1} X_i = W + \frac{P}{p_1} + R \qquad (2)$$

It is clear that, if relative prices in (2) depend on the money wage rate w and on the profit rate r, the value of the national product — when the physical output of the m commodities is considered as given — would be different in correspondence with different values assigned to the distributive variables w and r. The possibility of only apparent changes in the total product is, in Sraffa's words ((85), p. xlviii), 'particularly evident in the extreme case where the aggregate is composed of the same commodities in the same quantities, and yet its magnitude will appear to have changed as measured in value'. It would thus be difficult to ascertain the effects on profits (both in absolute terms and as a share of national income) of a change in money wages. In this context the problem of an 'unambiguous' measurement of national income (i.e. of the definition of relative prices independently of the distributive variables) is therefore logically prior to that of the analysis of the effects on profits of a change in wages.

The risk of circular reasoning pointed out by Sraffa may thus be seen as the main reason that led Ricardo to reject Adam Smith's cost of production theory of prices and to stand in favour of a labour-embodied theory of value.[12] Ricardo was, however, keenly aware of the limitations which, for the labour theory of value, stem from the existence of different ratios of fixed capital to labour in the various sectors of the economy as well as from the 'unequal durability of capital' and of the 'unequal rapidity with which it is returned to its employer' (Ricardo (68), ch. 1, sections 4 and 5).

Ricardo's long reflection on these difficulties has been differently interpreted. Some[13] maintain that the recognition of these problems necessarily implies the conclusion that Ricardo abandoned the labour ·theory of value as a rigorous analytical proposition on relative prices. Others[14] argue, on the contrary, that the changes introduced in the chapter 'On value' in the third edition of the *Principles* lend no support to 'the view of a retreat in Ricardo's position' (Sraffa (85), p. xxxviii) on the labour theory of value. Ricardo's efforts to arrive at a satisfactory definition of an invariable measure of value are, according to these authors, to be placed in this perspective.

The Ricardian problem of the effects on profits of a change in money wages can, however, be posed also in terms of consequences on the *rate* of profit.[15] This is the way in which Ricardo originally analysed the problem in the *Essay on Profits* and to which he later returned in the chapter 'On profits' of the *Principles*. The well-known arithmetical table of the *Essay* on the 'progress of rent and profit under an assumed augmentation of capital' ((67), p. 17) clearly distinguishes between the 'whole amount of profits' and 'profit per cent on the whole capital', and shows that, while the former may increase in the first stages of the process of accumulation, the latter *steadily* diminishes. The same type of distinction is made in the *Principles* and the same type of conclusion is arrived at (Ricardo (68), p. 123). In the light of the strongly reaffirmed divergence between the behaviour of the aggregate amount of profits and that of the rate of profit, the final sentence of the chapter − in which the conclusion of the whole argument is summarized (Ricardo (68), p. 127, italics added): 'I have endeavoured to show . . . that a rise of wages would not raise the price of commodities, but would *invariably* lower profits' − must necessarily refer to the *rate of profit*.

Ricardo's position is clearly confirmed in the following passage of the chapter 'On foreign trade', where he states ((68), p. 132, italics added): 'It has been my endeavour to show *throughout this work* that the *rate of profit* can never be increased but by a fall in wages, and that there can be no permanent fall of wages but in consequence of a fall of the necessaries on which wages are expended.'

The interpretation of Ricardo's argument in terms of the rate of profit is therefore legitimate and appears to be particularly significant since in the Ricardian growth model – as well as in other growth models based on the so-called 'extreme classical saving function' – the rate of profit coincides with the rate of capital accumulation and thus plays a key role in the study of the dynamics of the system.[16]

When Ricardo's problem is viewed in this perspective, the whole analytical question emerges in a different light and it becomes possible to grasp the fundamental relationship between technology and growth through the behaviour of the profit rate. The general results that can be achieved on this basis do not suffer from the limitations typical of the labour theory of value.

2.4 A theoretical framework for the analysis of price determination: a necessary prelude

Before undertaking the examination of the two lines of interpretation mentioned in the previous section, it is necessary to define a theoretical framework for the determination of prices and distributive variables, with reference to which Ricardo's problems may be more easily dealt with. Adam Smith's theory of natural prices may for this purpose represent a useful starting-point, in that the examination of some specific features of his logical scheme may help us to understand the origin of Ricardo's theoretical reflections on some basic issues.

In his definition of the natural price of commodities equal to their cost of production Smith assigns fundamental importance to the fact that in capitalist economies (characterized by 'the appropriation of land and the accumulation of stock') the value of commodities includes not only wages but also profit and rent. The natural price is thus determined by the 'adding up' of three separate components (Smith (80), p. 48, italics added):

> When the price of any commodity is neither more nor less than
> what is sufficient to pay the rent of the land, the wages of the
> labour, and the profits of the stock employed in raising, preparing,

and bringing it to the market, *according to their natural rates*, the commodity is then sold for what may be called its natural price.

The natural price is expressed in terms of *labour commanded*, i.e. in terms of the quantity of labour which a unit of each commodity can purchase on the market (Smith (80), p. 26):

> The value of any commodity . . . to the person who possesses it, and who means not to use or consume it himself, but to exchange it for other commodities, is equal to the quantity of labour which it enables him to purchase or command. Labour, therefore, is the real measure of the exchangeable value of all commodities.

Smith's choice of the unit of measure rests on the idea of a constant disutility of labour (Smith (80), pp. 28–9):

> Equal quantities of labour, at all times and places, may be said to be of equal value to the labourer. In his ordinary state of health, strength and spirits; in the ordinary degree of his skill and dexterity, he must always lay down the same portion of his ease, his liberty, and his happiness . . . . At all times and places that is dear which it is difficult to come at, or which it costs much labour to acquire; and that cheap which is to be had easily, or with very little labour. Labour alone, therefore, never varying in its own value, is alone the ultimate and real standard by which the value of all commodities can at all times and places be estimated and compared. It is their real price; money is their nominal price only.

Thus, contrary to what happens in the pre-capitalist stage of society, exchangeable values no longer depend solely on the quantity of labour bestowed on the production of the various commodities.

Some of the relevant problems of Smith's theory of value can be pointed out with reference to the following model of price determination:

$$
\left.
\begin{aligned}
p_1 &= (1+r)n_1 w + rk_1 n_1 p_m \\
p_2 &= (1+r)n_2 w + rk_2 n_2 p_m \\
\cdot \quad & \quad \cdot \quad \quad \cdot \\
\cdot \quad & \quad \cdot \quad \quad \cdot \\
\cdot \quad & \quad \cdot \quad \quad \cdot \\
p_m &= (1+r)n_m w + rk_m n_m p_m
\end{aligned}
\right\}
\tag{3}
$$

$$
w = 1 \tag{4}
$$

$$
w = p_1 x_1 \tag{5}
$$

where the n_is are the labour coefficients per unit of output and the k_is are the quantities of fixed capital per worker in each of the m sectors. Contrary to Smith's definition of natural prices, rent does not appear in the price equations. This exclusion – which in the

Ricardian theory is based on the familiar 'marginal' argument – is here justified by the purpose of a direct comparison between Smith's and Ricardo's theories.

In (3) the price of each commodity is set equal to the corresponding cost of production under the competitive hypothesis of the existence of a uniform rate of profit. The cost of production is the sum of two terms: labour cost (including profits on the wages advanced to the workers) and fixed capital cost, calculated as interest charged on the value of the machines used in production. The price equations (3) thus portray an economy in which production is carried out by means of labour and fixed capital – no intermediate inputs being required. This apparent limitation disappears, however, as soon as the general definition (1) of the money wage rate is introduced in the model of price determination.

For convenience, machines are here considered as non-perishable. If, on the contrary, one wished to consider the hypothesis of capital depreciation – the case, for example, of 'radioactive decay'[17] – a further cost element ($\sigma k_i n_i p_m$) must obviously be added in each of the price equations (3), σ representing the (constant) percentage physical wear and tear of machines. With the addition of this term the apparent asymmetry in the manner of expressing the two components of cost (labour and means of production) would disappear. This becomes particularly evident when $\sigma = 1$, i.e. when the means of production employed are totally worn out in each productive period.

Equation (4) defines Smith's choice of the unit of measurement of value: the quantity of labour commanded by every commodity. The exchange values defined by the model are thus what Smith calls 'real prices', i.e. commodity prices expressed in terms of wave units, as opposed to 'nominal prices', defined in terms of a money *numéraire* – 'silver' in Smith's words ((80), pp. 161 ff.). Equation (5) implicitly defines the *real* wage rate x_1, which we suppose here to be made up, for convenience, only of agricultural produce.

The model (3)-(5) – consisting of $m + 2$ equations in $m + 3$ unknowns (p_i, w, r, x_1) – helps in pointing out some of the difficulties of Smith's conception of natural prices. The existence of a solution for the model is in fact clearly inconsistent with the idea that the natural values of *both* the rate of profit *and* the real wage rate are given from outside. Only *one* of the two distributive variables (x_1 and r) can be exogenously given, but then nothing would warrant that the solution for the other variable should coincide with an otherwise defined natural level. The system of 'real prices' expressed by the model (3)–(5) is thus incompatible with the notion that the natural values of the distributive variables are logically prior to the determination of the natural prices of commodities.

This conclusion should not come as a surprise, if one considers that precise rules for the determination of the natural values of the distributive variables are not to be found in the *Wealth of Nations*.

As the idea of a constant subsistence wage may be said to be also present in Smith's theoretical construction of natural prices, the model can be closed, substituting for (5) the following equation:

$$w = p_1 \bar{x}_1 \tag{5a}$$

which is a special case of the general definition (1) of the money wage rate. With the assumption (5a) that a fixed real wage is exogenously given, the degree of freedom which is present in the model (3)-(5) is thus eliminated. The derived system (3), (4) and (5a) consists now of the same number $(m + 2)$ of equations and unknowns. The problem of the existence of economically meaningful solutions for this and similar models will be taken up later in this chapter. Assuming for the moment that a unique solution exists, some general remarks on the nature of the model can be made here.

(i) The model implies the existence of some sort of asymmetry between the price of the wage-good and the prices of all other commodities. Equations (4) and (5a) jointly considered entail that p_1 is always equal (given $w = 1$) to $1/\bar{x}_1$. The model thus excludes changes in p_1 even when changes in agricultural technology are considered – the burden of the adjustment rests entirely on the prices of the other commodities and on the rate of profit. This means, in other words, that, whereas in general the prices of non-wage-goods would assume different equilibrium values in relation to different states of technology as expressed by the coefficients n_i and k_i (as would happen if the production of one or more commodities exhibited increasing or decreasing returns to scale), the price of corn would on the contrary remain unchanged. It should be noted that, if a less restrictive assumption about the composition of the wage basket were adopted – if it were assumed that the wage basket consists of a variety of goods – the conclusion regarding the invariance of the price of corn would have to be replaced by that of the existence of a linear relation among the prices of all the wage-goods.

This feature of the model may be taken to reflect, carrying it to the extreme, Smith's belief on the 'secular' constancy of the price of corn ((80), p. 32, italics added): 'From century to century corn is a better measure than silver, because, from century to century, *equal quantities of corn will command the same quantity of labour* more nearly than equal quantities of silver.' This belief is based on what is essentially an assumption of constant returns to scale in agriculture, due to the balancing effects (Smith (80), pp. 161 ff.) of cost-reducing improvements in techniques and the rising price of cattle.

(ii) It is clear that a logical inconsistency would arise if we were to attribute to Smith the joint acceptance of three independent propositions about the choice of *numéraire* ($w = 1$), the constancy of the price of corn, and the fixity of the real wage at the subsistence level ($\bar{x}_1$). One of these propositions is bound to be derived from the other two.

The Smith-type model (3), (4) and (5a) implies the following logical sequence: from the choice of the unit of measurement and the assumption of a fixed subsistence wage, to the conclusion of the constancy of the price of corn. A different logical sequence is attributed to Smith by Blaug ((6), p. 53): given the unit of measurement and the assumed constancy in the long-term price of corn, the conclusion is drawn as to the secular constancy of the real wage rate. It must be said that both the assumption of the secular constancy of the subsistence wage (in the first approach) and that of the secular constancy of the price of corn (in the second approach) are scarcely supported by general empirical evidence. The choice made in our model − apart from its obvious Ricardian bias − seems to be more in line with a construction of a theory of natural prices.

A third logical sequence could in principle be envisaged: if both the price of corn and the real wage are supposed to be secularly constant, the conclusion is reached that the money wage rate is invariant. Smith's clear choice in favour of a labour-commanded theory of value seems, however, to support the opinion that he did not work with this logical sequence in mind.

(iii) The specific point of the risk of circular reasoning underlined by Sraffa can be easily shown considering the definition of one of the relative prices implicit in equations (3):[18]

$$\frac{p_2}{p_1} = \frac{n_2}{n_1} \cdot \frac{(1+r)w + rk_2 p_m}{(1+r)w + rk_1 p_m} \tag{6}$$

Acceptance of Smith's 'adding-up' theory of value implies, therefore, *in the general case* (i.e. when capital–labour ratios are different in the various sectors) the dependence of prices on distributive variables and thus the apparent risk that the measurement of the national product may depend on its distribution. The logical genesis of Ricardo's theoretical approach to the problems of 'value' – and in particular the role he seems to have assigned to a one-factor theory of relative values – may then be sought for in the need to eliminate the risk of a circular relation between distribution and measurement.

The formulation of a theory of value in which relative prices coincide with the ratios between the quantities of labour embodied in the commodities requires that it may be possible to ignore the effects resulting from the presence of fixed capital. It is clear that this can happen only if the capital–labour ratios are the same in all sectors. This is precisely the type of assumption on which Ricardo seems ultimately to rely. More complex situations are thus considered as mere sources of 'modification'[19] of a fundamental principle which, though analytically 'imperfect', makes it possible, in Ricardo's mind, to reach substantially valid conclusions.

(iv) When the money wage w is taken as *numéraire* (as is done in the Smithian-type model outlined above), the possibility is by definition ruled out of examining *both* the problem of the effects on prices of a change in money wages – a problem on which Smith's and Ricardo's opinions so markedly differed, as it will be stressed below in section 2.7 – *and* that of the effects on profits of a rise in money wages. It may be said, therefore, that the crucial Ricardian problem of the relation between diminishing returns in agriculture and the rate of profit – via changes in the level of money wages – cannot be posed in the Smithian framework. The basic reason for this is the fundamental difference between Smith's and Ricardo's assumptions as regards agricultural technology: constant returns for the former, diminishing returns for the latter.

An appropriate unit of measurement must be introduced in the model if the analysis of the Ricardian problems originating from changes in money wages is to be made possible.[20] As is well known, Ricardo's reflection on the issue of the choice of the *numéraire* has been particularly long and complex. This issue – with particular reference to the question of the role assigned to the standard of value – is discussed in Chapter 3. For the purpose of the present argument it is sufficient to focus on the first of the two requisites indicated by Ricardo for a perfect measure of value – that the same quantity of labour should at all times be required for its production. Assuming with Ricardo that gold is produced under constant returns to scale, we can choose this commodity as *numéraire*, letting for convenience:

$$p_2 = n_2 \tag{4a}$$

When this choice of unit of measurement is placed in a context in which the labour theory of value holds true, absolute prices of all commodities turn out to coincide with their respective direct labour inputs; for, combining (4a) with (6) when $k_i = k$ (uniform capital-labour ratio), we have:

$$p_i = n_i \tag{7}$$

This implies that the value of production per unit of labour is the same in all sectors and is equal to unity.

This result can be thought of as representing the extension of the labour theory of value from the realm of relative prices to that of absolute prices. Ricardo had perhaps in mind something similar when in the essay on *Absolute Value and Exchangeable Value* ((69), pp. 381-2) he wrote:

> Have we no standard in nature by which we can ascertain the uniformity in the value of a measure? It is asserted that we have, and that labour is that standard. The average strength of 1,000 or 10,000 men it is said is nearly the same at all times. A commodity produced in a given time by the labour of 100 men is double the value of a commodity produced by the labour of 50 men in the same time. All then we have to do it is said to ascertain whether the value of a commodity be now of the same value as a commodity produced 20 years ago is to find out what quantity of labour for the same length of time was necessary to produce the commodity 20 years ago and what quantity is necessary to produce it now. If the labour of 80 men was required a year then and the labour of 100 is required now we may confidently pronounce that the commodity has risen 25 [per cent].

2.5 The effects of a change in wages on the aggregate amount and on the share of profits: the first interpretation

When the solution of the Ricardian problem of the consequences on profits of a change in money wages is searched for along the first of the two interpretative approaches outlined above, a preliminary condition should apparently be fulfilled — the elimination of the risk of circularity between measurement of the national product and its distribution among social classes. To meet this requirement relative prices should be independent of the distributive variables – a result which is obtained with the labour theory of value. Since, however, this theory is valid only when specific technological circumstances are supposed to occur, its adoption entails a 'sacrifice' in the degree of realism of the assumptions on which the analysis is based. Our purpose is now to verify if, on the basis of this theory of value, it is possible to ascertain unambiguously the effects of a change in money wages on the aggregate amount of profits and on the profit share.

Given the real wage, $\bar{x}_1$, a change in money wages implies a corresponding change in the price of corn, p_1. This in turn presupposes, on account of (7), an equal variation in the labour input of corn, n_1, which is the inverse of the product of labour on the land which pays no rent.

Let us consider the case of a rise in the quantity of labour n_1 embodied in corn consequent upon diminishing returns in agriculture, while the labour inputs of the other commodities $(n_2, \ldots, n_m)$ remain unchanged. The relative prices appearing in the left-hand side of equation (2) will diminish. If it were then possible to suppose that both the physical quantities produced in the economy and total employment remained constant, the value of the national product, as expressed by the left-hand side of equation (2), would diminish. This would imply in the right-hand side of (2) – aggregate wages and rent being constant – an equal reduction in the absolute amount of profits. A fall would also occur in the share of profits in national income $(P/n_1)/\Sigma(n_i/n_1)X_i$ in connection with the rise in the share of wages-plus-rent $(W + R)/\Sigma(n_i/n_1)X_i$.

The hypotheses on which the validity of this conclusion depends appear, however, unacceptable even when the conditions for the labour theory of value to hold are met. An increase in n_1, given the assumption of diminishing returns in the production function of the agricultural sector, implies a movement along that function and, therefore, an increase in agricultural employment and in the output of corn X_1. This, in turn, entails an increase in rent,[21] and therefore – given Ricardo's hypotheses on the behaviour of the social classes – an increase in the production of luxury goods and in the corresponding levels of employment.

This result is of immediate evidence if reference is made to the case in which the value of rent (p_1R) is entirely spent on the purchase of gold (p_2X_2). Since we are assuming that the labour theory of value holds true, the increase in n_1 implies a corresponding increase in p_1, while p_2 remains unaltered on account of the hypothesis of constant returns in all non-agricultural production. The physical output of gold thus rises under the influence of the increase both in the price of corn and the amount of rent. In the case that landowners purchase other non-agricultural products, with the exception of machines $(\sum\limits_{i=2}^{m-1} p_i X_i)$, the production of all these commodities is bound to increase as a consequence of a rise in the value of rent provided that no change in the structure of rentiers' demand occurs. A parallel increase in employment must obviously accompany these changes in the physical quantities produced.

The logical sequence of events outlined above necessarily implies an increase in the production of machines (X_m) proportional to the increased levels of employment in the various sectors.

It may be said, therefore, that in the left-hand side of (2), while all the relative prices diminish as a consequence of the assumed rise in the labour input of corn, all the physical quantities increase. The 'extreme case', considered by Sraffa ((85), p. xlviii) for the purpose of exemplification, that the outputs of the various commodities remain unchanged in the presence of an increase in the labour input of corn, cannot, therefore, be envisaged. A significant aspect of the difficulties inherent in this exercise of comparative statics is represented by the resulting implications for the definition of rent. Given the agricultural production function implicit in the Ricardian framework, there exists a unique relation between the level of employment, the marginal product of labour, and rent. The possibility of considering different levels of rent with the same level of employment must therefore be ruled out, unless shifts in the production function are allowed for. Although admissible in principle, such shifts cannot be taken to be a constituent part of a model aiming to reconstruct Ricardo's theoretical framework.

The increase in all the physical quantities which accompanies the fall in all the relative prices thus makes it impossible to determine what change (if any) has occurred in the value of the national product expressed in corn as a result of an increase in n_1. A relevant conclusion can be drawn with reference to the right-hand side of (2): the increase in the wages fund (higher level of employment with a constant real wage) and in rent does not represent in general a sufficient condition to infer that a reduction in the value of aggregate profits has taken place. This type of conclusion is in full accordance with Ricardo's remarks in the *Essay on Profits* ((67), p. 17) and in the *Principles* ((68), p. 123) about the possibility of an increase in the aggregate amount of profits at some stage of the process of capital accumulation.[22]

An analogous conclusion holds for the share of profits in national income. Since the change in the value of the national product cannot be determined *a priori*, it is impossible to define the behaviour of the income shares of wages and rent even if it is known for certain that their absolute amounts have both increased. Nothing can thus be said, in general, as to the behaviour of the share of profits.[23]

It may be noted in passing that if the national product were expressed in terms of absolute prices, i.e. as $\Sigma n_i X_i$, rather than in terms of corn, as was done in (2), the preceding conclusion would obviously continue to hold; for, as a consequence of the increase in the price of corn — the price of the other commodities remaining unchanged — the value of the national product would now certainly show an increase. At the same time, in the right-hand side of (2), which would now read as $p_1 W + P + p_1 R$, there would be an increase in the wages fund and in rent. Thus neither in this case would it be possible to reach a general unambiguous conclusion about the type of changes taking place in the value of total profits (and in the share of profits).

We can therefore conclude in general that, even when prices are independent of the distributive variables (w and r), it is not possible to ascertain the effects of a change in money wages on the aggregate amount and on the share of profits. In other words, the independence of relative prices from distribution — obtainable on the basis of the labour theory of value, i.e. at the cost of accepting a highly unrealistic assumption about the productive technology — does not allow an unambiguous conclusion to be drawn along the first of the two interpretative approaches here considered.

2.6 The relation between money wages and the rate of profit: the second interpretation

As mentioned in section 2.3, the problem of the effects on profits of a change in money wages can also be examined according to a different interpretative approach: that is, in terms of consequences on the *rate of profit*. The legitimacy of this type of approach within the Ricardian theoretical framework has already been stressed. Its relevance in a model dealing with the problems of long-term growth can be immediately perceived when the crucial role of the rate of profit (coinciding here with the rate of capital accumulation) in shaping the path of the economic system over time is considered.

The problem can be analysed on the basis of what may be called the *'general' Ricardian price model* consisting of the definition of money wages (1), the price equations (3), and the unit of measurement (4a). The 'general' character of the model derives from the following circumstances: (i) m sectors are considered; (ii) capital-labour ratios are different in the various sectors; and (iii) no restrictions are introduced as to the definition of the basket of commodities constituting the real wage. The model is thus free from the limitations due to the consideration of only one (corn) or two (corn and gold) sectors, and therefore connected with the absence of fixed capital. Furthermore, with the assumption of different capital–labour ratios, the model escapes the strictures typically associated with the labour theory of value. Finally, with definition (1) account is taken of Malthus's criticism of the assumption that the wage rate may consist only of corn and that, as a consequence, in agriculture the 'same commodity, namely corn, forms both the capital . . . and the product' (Sraffa (85), p. xxxi). This criticism was addressed to the assumption that Ricardo was to adopt in the *Essay on Profits* – which made it possible to determine the rate of profit as a ratio of quantities of corn without reference to prices.[24] The general definition (1) adopted in the text is that which, according to Sraffa ((85), p. xxxii), Ricardo accepted in the *Principles*: 'he [Ricardo] was enabled to abandon the simplification that wages consist only of corn, which had been under frequent attack from Malthus, and to treat wages as composed of a variety of products (including manufactures), although food was still predominant among them'.

It should, however, be observed that intermediate goods other than those entering in the wage basket are not considered. This assumption implies some useful simplification in the structure of the model without affecting (on account of the differences in the k_is) the substantial generality of the argument.

The model (1), (3) and (4a) consists of $m + 2$ equations in an equal number of unknowns, and determines, as will be seen, a unique solution for the variables. As it stands, the model is thus unsuitable for the study of the behaviour of the rate of profit as a function of diminishing returns. To this end a degree of freedom must be acquired through the consideration either of the wage rate as an exogenous variable or of the labour input of corn as a variable parameter of the system. The former type of analysis is carried out in the present section as a sort of preliminary step for the latter, which is developed in section 2.8.

It is clear that for the study to be undertaken here, equation (1) must be dropped. The degree of freedom thus acquired can be used to investigate the solution of the model as a function of w and, in particular, the relationship between w and r which, in Hicksian terminology (Hicks (35), p. 140), may be called the 'wage equation'.[25]

It may be observed incidentally that the solution of the model along these lines shows close resemblance to Sraffa's analysis in *Production of Commodities* (86), where the solution for the prices of production and one of the distributive variables is obtained taking the value of the other distributive variable as given outside the model. When the exogenously given variable is the wage rate, resemblance could appear to turn into coincidence, were it not for the difference in the notion of wages used by Ricardo and Sraffa, and for the related difference in the context in which the analyses are developed. For, in the Sraffian scheme of 'production with a surplus', the key variables of the distributive antagonism are the profit rate and the wage rate as purchasing power ('real' wage), whereas in the Ricardian framework the relevant variables are, as already stressed above, the rate of profit and the *money wage* (the real wage being fixed at the subsistence level).

As we have seen, in the Ricardian theory the real wage of labour is conceived of as a necessary cost of production and is as such specified in its physical components. In the Sraffian scheme, on the contrary, the wage taken into consideration in the analysis of the distributive alternatives participates with profits in the division of the surplus. Sraffa's wage is thought of as purchasing power measured in terms of standard net product, which is the *numéraire* of the system. This wage has, in other words, the nature of a 'bill', which entitles the owner to purchase – in the actual, as opposed to the standard, system – a bundle of commodities corresponding in value to the given portion of the standard net product assigned to labour. As we may suppose that, with a given composition of expenditure, the quantities of the various commodities the labourers can purchase in the *actual* system vary in the same direction as the percentage of the *standard* net product assigned to labour, we can say that alternative levels of wages are to be taken, in the Sraffian context, as alternative values of the proportion of the actual national product going to labour. In this sense, Sraffa's wage is a *real* wage.

One might be led to think that the real wage could be defined in the Sraffian context also in physical terms, more specifically as a fixed percentage of *each* of the commodities of which the standard net product consists. This idea – clearly closer to Ricardo's – would run, however, into two kinds of difficulties. First, the vector of standard net quantities might well include non-wage-goods (as 'basic' commodities do not necessarily coincide with wage-goods). Second, it is by no means certain, in general, that the net quantities of the various commodities produced in the actual system are at least equal to the amounts of the commodities in the standard net product corresponding to the percentage exogenously assigned to labour.[26]

With this specification in mind, we may say that the different way in which the distributive antagonism is looked at by Sraffa and Ricardo clearly reflects a difference in the types of problems considered and in the analytical context in which the investigation is carried out.

Sraffa's analysis 'is concerned exclusively with such properties of an economic system as do not depend on changes in the scale of production or in the proportions of "factors"' (Sraffa (86), p. v), and concentrates on the study of distributive alternatives in their relation to the prices of commodities. On the assumption of a given technology, the feasible combinations of the profit rate and of the wage rate are determined, and the well-known linear relation between these variables defined. The analysis is thus basically static in nature.

A different point of view is expressed at this regard by Roncaglia, who argues ((76), p. 119) that, while the neoclassical equilibrium theories are static in that

> they are characterized by the fact that they are placed in an a-temporal context . . . Sraffa's analysis is not static, but rather represents a 'photograph' of a particular moment of a system's development. This is something rather different for it does not abstract from time. Instead, time is taken into account by the fact that any particular moment of time is determined by its past history, and serves as the determining factor of the next moment in time.[27]

Roncaglia's argument about the non-static nature of Sraffa's analysis cannot, however, be accepted. Neither the system's 'past history' nor the effects on 'the next moment in time' receive any kind of consideration in Sraffa's analytical framework. Naturally, nothing prevents one from thinking that the technical coefficients may somehow be the result of the past history of the economy (hence the consistency of Sraffa's scheme with the Keynesian analysis of income determination), nor that the possible investment of the surplus – or of part of it – may affect the structure, as well as the scale, of the economic system. All this, however, is left out of Sraffa's analysis, which must be evaluated *per se* and whose full relevance is in no way diminished by its qualification as static in nature.

Ricardo's analysis is based, on the other hand, as we have seen, on the key assumption that the real wage is fixed. The relation between the distributive variables is accordingly, in Ricardo, a relation between the money (not the real) wage and the profit rate. To this end, the possibility of alternative prices of wage-goods should be envisaged – a circumstance which, as already mentioned, requires that changes in technology should be allowed for. This is precisely the basic idea that lies behind the relation between w and r in the Ricardian scheme, where diminishing returns in agriculture (i.e. changes in coefficients of production *necessarily occurring over time* as a consequence of capital accumulation and population growth) determine a continuous increase in the price of corn and in the money wage. Contrary to Sraffa's analysis, Ricardo's approach is therefore essentially dynamic.

Having thus clarified what appears to be a significant distinction between two different (though often misleadingly identified) analytical issues, we can now turn to the study of the relation between w and r in the Ricardian model of price determination. Starting from the choice of *numéraire* (4a) and substituting for p_2 and p_m from (3), we obtain:

$$1 = \frac{(1+r)w\left[1 + rn_m\left(k_2 - k_m\right)\right]}{1 - rn_m k_m} \tag{8}$$

It is proved in the appendix to this chapter that – for r lying in the interval $[0, 1/n_m k_m]$, as required for the wage rate to be positive and for the prices of commodities to be meaningfully determined – (8) defines an inverse relation between the profit rate and the money wage rate, whatever the degree of capital intensity (k_2) of the gold-producing sector with respect to that (k_m) of the machine-producing sector. This shows that in a model of price determination, free of the limitations of the labour theory of value and without recourse to the use of *ad hoc numéraires* (such as Sraffa's standard commodity), the conclusion can be drawn that increasing levels of money wages are associated with declining values of the rate of profit. A first important answer to the Ricardian problem is thus obtained.

It may be interesting to note that the values of w corresponding to the interval of admissible values of r range from zero to one.[28] This means in particular that the maximum value the wage can assume in this model, given the specific choice of *numéraire* (4a), is one. It should, however, be clear from the preceding argument that this latter result − in spite of its formal similarity to that of Sraffa − does not justify any mechanical juxtaposition between the two schemes of Ricardo and Sraffa.

2.7 Wages and prices: Ricardo's criticism of Smith's theory

In connection with the preceding discussion we can also consider the problem of the effects of a change in money wages on the prices of commodities − an issue on which Ricardo severely criticized Smith's position. When the conditions obtain for the labour theory of value to hold, a very strong − though obvious − result emerges. Since relative prices are equal to the ratios between the quantities of direct labour inputs, and absolute prices are proportional − equal with the choice of *numéraire* (4a) − to the same labour inputs, changes in money wages have no effect on prices, so that the burden of adjustment falls entirely on the rate of profit.

When, on the contrary, the general case is considered − as in the price equations (3) − relative and absolute prices depend on w. In order to assess the consequences of changes in money wages on prices, two effects must be jointly considered: (i) the effect on the labour component of cost, proportional to the variation in money wages; and (ii) the effect in the opposite direction on the profit component of cost connected with the inverse relation between w and r. These two effects exactly balance out only in the case of the commodity chosen as *numéraire*, whose price is by definition constant. In all other cases, the situation is more complex and the net effect of a change in w may be either positive, nil, or negative. A general result may none the less be established with reference to the degree of capital intensity prevailing in the production of each commodity as compared with that of the *numéraire*. As is proved in the appendix, this general result is:

$$\text{sign} \left\{ \frac{dp_i}{dw} \right\} = \text{sign} \{ k_2 - k_i \} \tag{9}$$

In other words, if the productive technique of commodity i is less capital intensive than that of the *numéraire*, a rise in money wages will be associated with an increase in its price, and vice versa.

It is interesting to note that this substantially confirms Ricardo's opinion as regards the effects of a change in money wages on the price of commodities (Ricardo (68), p. 43, italics added):

> It appears . . . that in proportion to the durability of capital [the
> first edition of the *Principles* reads: 'in proportion to the quantity
> and durability of the fixed capital'] employed in any kind of pro-
> duction, the relative prices of those commodities on which such
> durable capital is employed, will vary inversely as wages; they will
> fall as wages rise, and rise as wages fall; and, on the contrary, those
> which are produced chiefly by labour with less fixed capital, or with
> fixed capital of a less durable character than the *medium* in which
> price is estimated, will rise as wages rise, and fall as wages fall.

Since it is clear that the notion of 'durability' of capital is to be
subsumed in the context of the present model under the concept of
capital intensity, it can be said that, if the word 'medium' were to be
interpreted as equivalent to '*numéraire*', Ricardo's conclusion would
exactly coincide with the result expressed by (9). But in the context
of the above cited passage of the *Principles*, the word 'medium' has
the very specific (though analytically vague) meaning of 'social average',
i.e. of a commodity whose productive technique implies a degree of
capital intensity equal to the 'average' of the system, and is for this
very reason chosen as *numéraire*. The medium in which price is
estimated is thus a standard of value whose essential feature is that
of being 'produced with such proportions of the two kinds of capital
[fixed and circulating] as approach nearest to the average quantity
employed in the production of most commodities' (Ricardo (68),
p. 45).

This interpretation is confirmed by a letter to McCulloch of 13
June 1820 in which Ricardo writes (Sraffa (84), vol. 8, p. 193, italics
added):

> perhaps the best [standard of absolute value] adapted to the general
> mass of commodities [is] the *medium* [between the] two extremes
> . . . one, where the commodity is produced without delay and by
> labour only, without the intervention of capital; the other where it
> is the result of a great quantity of fixed capital, contains very little
> labour, and is not produced without considerable delay.

Ricardo's conclusion as to the effects of a change in wages on the
price of commodities differs therefore from (9), only in that Ricardo
refers to a commodity which is selected as *numéraire* by virtue of its
peculiar technological features. Expression (9), on the contrary, establishes a property with regard to any *numéraire as such*, whatever
its technological structure of production may be.

With the same proviso, we may conclude that Ricardo's criticism
of Smith's theory on this issue finds substantial support in the ana-

lytical properties of the present model (Ricardo (68), p. 46):

> Adam Smith, and all the writers who have followed him, have, without one exception that I know of, maintained that a rise in the price of labour would be uniformly followed by a rise in the price of all commodities. I hope I have succeeded in showing, that there are no grounds for such an opinion, and that only those commodities would rise which had less fixed capital employed upon them than the medium in which price was estimated, and that all those which had more, would positively fall in price when wages rose.

2.8 The relation between the labour input in the production of corn and the rate of profit

The analysis carried out in the previous sections is to be considered only as a preliminary step in the study of the Ricardian problem in that it disregards the reason why money wages tend to increase in the process of growth, i.e. the crucial connection between money wages, the price of corn and diminishing returns in agriculture. The key variable with respect to which the behaviour of the profit rate has to be analysed is therefore the quantity of labour necessary to produce a unit of corn in the less favourable conditions. This means that it is now the labour coefficient n_1 that must be considered as a parameter, assuming different values increasing in time. The model (1), (3) and (4a) must then be viewed as yielding a solution for each of the values of n_1 — the relation directly relevant for Ricardo's problem being obviously that between n_1 and r. This relation — with an expression analogous to the Hicksian 'wage equation' — will be indicated as the 'profit equation'.

Substituting the general definition of money wages (1) in the price equations (3), we have:

$$p_1 = (1 + r)n_1 (p_1\bar{x}_1 + p_2\bar{x}_2 + \ldots + p_{m-1}\bar{x}_{m-1}) + rk_1 n_1 p_m$$
$$p_2 = (1 + r)n_2 (p_1\bar{x}_1 + p_2\bar{x}_2 + \ldots + p_{m-1}\bar{x}_{m-1}) + rk_2 n_2 p_m$$

$$\qquad \qquad \qquad \cdot \qquad \qquad \cdot \qquad \qquad \cdot \qquad \qquad \cdot$$
$$\qquad \qquad \qquad \cdot \qquad \qquad \cdot \qquad \qquad \cdot \qquad \qquad \cdot$$
$$\qquad \qquad \qquad \cdot \qquad \qquad \cdot \qquad \qquad \cdot \qquad \qquad \cdot$$

$$p_m = (1 + r)n_m (p_1\bar{x}_1 + p_2\bar{x}_2 + \ldots + p_{m-1}\bar{x}_{m-1}) + rk_m n_m p_m$$

$$(10)$$

Since the labour theory of value does not hold for the 'general' Ricardian model, as simple inspection of (10) shows, the relation between r and n_1 cannot be given explicit algebraic form but can be identified only through the complete solution of the model. The appendix to this chapter shows: (i) that the model (10)-(4a) has a unique positive solution for each of the values assignable to n_1; and (ii) that, as n_1 increases, r continually decreases. The model thus defines, in general, an inverse relation between n_1 and r, showing that the central problem of Ricardo's analysis finds an unambiguous solution, not subject to any of the limitations of the labour theory of value.

Similar results as to the determination of the rate of profit in the Ricardian system have been reached by Dmitriev (19), who shows that r can be determined directly (i.e. without the need for the prior determination of prices) from the technological conditions of production of the wage-goods, given the physical composition of the wage basket. Since, however, Dmitriev's model, which is based on the assumption that intermediate products can be reduced to a finite sequence of dated quantities of labour, substantially disregards fixed capital, a significant difference emerges from this point of view with respect to the Ricardian price model examined in this chapter. The latter can therefore be considered, with regard to the relation between diminishing returns and the rate of profit, as a step towards generalization.

A further difference *vis-à-vis* Dmitriev should be noted. It concerns the evaluation of Ricardo's awareness of the analytical results obtainable within his theoretical framework. In the above-mentioned letter to McCulloch, Ricardo writes (Sraffa (84), vol. 8, pp. 194-5, italics added):

> The greater the portion of the result of labour that is given to the labourer, the smaller must be the rate of profits, and vice versa. Now this portion must essentially depend on the facility of producing the necessaries of the labourer – if the facility be great a small portion of any commodity . . . will be sufficient to furnish the labourer with the necessaries, and consequently profits will be high. *The truth of this doctrine I deem to be absolutely demonstrable.*

While Dmitriev ((19), p. 58) credits Ricardo with the 'immortal contribution' of the 'brilliant solution' of the 'seemingly insoluble problem' of the profit rate, it is our opinion that the belief expressed by Ricardo in the above-cited letter to McCulloch is not matched by the achievement of adequate analytical results. His open admission in the *Principles* of the limited validity of his propositions on value and his consequent, endless research for the invariable measure are clear evidence of this circumstance.

2.9 The rate of profit in the Ricardian model

The conclusion arrived at in the preceding section has relevant implications for the following three issues: (i) the relation between the rate of profit and the agricultural sub-system; (ii) the definition of the rate of profit as a ratio between quantities of labour; and (iii) the problem of logical circularity between measurement and distribution.

(i) As we have seen, the rate of profit cannot in general be determined with exclusive reference to the technical conditions of agricultural production; it depends instead on the technical conditions of production of all the commodities entering the wage basket and of machines – the only possible exclusion being represented by the commodities consumed exclusively by rentiers and capitalists.

The only special case in which the rate of profit can be determined with the exclusive consideration of the technical conditions ruling in the agricultural sector is what we have learned to call, with Sraffa, the *corn model*. This is the model of an economy which, even if consisting of *m* sectors, is characterized by the fact that in agriculture the same commodity, namely corn, forms both the capital (by definition consisting here of the subsistence necessary for workers) and the product (Sraffa (85), p. xxxi) – fixed capital and other means of production are not used and the real wage is represented only by corn. As soon as less simplified (though still not general) models are considered, this possibility disappears, as in the following cases:

(a) An economic system in which no fixed capital is used, but the wage basket consists of a 'variety of products' including manufactures, as in definition (1). Reference to Malthus's criticism of Ricardo's initial assumption as to the 'nature' of the 'capital advanced' may justify, for this case, the use of the label *Malthusian wage model*.

(b) An economic system in which, whatever the composition of the wage basket, fixed capital is required in the production of all commodities and capital-labour ratios are uniform throughout the economy. Reference to a large (and consistent) part of Marx's analysis based on the assumption of a uniform organic composition of capital[29] may justify, in this instance, the use of the label *Marxian-type model*.

From the point of view of the determination of the rate of profit, the Malthusian wage model and the Marxian-type model thus exhibit the same characteristics of what has been previously called the 'general' Ricardian model, in the sense that *r* turns out to depend on the technical conditions of production of all 'basic' commodities.

From the point of view of the determination of prices, a relevant difference arises, however, between the special cases (corn model, Malthusian wage model and Marxian-type model) on the one hand, and the general case (Ricardian model) on the other. In the former group of models the labour theory of value holds; prices, therefore, are independent of distribution and can be determined prior to the definition of the rate of profit. (In the corn model, in particular, prices and distribution are mutually independent.) In the latter prices and the rate of profit are arrived at simultaneously through the solution of the model.[30]

It can thus be said in general that the thesis[31] according to which the problems relating to the definition of the profit rate and to its behaviour through time can be solved with exclusive reference to the agricultural sector does not hold. This thesis, however, is not to be confused with that of the dependence of the general profit rate on the phenomenon of diminishing returns in agriculture.

The former thesis would imply the possibility of defining the rate of profit in a sub-system (the agricultural sector) independent of the rest of the economy. The latter, on the contrary, denies this possibility in general and maintains that the impact of diminishing returns in agriculture on the rate of profit can only be assessed through the solution of the whole model of prices and distribution. In Sraffa's words ((85), pp. xxxi–xxxiii):

> [the] basic principle . . . that 'it is the profits of the farmer that regulates the profits of all other trades'[32] . . . [a]fter the *Essay* disappears from view, and is not to be found in the *Principles* . . . In the *Principles* . . . it became possible for Ricardo to demonstrate the determination of the rate of profit in society as a whole instead of through the microcosm of one special branch of production . . . . (But while the theory that the profits of the farmer determine all other profits disappears in the *Principles*, the more general proposition that the productivity of labour on land which pays no rent is fundamental in determining general profits continues to occupy a central position.)

The fact that the latter proposition is deeply rooted in Ricardo's mind is clearly shown by the following passage of the *Principles*, where Ricardo neatly distinguishes between the effects on profits of changes in conditions of production of agricultural products as opposed to those of luxury goods ((68), p. 132):

> If . . . by the extension of foreign trade, or by improvements in machinery, the foods and necessaries of the labourer can be brought to market at a reduced price, profits will rise . . . but if the com-

modities obtained at a cheaper rate, by the extension of foreign commerce, or by the improvement of machinery, be exclusively the commodities consumed by the rich, no alteration will take place in the rate of profits. The rate of wages will not be affected, although wine, velvets, silks and other expensive commodities should fall . . . and consequently profits would continue unaltered.

(ii) It may be of some interest to compare the results here obtained with Ricardo's statement that profits depend upon the 'proportion of the annual labour of the country [which] is devoted to the support of the labourers' ((68), pp. 48-9) and with Sraffa's consequent interpretation which assigns to this statement a key role in the analytical apparatus of the *Principles* ((85), p. xxxii):

> In the *Principles* . . . with the adoption of a general theory of value, it became possible for Ricardo to demonstrate the determination of the rate of profit in society as a whole . . . . It was now labour, instead of corn, that appeared on both sides of the account – in modern terms, both as input and output: as a result, the rate of profit was no longer determined by the ratio of the corn produced to the corn used up in production, but, instead, by the ratio of the total labour of the country to the labour required to produce the necessaries for that labour.

The solution of the model (1), (3) and (4a) makes it clear that the rate of profit cannot in general be determined as a ratio between quantities of labour. Sraffa's claim that this type of result stems from Ricardo's adoption of a *general* theory of value is therefore not supported by the analytical properties of the model. Only when the labour theory of value holds true can the rate of profit be consistently defined as a ratio between quantities of labour, but not in all cases are the quantities of labour involved those indicated by Sraffa.

Let us for this purpose consider the definition of the rate of profit in the above-mentioned three classes of models representing the 'special cases' considered. In the *corn model*, which can be obtained from the general model setting $\bar{x}_i = 0$ for $i \neq 1$ and $k_i = 0$, solving the first of the price equations (3) for r we have:

$$r = \frac{\dfrac{1}{n_1} - \bar{x}_1}{\bar{x}_1} \tag{11}$$

where obviously $1/n_1$ represents the physical output of corn obtained by a unit of labour in the 'less favourable conditions', i.e. on the land which pays no rent. The rate of profit thus turns out to be a ratio between quantities of corn without any reference to prices. The definition of r given by (11) can be easily transformed into a ratio between quantities of labour multiplying all terms by n_1 – the quantity of labour required to produce a unit of corn:

$$r = \frac{1 - n_1 \bar{x}_1}{n_1 \bar{x}_1} \tag{12}$$

The interpretation of (12) is straightforward: $n_1 \bar{x}_1$ is the quantity of *unassisted* labour required to produce the necessaries for one labourer and $(1 - n_1 \bar{x}_1)$ is 'surplus labour', i.e. the difference between the total quantity of labour supplied by each worker (the unit of labour) and the fraction of it which is necessary for his support. In this case the rate of profit – or, to be painstakingly exact, $(1 + r)$ – as Sraffa suggests, is 'the ratio of the total[33] labour of the country to the *labour required to produce the necessaries for that labour*' (italics added).

In the *Malthusian wage model*, which can be derived from the general model letting $k_i = 0$, the profit rate can be determined solving any one of the price equations (3):

$$r = \frac{\dfrac{p_i}{n_i} - \Sigma p_i \bar{x}_i}{\Sigma p_i \bar{x}_i} \tag{13}$$

where p_i/n_i is the value of the output of one labourer in any sector i of the economy and $\Sigma p_i \bar{x}_i$ is the value of the (given) subsistence wage when the wage basket consists of a variety of products. The rate of profit, as defined by (13), is thus a ratio between two values – the value of the net output of each worker above his subsistence and the value of the circulating capital employed in production (the advances to each labourer). Since in this case (with the particular choice of the *numéraire* (4a)) prices are identical to labour inputs, (13) can be transformed into a ratio between quantities of labour:

$$r = \frac{1 - \Sigma n_i \bar{x}_i}{\Sigma n_i \bar{x}_i} \tag{14}$$

which is the obvious generalization of (12) – the economic meaning of the terms remaining unchanged. It is thus true that here, with a general definition of wages, implying a significant departure from the basic feature of the corn model, the profit rate is a ratio between quantities of labour, and that these quantities are exactly those indicated by Ricardo and Sraffa.

A different conclusion holds, on the contrary, for the *Marxian-type model*, whose distinguishing feature from the preceding models is the presence of fixed capital, even though the simplified assumption is made of a uniform ratio of fixed capital to labour ($k_i = k$ in (3)). Solving again any one of the price equations for r, we have:

$$r = \frac{\dfrac{p_i}{n_i} - \Sigma p_i \bar{x}_i}{p_m k + \Sigma p_i \bar{x}_i} \tag{15}$$

The numerator of (15) represents, as in (13), the value of the net output of one labourer above subsistence (profits per labourer), while the denominator is the value of all the means of production employed − the sum of the value of the k machines with which each worker must be equipped (fixed capital) and the value of the advances to each labourer (circulating capital).

As also in this case the labour theory of value holds true, (15) may be rewritten as:

$$r = \frac{1 - \Sigma n_i \bar{x}_i}{n_m k + \Sigma n_i \bar{x}_i} \tag{16}$$

The numerator of (16) remains formally unchanged with respect to (14) and (12); the denominator, on the contrary, now consists of the quantity of labour that must be used (*together with the appropriate amount of fixed capital*) to produce the machines k and the necessaries $\bar{x}_i$ with which each labourer must be equipped and supported.

As in (14), r is expressed as a ratio between two quantities of labour ('labour . . . appear[s] on both sides of the account . . . both as input and output'), but the amounts of labour involved are not those indicated by Sraffa. For this purpose, two cases can be distinguished according to the meaning that may be attributed to Sraffa's expression of 'labour required to produce the necessaries'.

The first alternative is to interpret this notion as referring to the quantity of *direct* labour − obviously to be assisted by machines in the model here considered − necessary to produce the advances for one labourer ($\Sigma n_i \bar{x}_i$). The numerator of (16) would then represent the excess of the quantity of labour supplied by each worker over that quantity which − given the technical conditions of production − is necessary to bestow directly for the production of the subsistence wage. The denominator of (16) would not, however, coincide with the concept of (direct) 'labour required to produce the necessaries', because in addition to the term $\Sigma n_i \bar{x}_i$ we now have also the term $n_m k$.

The second alternative is to interpret the concept of 'required' labour used by Sraffa as referring to the quantity of both direct and indirect labour necessary to produce the real wage – where indirect labour may be defined, with Marx, as consisting of the quantity of labour 'embodied' in the machines that are used up in the production of the subsistence basket.

As in our model machines are supposed to be non-perishable, we may say that their current and repeated use does not reduce their efficiency. No transfer of a fraction of the quantity of labour embodied in the machines to the value of the wage basket can be said to occur. The concept of indirect labour appears, therefore, difficult to grasp in this context.

If, on the other hand, depreciation of machines were allowed for, e.g. in the form of 'radioactive decay', the concept of indirect labour necessary to produce the subsistence wage could be identified with the depreciation of machines, i.e. with the fraction of machines used up in current production. (Circulating capital clearly represents the 'extreme case' where value is entirely transferred to the final product and 'depreciation' is equal to one.) Neither in this case, however, would Sraffa's definition coincide with the result of this new version of the price model.

Indeed, in the case now considered the definition of the rate of profit corresponding to (16) would require in the numerator a further deduction besides the quantity of labour necessary to produce the wage basket – the quantity of labour necessary to replace the fraction of machines used up in the production of that wage basket. No change with respect to (16) would occur in the denominator.

When Sraffa's concept of 'required' labour is taken to refer to the quantity of direct and indirect labour (in the sense defined above) necessary to produce the wage basket, his definition of the profit rate would diverge from the appropriately modified (16). While the numerator would be the same, a difference would emerge in the denominator, where, for Sraffa, depreciation (i.e. a fraction of the value of the k machines necessary to equip one labourer) would appear instead of the total value of these k machines.

It may be said in conclusion that Sraffa's interpretation of Ricardo's theory of the rate of profit in the *Principles* thus appears to be: (i) not valid in the general case, i.e. when the ratios of fixed capital to labour are different; and (ii) inapplicable to the case of a uniform ratio of fixed capital to labour. This latter circumstance seems to be of particular significance as it means that Sraffa's definition of the rate of profit as 'the ratio of the total labour of the country to the labour required to produce the necessaries of that labour' does not apply to *all* the cases of validity of the labour theory of value.

(iii) The existence of a unique significant solution for the model (1), (3) and (4a) has direct relevance for the delicate problem of the relation between distribution and measurement. The risk of circularity − certainly present in Ricardo's reflections and in some of the interpretations of the development of his analysis − is proved to be only apparent. The problems relating to the determination of the rate of profit and to its behaviour can find an unambiguous answer on the basis of the simultaneous solution of the price model.

It may be useful to add that this conclusion carries no implications as to the neoclassical character of the solution arrived at. It moves instead within the 'classical' framework of value and distribution, whose general feature is that income distribution is not part of the general pricing process.[34]

The distinguishing feature of the classical, as opposed to the neoclassical, approach is represented in fact by the idea that one of the two distributive variables (w or r) is taken from outside the model as a socio-historical datum. If this variable is the wage rate, two roads are opened for the solution of the model: (i) the *aggregative approach* in which the determination of the rate of profit − and thus the definition of the entire distributive set-up − precedes that of prices; (ii) the *simultaneous approach*, in which the rate of profit and prices are determined *together* as parts of the simultaneous solution of the model.[35] While Ricardo's *corn model* and Sraffa's scheme with the choice of the standard commodity as *numéraire* belong to the former approach, the type of solution of the general Ricardian price model arrived at here clearly moves within the latter approach.

To sum up, it may be said that Ricardo's theoretical framework contains all the elements that appear to be necessary for the analytical definition of the central issue of his investigation − the long-term behaviour of the rate of profit on the assumption that a key sector of the economy operates under the law of diminishing returns. His ingenious attempts to overcome (through the construction of a perfect standard of measurement) the limitations of the labour theory of value seem, therefore, to stem, as we have stressed above, from his incomplete awareness of the analytical implications of his own theoretical model.

2.10 Technological improvements and the declining rate of profit

The inverse relation between the rate of profit and diminishing returns in agriculture may be taken to represent, as we have repeatedly pointed out, Ricardo's main conclusion on the issue of the long-term prospects of a capitalist system, whose essential features were meant to depict England's economy at the time of the industrial revolution.

This conclusion clearly implies an important underestimation of the role of technological improvements which for Ricardo could only postpone, but not avoid, the final outcome of the stationary state. The label of 'pessimist' pinned on Ricardo originates from this circumstance. The stand he took in the debate on the corn laws may, however, help to clarify the real meaning of his thesis about the final outcome of the capitalist economy. In Ricardo's argument the idea is implicit that the adoption of the free-trade measures for the import of corn advocated by him might have changed the foreseeable sequence of events and made it possible for the process of economic growth — presumably based on the expansion of the industrial sector — to continue indefinitely. His pessimism may thus be viewed as playing an 'instrumental' role in the policy debate he was engaged in.

The profit equation, derived on the assumption that no technological progress takes place in the economy, is — as we mentioned — a tool of comparative statics because it defines alternative combinations of the rate of profit and of the labour input of corn. With the assumption of diminishing returns in mind, this equation acquires a substantially dynamic meaning in that it clearly implies the direction of movement of the rate of profit.

The exact definition of the time path of this variable (as well as of the other variables of the system) requires, however, the use of a truly dynamic model in which the sequence of events can be analysed and the feed-back effect of accumulation on diminishing returns fully appreciated. This type of analysis may be viewed, for the aspect referring to the definition of the natural equilibrium path, as an explanation of the movement of the system along the 'profit equation' associated with the specific versions of the Ricardian dynamic model considered in Part II.

Appendix   Properties of the Ricardian price model

Existence and uniqueness of the solution

Substituting the definition (1) of the money wage rate in the price equations (3) (as already done in the equations (10) of section 2.8), the Ricardian price model can be conveniently expressed in matrix notation as follows:

$$p[\lambda I - D(\lambda)A] = 0 \tag{A.1}$$

$$p_2 = n_2 \tag{A.2}$$

where p is a $(1 \times m)$ vector of commodity prices, λ is the scalar

$$\lambda = \frac{1}{1+r} \tag{A.3}$$

and A and $D(\lambda)$ are the $(m \times m)$ square matrices:

$$A = \begin{bmatrix} n_1\bar{x}_1 & n_2\bar{x}_1 & \dots & n_m\bar{x}_1 \\ n_1\bar{x}_2 & n_2\bar{x}_2 & \dots & n_m\bar{x}_2 \\ \cdot & \cdot & & \cdot \\ \cdot & \cdot & & \cdot \\ \cdot & \cdot & & \cdot \\ n_1k_1 & n_2k_2 & \dots & n_mk_m \end{bmatrix} \tag{A.4}$$

$$D(\lambda) = \begin{bmatrix} 1 & 0 & \dots & & 0 \\ 0 & 1 & \dots & & 0 \\ \cdot & \cdot & & & \cdot \\ \cdot & \cdot & & & \cdot \\ \cdot & \cdot & & & \cdot \\ 0 & 0 & \dots & & (1-\lambda) \end{bmatrix} \tag{A.5}$$

Let us recall that the system of m equations (A.1) defines, for each one of the m commodities considered ($m - 1$ consumption goods and *one* capital good), prices as equal to the corresponding costs of production, given the assumption of a uniform rate of profit; and that (A.2) specifies the choice of *numéraire*. The unknowns of the model are the price vector p and the scalar λ, which is related to the rate of profit r through the definition (A.3).

The condition for the solution to be economically meaningful is that prices and the rate of profit should be non-negative. Taking account of (A.3), the non-negativity constraint on r is transformed into a constraint on λ, which must assume values in the closed interval $[0,1]$.

To prove the existence and the uniqueness of the solution, it is convenient to rewrite (A.1) in the form

$$p[\mu I - D(\lambda)A] = 0 \qquad (A.6)$$

where μ is the eigen value of the matrix $D(\lambda)A$ for given λ.

Let us consider n_1 as given. A is by definition a non-negative indecomposable matrix so that, for λ in the interval $[0, 1]$, also $D(\lambda)A$ is a non-negative indecomposable matrix. We can therefore conclude, on the basis of Perron–Frobenius theorems,[36] that the dominant root of $D(\lambda)A$ — which we shall indicate as $\mu(\lambda; n_1)$ — is positive and that the characteristic vector associated with this root is also positive. The existence of an economically meaningful characteristic vector of prices satisfying (A.1) and (A.2) thus depends on the existence of a fixed point for the mapping $\mu(\lambda; n_1)$ in the interval $[0, 1]$.

Note, first of all, that $\mu(\lambda; n_1)$ is a continuous and increasing function of the elements of $D(\lambda)A$. We have therefore from (A.4) and (A.5):

$$\frac{\partial \mu(\lambda; n_1)}{\partial \lambda} < 0 \qquad (A.7)$$

$$\frac{\partial \mu(\lambda; n_1)}{\partial n_1} > 0 \qquad (A.8)$$

Let us then determine the values of $\mu(\lambda; n_1)$ corresponding to the extreme points (zero and one) of the interval of admissible values of λ, so that we define the range of possible values of $\mu(\lambda; n_1)$.

For $\lambda = 0, D(0)A = A$. $\mu(0; n_1)$ is the dominant root of A and we know it is positive.

For $\lambda = 1$, we have

$$D(1)A = \begin{bmatrix} n_1 \bar{x}_1 & n_2 \bar{x}_1 & \dots & n_m \bar{x}_1 \\ n_1 \bar{x}_2 & n_2 \bar{x}_2 & \dots & n_m \bar{x}_2 \\ . & . & & . \\ . & . & & . \\ . & . & & . \\ 0 & 0 & \dots & 0 \end{bmatrix} \qquad (A.9)$$

The characteristic equation of this matrix is:[37]

$$\phi(\mu) = (-\mu)^m + (-\mu)^{m-1} \sum_{i=1}^{m} b_{ii} + (-\mu)^{m-2} B_2 + \ldots$$
$$+ (-\mu)B_{m-1} + B_m \tag{A.10}$$

where for convenience we have set $D(1)A = B = [b_{ij}]$ and denoted as B_s $(s = 2, \ldots, m)$ the sum of the sth order minors of B, with $B_m =$ determinant (B).

Since the rank of $D(1)A$ is one, all the minors of order greater than one are nil. The characteristic equation thus turns out to be

$$\phi(\mu) = (-\mu)^m + (-\mu)^{m-1} \sum_{i=1}^{m-1} n_i \bar{x}_i \tag{A.11}$$

The characteristic roots of $D(1)A$ are then $\mu = 0$, with nullity $m - 1$, and

$$\mu(1; n_1) = \sum_{i=1}^{m-1} n_i \bar{x}_i \tag{A.12}$$

which is clearly the dominant root.

This means that if the condition

$$\sum_{i=1}^{m-1} n_i \bar{x}_i \leqslant 1 \tag{A.13}$$

is satisfied, $\mu(\lambda; n_1)$ has a unique fixed point[38] in the interval $[0, 1]$ — as illustrated in Figure 1 — and there exists, therefore, a unique (economically meaningful) solution of the system of equations (A.1)–(A.2).

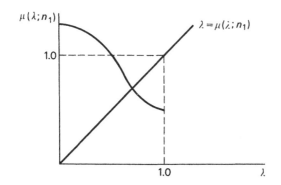

Figure 1

The economic interpretation of the constraint (A.13) is quite straightforward. Since $\Sigma n_i \bar{x}_i$ is the quantity of (assisted) labour required to produce the necessaries for each labourer, (A.13) simply states a condition for the economy to be 'viable'. For a (closed) economy cannot be viable unless the quantity of labour supplied by each worker (the unit of labour) is at least equal to the quantity of labour required to produce the necessaries for the same worker. More specifically, when the quantity of labour required to produce the necessaries is less than one, the technological structure of production implies the existence of a surplus and thus of positive profits. When, on the contrary, the quantity of labour required to produce the necessaries is exactly equal to one, no such surplus exists and profits are accordingly nil. In this latter case, as (A.12) shows, the fixed point of the function $\mu(\lambda; n_1)$ is $\lambda = 1$.

Inverse relation between r and n_1

The proof of the proposition that there exists an inverse relation between the rate of profit and the labour input in the production of corn is already contained in the derivative (A.8). This shows that the dominant root of the matrix $D(\lambda)A$ is positively related to n_1. Taking then into account the definition (A. 3), the inverse relation between r and n_1 is established.

An intuitive explanation of the direction of movement in the process of growth can be proposed with reference to Figure 1. As (A. 8) shows, a rise in n_1 is associated – in the plane $[\lambda, \mu(\lambda; n_1)]$ – with a shift to the right of the function $\mu(\lambda; n_1)$. This implies that the fixed point of $\mu(\lambda; n_1)$ moves, so to speak, over time along the 45-degree line, finally reaching – with the progressive increase of n_1 – the point $\lambda = 1$ (i.e. $r = 0$), in which the movement (process of growth) comes to an end.

Inverse relation between r and w

To prove the existence of an inverse relation between the rate of profit and the wage rate, let us rewrite equation (8) of section 2.6 as

$$1 = (1 + r)w\frac{f(r)}{g(r)} \tag{A.14}$$

where

$$f(f) = 1 + rn_m (k_2 - k_m) \tag{A.15}$$

$$g(r) = 1 - rn_m k_m \tag{A.16}$$

These definitions show that the condition for the wage rate to be positive is $g(r) > 0$, which implies $0 \leqslant r < 1/n_m k_m$. For r in this interval the price of machines

$$p_m = \frac{(1+r)n_m w}{1 - r n_m k_m}$$

is also positive, and so are the prices of all other commodities. The value $r = 1/n_m k_m$ must be excluded from the range of the admissible values of r, as in this case the price of machines (and all other prices) would become indeterminate. Note, furthermore, that $w = 1$ when $r = 0$, and that w tends to zero as r tends to $1/n_m k_m$.

The derivative of r with respect to w is

$$\frac{dr}{dw} = -\frac{1}{w\left[\dfrac{1}{1+r} + \dfrac{f'(r)g(r) - f(r)g'(r)}{f(r)g(r)}\right]} \qquad (A.17)$$

where $f'(r)$ and $g'(r)$ denote the first derivatives of the corresponding functions. The derivative in (A.17) is certainly negative if

$$f'(r)g(r) - f(r)g'(r) > 0 \qquad (A.18)$$

With appropriate substitutions from (A.15) and (A.16) in (A.18), we have

$$n_m (k_2 - k_m)(1 - r n_m k_m) + [1 + r n_m (k_2 - k_m)] n_m k_m$$
$$= n_m k_2 > 0 \qquad (A.19)$$

We can conclude, therefore, that dr/dw is always negative.

Effects on prices of a change in w

The price equations (3) of section 2.4 can be rewritten in matrix notation as

$$p[I - rC] = (1+r)wn \qquad (A.20)$$

where n is the $(1 \times m)$ vector of labour inputs n_i and C is the $(m \times m)$ matrix

$$C = \begin{bmatrix} 0 & 0 & \ldots & 0 \\ 0 & 0 & \ldots & 0 \\ \cdot & \cdot & & \cdot \\ \cdot & \cdot & & \cdot \\ \cdot & \cdot & & \cdot \\ n_1 k_1 & n_2 k_2 & \ldots & n_m k_m \end{bmatrix} \qquad (A.21)$$

For $0 \leqslant r < 1/n_m k_m$, the matrix $[I - rC]$ is non-singular and, on account of Perron–Frobenius theorems, the elements of the inverse $[I - rC]^{-1}$ are non-negative. There exists, therefore, a non-negative price vector satisfying (A.20), namely

$$p = (1 + r)wn \, [I - rC]^{-1} \tag{A.22}$$

Taking the derivative of (A.22) with respect to w, we have

$$\frac{dp}{dw} = (1 + r)n \, [I - rC]^{-1} + w \, \{n[I - rC]^{-1} + $$

$$(1 + r)n \, [I - rC]^{-1} C[I - rC]^{-1}\} \, \frac{dr}{dw} \tag{A.23}$$

where $\{n[I - rC]^{-1}\}$ and $\{n[I - rC]^{-1} C \, [I - rC]^{-1}\}$ are $(1 \times m)$ row vectors with elements

$$\left[n_i \left(1 + \frac{rn_m k_i}{1 - rn_m k_m} \right) \right] \quad \text{and} \quad \left[n_m \frac{n_i k_i}{(1 - rn_m k_m)^2} \right]$$

respectively.

Let us now consider the ith derivative in (A.23), which is

$$\frac{dp_i}{dw} = n_i \left(1 + \frac{rn_m k_i}{g(r)} \right)$$

$$\left\{ (1 + r) + w \left[1 + (1 + r) \frac{n_m k_i}{f_i(r)g(r)} \right] \frac{dr}{dw} \right\} \tag{A.24}$$

where $g(r)$ is defined as in (A.16), and, with obvious extension of (A.15) to any commodity i,

$$f_i(r) = 1 + rn_m \, (k_i - k_m) \tag{A.25}$$

so that (A.15) is now to be read as $f_2 (r)$.

Substituting in (A.24) for dr/dw from (A.17) and taking account of (A.19), we have

$$\text{sign} \left\{ \frac{dp_i}{dw} \right\} = \text{sign} \left\{ (1 + r) - w \left[1 + (1 + r) \frac{n_m k_i}{f_i(r)g(r)} \right] \right.$$

$$\left. \cdot \frac{1}{w \left[\dfrac{1}{1 + r} + \dfrac{n_m k_2}{f_2 (r)g(r)} \right]} \right\}$$

$$= \text{sign} \, \{k_2 f_i(r) - k_i f_2 (r)\} = \text{sign} \, \{(k_2 - k_i)g(r)\}$$

$$= \text{sign} \, \{k_2 - k_i\} \tag{A.26}$$

This shows, as already mentioned in section 2.7, that a rise in money wages determines an increase in the price of the commodities produced with a technique more capital intensive than that of the *numéraire* and, conversely, a decrease in the price of the commodities produced with a technique less capital intensive than that of the *numéraire*.[39] It is clear, as (A.26) confirms, that the price of the *numéraire* is invariant to changes in the money wage rate, that is in distribution.

3 Sraffa's standard commodity and Ricardo's theory of value and distribution

3.1 Ricardo's search for an invariable standard of value

The results arrived at in the preceding chapter show that the central problem of the Ricardian theoretical investigation — the relation between technology and the rate of profit — finds a general solution subject to none of the limitations typical of the labour theory of value. As it has been maintained, Ricardo, however, was not fully aware of the analytical implications of his own model and was therefore unable to reach the general results he was aiming for.

An unambiguous answer to his problem could have been obtained with the labour theory of value — had this theory attained general validity. In this case, as equation (16) of Chapter 2 clearly shows, the rate of profit would have turned out to be a ratio between two quantities of labour, and its connection with diminishing returns could have been immediately established — for an increase in n_1 would have implied a parallel increase in the money wage expressed in terms of labour, leading to a reduction in the value of net output above subsistence and to a rise in the value of circulating capital, both measured in terms of labour.

Ricardo certainly considered the labour theory of value a good approximation to a valid analytical construction and thus as an acceptable tool for the interpretation of the real world (Ricardo (68), pp. 36–7):

> In estimating . . . the causes of the variations in the value of commodities, although it would be wrong wholly to omit the consideration of the effect produced by a rise or fall of labour, it would be equally incorrect to attach much importance to it; and consequently . . . though I shall occasionally refer to this cause of variation, I shall consider all the great variations which take place in the relative value of commodities to be produced by the greater

or less quantity of labour which may be required from time to time to produce them.

But at the same time – as we have mentioned in section 2.3 of Chapter 2 – Ricardo was fully aware of the limitations of the labour theory of value *on the analytical plane*. Sections 4 and 5 of the chapter 'On value' of the *Principles* are devoted precisely to the discussion of the 'considerable modifications' of the principle that relative prices are regulated only by the quantities of labour bestowed on the production of commodities.

Thus it seems plausible to argue that Ricardo's efforts to define an invariable measure of value stem from his awareness of these logical difficulties and aim at restoring general validity to the proposition that exchange values are determined solely by relative labour inputs. The role envisaged by Ricardo for the perfect standard of value was, in other words, that of establishing in general the same straightforward connection between diminishing returns and the rate of profit – to the exclusion of the 'confusing' effects of movements in relative prices due to changes in distribution consequent upon technological changes occurring in agriculture – that the labour theory of value made possible, in its limited sphere of validity.

3.2 The requisites of the invariable measure of value

Mention has already been made to the requisites of the invariable standard in the context of the discussion of the relation between changes in money wages and the rate of profit as an essentially dynamic issue in the Ricardian theoretical framework.[1] The problem must now be examined in greater detail.

Two requisites of the standard of measurement are clearly indicated by Ricardo in section 6 of his chapter 'On value' in the context of the argument aiming to point out the difficulties involved in the definition of a perfect standard of value. The first is that the commodity to be chosen as 'measuring rod' should at all times require for its production the same quantity of labour. The second is that this commodity should be such as to make the prices of the other commodities (expressed in terms of this unit of measurement) invariant to changes in distribution (Ricardo (68), pp. 43–4, italics added):

> [The] invariable standard measure of value . . . should itself be subject to none of the fluctuations to which other commodities are exposed. Of such a measure it is impossible to be possessed,

because there is no commodity which is not itself exposed to the same variations as the things, the value of which is to be ascertained; that is, there is none which is not subject to require more or less labour for its production. But if this cause of variation in the value of a medium could be removed – if it were possible that in the. production of our money, for instance, the same quantity of labour should at all times be required, still it would not be a perfect standard or invariable measure of value, because, as I have already endeavoured to explain, it would be subject to *relative* variations from a rise or fall of wages, on account of the different proportions of fixed capital which might be necessary to produce it, and to produce those other commodities whose alteration of value we wished to ascertain.

Differences in the degree of durability of fixed capital and in the time required to bring the commodities to the market obviously imply, as Ricardo points out, the same type of difficulties.

With reference to the second requisite of the measure of value, Ricardo points out that any commodity – gold for instance (Ricardo (68), p. 45) – 'would be a perfect measure of value for all things produced under the same circumstances [i.e. with the same combination of fixed and circulating capital] precisely as itself, but for no others'.

The difficulties encountered by Ricardo in the definition of the invariable standard of value – from the point of view of the possibility of eliminating the 'disturbances' which originate in the sphere of distribution – thus turn out to be exactly of the same nature as those preventing the labour theory of value from attaining general validity. It may therefore appear curious that Ricardo's attempt to. overcome the limitations of the labour theory of value should be based on the construction of an analytical tool exposed to the same type of criticism. The point is lucidly stressed by Sraffa ((85), p. xli): 'the same exceptions which he had discovered in the fundamental rule determining value cropped up again in attempting to define the qualities of an invariable standard'.

Ricardo in fact draws from his argument the only possible and correct analytical conclusion (Ricardo (68), p. 45): 'Neither gold then, nor any other commodity, can ever be a perfect measure of value for all things.'

The awareness of the impossibility of defining a perfect measure of value induces Ricardo to settle on an approximate solution for his problem (Ricardo (68), p. 45):

I have already remarked, that the effect on the relative prices of things, from a variation in profits, is comparatively slight; that by

far the most important effects are produced by the varying
quantities of labour required for production; and therefore, if
we suppose this important cause of variation removed from the production of gold, we shall probably possess as near an approximation to a standard measure of value as can be theoretically
conceived.

The impossibility of satisfying the second of the 'requisites' of a
perfect standard of value thus leads Ricardo to concentrate on the
first and to accept as an adequate (not perfect) measure a commodity
produced at all times with the same quantity of labour. The invariance
of the standard of value accepted by Ricardo refers, therefore, only
to the technological conditions of production of the standard itself.
The conclusion is (Ricardo (68), p. 46):

although I fully allow that money made of gold is subject to most
of the variations of other things, I shall suppose it to be invariable,
and therefore all alterations in price to be occasioned by some
alteration in the value of the commodity of which I may be
speaking.

Ricardo also points out that the commodity (gold) chosen as
numéraire should have the property of being produced with a degree
of capital intensity equal to the 'social average'. This property, which
has already been mentioned in the discussion of the effects on prices
of changes in money wages, plays the role of minimizing the 'deviations
from truth' (Ricardo (69), p. 405) occasioned by changes in distribution. For the choice of one of the two extremes – 'the one where
little fixed capital is used, the other where little labour is employed'
(Ricardo (68), pp. 45-6) – would obviously magnify the deviations
of relative prices from the ratios between labour inputs.

With the addition of the emphasis on the notion of *absolute value* –
the quantity of labour required for the production of commodities –
Ricardo's position on the issue of the invariable measure of value is
fully retained in his unfinished 1823 essay on *Absolute Value and
Exchangeable Value* ((69), p. 404):

It must then be confessed that there is no such thing in nature as
a perfect measure of value, and that all that is left to the Political
Economist is to admit that the great cause of the variation of commodities is the greater or less quantity of labour that may be necessary to produce them.

This proposition, concerning the impossibility of having a perfect
measure of value, is followed by the repetition of the idea that the
acceptable measure should be a 'mean between the two extremes of
commodities produced on one side by labour and advances for much

more than a year, and the other by labour employed for a day only without any advances' (Ricardo (69), p. 405).

Ricardo's search for the invariable measure of value is thus unsuccessful. The aim to restore in the general case the simple relation between technology and the rate of profit, which is obtained when the labour theory of value holds true, is not achieved. The reason for this failure is clearly analysed by Ricardo. It is represented by the logical impossibility of defining a commodity such that relative prices, when measured in terms of it, are not affected by the changes in distribution ensuing from the working of diminishing returns.

The difficulties encountered by Ricardo led him, as we have seen, to give up the search for a measure of value fulfilling the second requisite — namely, the invariance of relative prices with respect to changes in distribution — and to settle on a *numéraire* invariant only with respect to its own technology. It is clear, however, that this type of standard is logically *acceptable* only if we ultimately believe that relative prices are regulated exclusively by relative labour inputs, i.e. only if we are convinced that the labour theory of value is valid. But in this case the problem itself of the search for an invariable measure of value would disappear, since the relation between technology and the rate of profit would be straightforward, undisturbed by distribution effects working through the prices of commodities.

If, on the other hand, one recognizes, as Ricardo does, the existence of 'deviations' from labour values, it is quite difficult to understand what is the analytical role of an 'admittedly imperfect standard'; for the adoption of such a standard would *not* make it possible to obtain a direct relation between diminishing returns and the rate of profit similar to equation (16) of Chapter 2. The problem is, in other words, unresolvable. The very reasons from which it originates are those which prevent it from finding a solution.

The analytical difficulties met by Ricardo in his search for an invariable measure of value are at the origin of Sraffa's reflections on the 'contradictory' nature of the whole question. It is to the examination of this issue that the following section is addressed.

3.3 The invariable measure of value in the interpretation of Sraffa's 'Introduction'

As we have mentioned in Chapter 2 (section 2.2), Sraffa's 'Introduction' supplies the basis of an interpretation according to which the two requisites indicated by Ricardo for the invariable measure of value imply the existence of two separate analytical problems – an interpretation which we have maintained is in contrast with Ricardo's main line of theoretical investigation, centred upon the notion of natural equilibrium.

The key passages of Sraffa's 'Introduction' on which the above-mentioned interpretation is constructed are the following (Sraffa (85), pp. xlvi–xlvii):

Ricardo starts (in ed. 1 of the *Principles*) by applying the concept [of absolute value] to the problem of two commodities which have changed in relative value as a result of a change in the difficulty of production: absolute value is then the criterion for deciding in which of the two the real change has occurred. He ends (in his last paper on value) by bringing this criterion to bear upon another problem, namely the distinction between two causes of changes in exchangeable value: for, 'difficulty or facility of production is not absolutely the only cause of variation in value [,] there is one other, the rise or fall of wages', since commodities cannot 'be produced and brought to market in precisely the same time'. Absolute value, however, reflects only the first type of change and is not affected by the latter. . . .

In his attempt to extend the application of absolute value to the second problem (that of distinguishing the two sorts of changes in exchangeable values) Ricardo was confronted with this dilemma: whereas the former application presupposes an exact proportionality between relative and absolute value, the latter implies a variable deviation of exchangeable from absolute value for each individual commodity. This contradiction Ricardo never completely succeeded in resolving.

The thesis of the *contradiction* is based on the idea that the two problems – (i) that of ascertaining in which of the two commodities (whose relative values have changed) the variation in technology has occurred, and (ii) that of distinguishing this cause of change in relative prices from the other cause, changes in distribution – are logically autonomous. It consequently implies that the problem of the effect on relative prices of changes in distribution can be posed in Ricardo independently of changes in technology and, on the other hand, that the question of variations in the difficulties of production can be raised independently of changes in distribution. A solution, if any, of these allegedly separate problems must, then, be searched for along different lines.

Some passages of Ricardo's writings undoubtedly seem to support the view that he considered the effects of changes in distribution unaccompanied by changes in the techniques of production. In section

4 of the chapter 'On value' of the *Principles*, he writes (Ricardo (68), p. 45):

> every alteration in the permanent rate of profit would have some effect on the relative value of all these goods [the commodities produced with either a less or a greater proportion of fixed capital with respect to the *numéraire* gold], independently of any alteration in the quantity of labour employed on their production.

In a draft letter of 15 August 1823 to McCulloch, Ricardo says (Sraffa (84), vol. 9, pp. 355–6):[2]

> The two commodities change in relative value . . . . Can it be said that the proportions of capital we employ are in any way altered? or the proportion of labour? certainly not, nothing has altered but the rate of distribution between employer and employed . . . this and this only is the reason why they alter in relative value.

A similar concept is put forward in *Absolute Value and Exchangeable Value* (Ricardo (69), p. 403):

> if profits fell from 10 [per cent] to 5 [per cent], the proportions between the value of wine, of cloth and of shrimps [whose circumstances of production are supposed to be different] would alter accordingly, although no alteration whatever took place in the quantity of labour necessary to produce these commodities respectively.

Before commenting on these passages, it may be of some interest to note that in this context Ricardo seems to tackle the problem of changes in relative prices from a different point of view with respect to that which he takes in his main line of theoretical investigation. In the study of the long-term prospects of the economy, Ricardo's logical approach goes from changes in technology, which are assumed to be known (diminishing returns in agriculture), to the determination of relative prices, of the rate of profit and of the rate of accumulation. When discussing the question of the invariable measure of value, Ricardo, instead, appears to take as the starting-point of his reasoning a change in relative prices; he then seems to pose the question of ascertaining in which of the two commodities the technological change (i.e. variation in the quantity of labour needed to produce it) has occurred. In other words, while his main theoretical argument runs from technology to relative prices (and to profits), Ricardo's line of thought seems here to run in the opposite direction, from relative prices to technology (Ricardo (68), p. 43, itálics added):

> *When commodities varied in relative value*, it would be desirable to have the means of *ascertaining which of them fell and which rose in real value*, and this could be effected only by comparing them one after another with some invariable standard measure of value.

This fact should not be interpreted to imply that Ricardo, when discussing the invariable measure of value, opened a new line of theoretical investigation, totally different — indeed opposite — with respect to that started in the *Essay on Profits* and consistently carried on in the *Principles*. It is, on the contrary, to be viewed solely as a logical step in the construction of an analytical tool — the invariable standard — which should, in his intentions, perform the task of isolating changes in the circumstances of production (net of the disturbing effects of changes in distribution).

Reverting to Sraffa's thesis of the 'contradiction', let us now consider its first implication: that the effect on relative prices of changes in distribution can be posed in Ricardo independently of changes in technology. As to the general validity of this approach, it seems necessary to recall, as has been shown in Chapter 2, that the Ricardian price model defines, for each state of technology (i.e. for each given level of the labour input in agriculture), a unique natural equilibrium solution for the prices of commodities and for the distributive variables — given the bundle of commodities constituting the real wage of the labourers. Changes in distribution cannot therefore be envisaged in the context of the natural equilibrium positions of the economy but rather as a consequence of changes in technology.

With this general warning in mind, the above-cited passages in which Ricardo seems to consider the possibility of changes in distribution unaccompanied by changes in technology can be interpreted in two different ways: one fully compatible with the Ricardian natural equilibrium analysis, the other lying totally outside this type of approach.

Within the natural equilibrium context, the situation considered by Ricardo can be easily comprehended on the basis of the distinction, crucial for Ricardo, of commodities produced under conditions of diminishing returns and commodities characterized by constant returns to scale. A change in the relative price of two commodities, neither of which has experienced a change in the circumstances of production, can thus emerge as a consequence of a change in technology of a third commodity; for if we suppose that Ricardo had in mind two non-agricultural commodities, a change in their relative price can occur in general as a consequence of the variation in distribution brought about by the assumed change in the conditions of production of 'corn'. The only instance in which this would not occur is when the two non-agricultural commodities are produced exactly under the same technological conditions, i.e. in terms of our price model with

61

the same ratio of fixed capital to labour. This instance being the exception, the situation envisaged by Ricardo — the possibility of a modification in the relative prices of commodities produced in conditions of constant returns — should then be considered the normal outcome of the working of diminishing returns in agriculture. It is clear that this outcome is fully consistent with the idea that each state of technology generates a unique set of natural equilibrium values of prices and distributive variables.

In this perspective Ricardo's cited propositions cannot be taken to mean that he had in mind a situation in which changes in relative prices could take place without *any* change in technology, i.e. as a consequence of *pure* distributive effects. In other words, the situation described by Ricardo is only apparently the outcome of a pure change in distribution; it is, in fact, the ultimate outcome of a phenomenon originating in a technological change that takes place *elsewhere* in the economy and the impact of which is transmitted on all relative prices via changes in distribution.

If, on the contrary, changes in technology of *all* commodities are, by definition, ruled out, the possibility of alternative values of the distributive variables would depend on the admissibility of alternative levels of the *real* wage. This, however, as we pointed out in the preceding chapters,[3] clearly conflicts with the Ricardian notion of a given subsistence wage — which is central to the concept of natural equilibrium. The study of 'changes' in distribution unaccompanied by changes in technology — though conceivable in a Sraffa-type static framework of analysis — would therefore lie outside Ricardo's main line of theoretical investigation.

The second implication of Sraffa's thesis of the 'contradiction' — that changes in technology can be considered independently of distribution — must, on the other hand, be equally ruled out, since the solution of the Ricardian price model makes it clear that variations in the condition of production imply, in general, changes in distribution. As Ricardo clearly perceived, the effect on relative prices of these changes in distribution cannot be eliminated; it is therefore impossible in general to isolate the effects of changes in technology from those in distribution.

In conclusion, while a 'contradiction' exists in Ricardo, as Sraffa points out, between absolute values (i.e. labour inputs) and relative values (i.e. relative prices, depending in general on the distributive variables as well as on the labour inputs), no clear-cut distinction seems to be possible between the problem of finding out where the change in the difficulty of production has taken place and the problem of distinguishing this cause of change in relative prices from that represented by changes in distribution. No 'contradiction' between these problems can thus be logically conceived. The substantial unity of the analytical question tackled by Ricardo does not permit the interpretation of the two requisites for the invariable measure of value as two separate analytical functions aimed at answering two separate analytical problems.

Ricardo correctly felt that the fundamental relation between diminishing returns in agriculture and the rate of profit somehow involved in general distribution effects working through the prices of commodities. This 'passage through distribution' could not, however, be achieved by means of a logical approach based upon the construction of an invariable measure of value. It should be effected, instead, through the 'simultaneous' solution of the whole price model.

3.4 Sraffa's standard commodity and Ricardo's invariable measure of value

The particular *numéraire* defined in *Production of Commodities* – the standard commodity – is considered by Sraffa as a 'development' of Ricardo's idea of the invariable measure of value (Sraffa (86), p. 94): 'The conception of a standard measure of value as a medium between two extremes . . . belongs to Ricardo and . . . the standard commodity . . . has been evolved from it'.

The idea that the standard commodity is to be viewed as staging a comeback of Ricardo's problems concerning the definition of an invariable standard and as a solution of these problems has been largely accepted in the literature. In Pasinetti's words ((66), pp. 18 and 120 respectively):

> The problem of the search for an 'invariable standard of value' was never solved by Ricardo. It may be of interest to add, however, that one of the most rigorous theoretical schemata of production . . . – that of Piero Sraffa – has recently sprung from precisely the attempt to solve this Ricardian problem.

> After a century and a half, Sraffa's standard commodity has . . . fulfilled Ricardo's dream of an 'invariable measure' of value.

The remaining part of the present chapter aims at clarifying, in the light of the arguments developed above, the relationship between Ricardo's measure of value and Sraffa's standard commodity. For this purpose, the relevant properties of the standard commodity will be first recalled; these properties will then be compared with Ricardo's requisites for an invariable measure; finally an attempt will be made to answer the question concerning the possibility of using the standard commodity in the analysis of the crucial Ricardian problem – the connection between technology and capital accumulation.

3.5 The standard system

Using matrix notation, Sraffa's standard system is expressed by the following equations:

$$[I - A]x^* = RAx^* \tag{1}$$
$$nx^* = 1 \tag{2}$$

where x^* is the column vector of gross physical outputs of the m single-product industries; n is the row vector of the direct labour coefficients; R is the physical rate of surplus for each of the m commodities (standard ratio); and A is the $(m \times m)$ indecomposable and non-negative matrix of inter-industry coefficients a_{ij}.

The m equations (1) define the standard system on the basis of the peculiar property of the uniformity of the rate of physical surplus R for each of the m goods – i.e. of the uniformity of the ratio between the net output of each commodity and the quantity of the same commodity used up in production in the system as a whole. With equation (2) the assumption is made that the total quantity of labour employed in the standard system is equal to one.

Perron-Frobenius theorems for non-negative square matrices guarantee the existence and uniqueness of a positive solution for the $m + 1$ unknown variables of the system (1)–(2), x^* and R.

The definition of the standard system implies that R represents 'also the rate by which the total product of the standard system exceeds its aggregate means of production, or the ratio of the net product to the means of production of the system' (Sraffa (86), p. 21). It follows for the standard system a relevant property typical, as we have seen, of Ricardo's *corn model* (Sraffa (86), ibid.):

> the possibility of speaking of a ratio between two collections of miscellaneous commodities without need of reducing them to the common measure of price arises of course from the circumstance that both collections are made up in the same proportions – from their being in fact quantities of the same composite commodity.

Let $y*$ be the gross quantity of the composite commodity produced by the standard system and $ay*$ be the quantity of the same composite commodity used up in production – where the 'technical coefficient' a obviously lies between zero and one. The standard ratio may then be expressed as

$$\frac{(1-a)y*}{ay*} = R \tag{3}$$

If the net standard product $(1 - a)y*$ is distributed between wages and profits, assigning to the former the proportion ω, (3) becomes

$$\frac{(1-\omega)(1-a)y*}{ay*} = R(1-\omega) \tag{4}$$

As the left-hand side of (4) is the rate of profit r of the standard system defined as a ratio between physical quantities,[4] (4) turns out to be a linear relation between the rate of profit and 'wages (as a proportion of the Standard net product)' (Sraffa (86), p. 22).

Taking now into account equation (2) and assuming that the *numéraire* is the net standard product, (4) becomes a linear relation between the rate of profit and the wage rate $w*$, i.e. the wage rate expressed as a proportion of the standard net product in physical terms $(1 - a)y*$:

$$r = R(1 - w*) \tag{5}$$

It is clear, as Sraffa points out ((86), ibid.), that '[s]uch a relation is of interest only if it can be shown that its application is not limited to the imaginary standard system but is capable of being extended to the actual economic system of observation'.

It is precisely this result that can be obtained with the choice of the standard net product as *numéraire* of the actual system. Simple manipulation[5] shows, in effect, that (5) holds true for the actual system represented by the price equations

$$p = (1 + r)pA + nw \tag{6}$$

and by the choice of *numéraire*

$$p[I - A]x* = 1 \tag{7}$$

The validity of (5) for the actual system implies that with this particular choice of the unit of measurement the relation between the rate of profit and the rate of wages appears to be defined independently of prices. (However, a warning on a possible limitation of this concept of 'independence' will be mentioned later.)

3.6 The intrinsic properties of the standard commodity

On the basis of the definitions given above, some intrinsic – i.e. not depending on its choice as *numéraire* of the system – analytical properties of the standard commodity can now be pointed out.

(i) The rate of physical surplus R defined above represents, as we have recalled, the ratio between net product and means of production for the standard system. The physical homogeneity of these quantities, consisting of the 'same composite commodity', implies that the ratio between the *value* of the net standard product and the *value* of its means of production is independent of prices and hence of distribution.

Multiplying (1) by p, we obtain:

$$R = \frac{p[I-A]x^*}{pAx^*} \tag{8}$$

In spite of it being defined here as a ratio between *values*, R is independent of prices because prices 'cancel out', as a consequence of the fact that the quantities of each commodity in the numerator and in the denominator are proportional. In Sraffa's words ((86), p. 21):

> The result [the definition of R as the ratio of the net product to the means of production of the system] would therefore not be affected by multiplying the individual component commodities by their prices. The ratio of the values of the two aggregates would inevitably be always equal to the ratio of the quantities of their several components. Nor, once the commodities had been multiplied by their prices, would the ratio be disturbed if those individual prices were to vary in all sorts of divergent ways. Thus in the Standard system the ratio of the net product to the means of production would remain the same whatever variations occurred in the division of the net product between wages and profits and whatever the consequent price changes.

The independence of R with respect to distribution is a relevant property that other commodities do not possess. This circumstance can be easily seen considering, for any commodity j, the ratio R_j between the price p_j and the value of the means of production required to produce a unit of the same commodity:

$$R_j = \frac{p_j}{\sum_i p_i a_{ij}} = \frac{1}{\sum_i \frac{p_i}{p_j} a_{ij}} \tag{9}$$

The dependence, in general, of relative prices on distribution implies for R_j the same type of dependence. The only instance in which this would not occur is clearly the case when the labour theory of value holds true.[6]

(ii) As Sraffa points out ((86), ch. 6), the prices of commodities can be expressed, in general, as 'dated quantities of labour':[7]

$$p = n[I - (1 + r)A]^{-1} w = nw + (1 + r)nAw +$$
$$(1 + r)^2 nA^2 w + \ldots \tag{10}$$

The quantities of labour $(n, nA, nA^2, \ldots)$ appearing in (10) do not exhibit any specific 'regularity', in the sense that the ratio between the quantity of labour employed in any one 'layer' and that employed in the successive 'layer' is not the same for the various stages of the sequence. The standard commodity, on the contrary, shows from this point of view the peculiar property that the quantity of labour employed in each layer of production is always equal to $1/(1 + R)$ times the quantity of labour employed in the preceding layer:[8]

$$p[I - A]x^* = \frac{R}{1+R} w \left[1 + \frac{1}{1+R}(1 + r) + \left(\frac{1}{1+R} \right)^2 (1 + r)^2 + \ldots \right] \tag{11}$$

The terms in square brackets denote the sequence of dated quantities of labour, with a first term (direct labour) equal to one in accordance with equation (2). It is clear that the regularity of the layers depends in particular on the assumed homogeneity between input and output for a given technology.

(iii) The regularity of the layers from the point of view of the quantity of labour employed finds, for the standard commodity, an immediate counterpart in the regularity of the layers from the point of view of the means of production. The value of the means of production directly required to produce the net standard output is pAx^*. To produce these means of production, a value of $pA(Ax^*)$ means of production is clearly necessary. From the definition (1) of the standard system, Ax^* is equal to $[1/(1 + R)]x^*$, so that

$$pA(Ax^*) = \frac{1}{1+R} pAx^* \tag{12}$$

with obvious extension to all other layers. This also means that the value of the means of production employed in each layer is always equal to $1/(1 + R)$ times the corresponding value in the preceding layer.

It clearly follows that the ratio of the value of the means of production to the quantity of labour − henceforth denoted by k_{sc} − is the same in all layers and is equal to

$$k_{sc} = pAx^*$$ (13)

3.7 The properties of the standard commodity *qua numéraire*

The analysis of the intrinsic properties of the standard commodity must now be supplemented with the consideration of some relevant properties obtaining for the standard commodity *when it is used as* numéraire *of the system.*

(i) The ratio of the value of the means of production to the labour employed in the standard system, which − as we have just mentioned − is equal to pAx^*, turns out to be constant and thus independent of distribution. As it can be immediately seen from (8), when $p[I − A]x^*$ is set equal to one, (13) becomes

$$k_{sc} = \frac{1}{R}$$ (14)

(ii) As we have mentioned with reference to (5), when the standard commodity is taken as *numéraire* of the system, the relation between the two distributive variables is particularly simple in that a given change of wages implies, independently of the initial value considered, the same change in the rate of profit.

This characteristic of the relation between w and r is not to be found when a different *numéraire* is chosen. In this case, a given change in wages is associated with a change *in the opposite direction* of the rate of profit, a change whose magnitude varies according to the initial value of the wage rate. In other words, the relation between w and r is, in general, not linear. It must be noted, however, that this circumstance does not imply that the inverse relation between the wage rate and the profit rate is, in the general case, incapable of being fully determined from the analytical point of view.

It can be easily seen with reference to (10) that, when any commodity i is chosen as *numéraire*, the relation between w and r is necessarily negatively sloped. If, for instance, commodity 1 is taken to be the unit of measurement, we have from (10):

$$1 = p_1 = n_1^0 w + (1 + r)n_1^1 w + (1 + r)^2 n_1^2 w + \ldots$$ (15)

where n_1^0 is the quantity of direct labour employed in the production of a unit of commodity 1, and $n_1^s (s = 1, 2, \ldots)$ is the quantity of labour required to produce the means of production needed in any one of the s layers in which the production of commodity 1 can be analysed. Since the right-hand side of (15) can be rewritten as $[f(r)]\, w$, where $f(r)$ is an increasing function of r because all the coefficients n_1^0 and n_1^s are positive, it is clear that dr/dw is negative.[9]

It may be of interest to compare the relation w–r obtained when the standard commodity is chosen as *numéraire* with that resulting from the choice of a different *numéraire* such as, for instance, commodity 1. When (15) is compared with (11) only one difference, apart from the methodological implications, can be perceived – namely the circumstance that the sequence of the dated quantities of labour is 'regular' in (11), and 'irregular' in (15). In other words, the coefficients appearing in (15) are not in general proportional to each other, while – as we have already pointed out – each dated quantity of labour in (11) is equal to a constant proportion of that employed in the preceding layer.

This fact does not justify, in our opinion, the claim (Pasinetti (66), pp. 118-20, and Eatwell (24), p. 545) of a difference in the *quality* of the results obtained in the two cases considered, and, therefore, the idea that the perception of the relation between the distributive variables is, without the standard commodity, 'disturbed' by 'the peculiarities of the methods of production of the *numéraire* – commodity' and instead free of any such disturbance when the standard commodity is taken as *numéraire*.[10] An unambiguous analysis of the distributive 'antagonism' between profits and wages is thus equally possible with the standard commodity and without it.

(iii) When the standard commodity is the *numéraire*, the standard system performs the same role as Ricardo's corn model. As we have seen in Chapter 2, Ricardo's corn model is built on the assumption of physical homogeneity between input and output in the agricultural sector when corn is the only wage-good. In this case the rate of profit can be determined in the corn-producing sector without any reference to prices (which will then adjust so as to make it possible for that rate of profit to prevail in all the other sectors of the economy) *independently of the choice of corn as* numéraire.

It has been maintained that Sraffa's construction of the standard system represents a generalization of Ricardo's corn model[11] to a multi-sector model in which physical homogeneity between input and output does not occur in any sector of the actual economy. The construction of a 'physical analogue' to the corn model requires that the output of the system, its means of production and the wages of labour be homogeneous. This requirement is met by the definition of the standard system with respect to the output and the produced means of production but – contrary to what happens in Ricardo's corn model – only when the net standard product is chosen as *numéraire* with respect to the wages of labour.[12] Since in Sraffa's model the wage cannot, in general, be expressed as a bundle of commodities with the same composition as the net standard product,[13] the requirement of homogeneity can only be met if the wage is expressed as a percentage of the value of the net standard product. This procedure clearly implies the choice of the net standard product as *numéraire*.

The analogy drawn here between Ricardo's corn model and Sraffa's standard system should not be taken to imply that the analytical role of the former is directed to the study of the Sraffa-type problem, i.e. of the effect on the rate of profit (and prices) of changes in real wages, given the state of technology. Clearly, the corn model can also be used to analyse this type of problem, but, as we maintained in Chapter 2, section 2.9, its main analytical function is that of making it possible to establish a straightforward connection between diminishing returns and the rate of profit, given the real wage. While this function belongs to the natural equilibrium approach, the role connected with the study of the Sraffa-type problem obviously does not.

(iv) The use of the standard commodity as a unit of measurement has a relevant methodological implication with regard to the process of solution of the price model. With reference to the distinction between the *aggregative* and the *simultaneous* approaches, mentioned in the preceding chapter,[14] it can be said that Sraffa's standard commodity makes it possible to determine the rate of profit (given the wage rate) prior to, and independently of, prices.[15] This result stems from the fact that the linear relation (5) between the distributive variables holds for the actual system as well, provided that the standard commodity is chosen as *numéraire*. The aggregative approach would thus consist of: (a) the determination of the rate of profit (given the wage rate) through (5), where R – as an 'expression' of technology – is known once the matrix A is given; and (b) the determination of the prices of commodities – given in this case the wage rate *and* the profit rate – through (6).

With reference to this methodological result, it seems, however, legitimate to raise the question of the logical role to be assigned to the 'institutional rules' of price determination.

It is clear, on the one hand, that the determination of the *w–r* relation in the standard system requires the prior definition of the rules according to which the payment of the productive resources (labour and produced means of production) is to be made. In other words, the rule must be defined as to the *anticipation or not* of this payment. Several possibilities can in fact be envisaged. It may be assumed (as in Ricardo and in Marx) that wages are paid at the outset of the productive process, or it may be supposed (as in Sraffa) that workers are paid *post factum*, participating with profit receivers in the division of the net output. The productive process may be further thought of as an instantaneous process (with no anticipation of the means of production), or as a process occurring through time (thus requiring the prior availability of the means of production). Although this latter alternative may be considered to be abstract (in that it appears highly unrealistic to suppose that the productive process can be carried out instantaneously), the former alternative is fully admissible; as we have mentioned, both possibilities have in fact been considered in the construction of economic models. It may thus be said that the 'institutional rule' regarding the payment of wages on which Sraffa's formulation of the price system is based is only one of the possible choices – though, in fact, the only choice consistent with Sraffa's notion of wages.

It is clear, on the other hand, that the 'institutional rules' adopted must be the same both for the standard and for the actual system, if the $w-r$ relation defined for the former is also to be found in the latter. If we introduce, for instance, in Sraffa's scheme the typically Ricardian and Marxian assumption that wages are anticipated, the relation between the distributive variables for the standard system ceases to be linear and becomes hyperbolic (Pasinetti (66), p. 132). The same hyperbolic relation is then found in the actual system, defined on the basis of the same 'institutional rules'.

Thus, in order to define the $w-r$ relation for the standard system a given set of 'institutional rules' must be assumed and, for the very same $w-r$ relation to hold in the actual system, it is necessary that the price equations be defined on the basis of the very same set of rules. If, then, each set of 'institutional rules' is associated with a specific $w-r$ relation independent of commodity prices and with a specific definition of prices for the actual system, it seems admissible to raise the question of the relevance of these 'institutional rules' as regards the *logical* problem of the independence of the rate of profit from prices. The answer would seem to depend upon the function assigned to these 'rules' in the model – namely, upon the choice between taking them as necessary *data* for the resolution of the problem and considering them as assumptions for the definition of which there exists a degree of freedom. The claim as to the independence of distribution from prices certainly would be valid in the first case but not in the second.

In this respect Pasinetti's argument about the autonomy of the 'physical quantity system' (standard system) and of the 'price system' (actual system) does not appear to be decisive (Pasinetti (66), p. 111):

> the system of prices and the system of physical quantities are two separate systems, neither of which carries any implications for the other. The standard system, for example, is a logical construction which relates to physical quantities and which implies nothing about the price system. Although, from a formal point of view, the particular system of prices in which $w = 0$ appears as 'dual' to the standard system, the former in no way implies the latter and, similarly, the latter in no way implies the former. If, for example, a certain economic system were actually to be in the standard proportions, that would not imply that the system of prices would necessarily have to be that for which $w = 0$. Any other system of prices would be perfectly possible. Similarly, if the (surplus) wage were actually zero in an economic system, that would in no way imply that the proportions of the [actual] physical system would necessarily have to be those of the standard system. Any other set of proportions would be possible.

This argument is certainly correct, but it does not seem to touch upon the logical problem raised above of the independence of the rate of profit from prices. It is true that the unknown variables of the standard system, R and x^*, are totally independent of all possible definitions of the 'institutional rules' and therefore of prices; this, however, does not apply to the w-r relation in the standard system that can be determined only on the basis of such 'rules'.

3.8 The standard commodity and the analysis of price changes

The standard commodity is conceived of by Sraffa not only as a tool for attaining the independence of distribution from prices, but also as a device which makes it possible to identify the origin of changes in relative prices due to changes in distribution. This latter function is clearly connected with a similar (and, in our opinion, secondary)[16] problem raised by Ricardo in the discussion of the invariable measure of value. The function referred to is thus specified by Sraffa ((86), p. 18):

It is true that, as wages fell, such a commodity [the standard commodity] would be no less susceptible than any other to rise or fall in price relative to other individual commodities; but we should know for certain that any such fluctuation would originate exclusively in the peculiarities of production of the commodity which was being compared with it, and not in its own . . . we should therefore be in possession of a standard capable of isolating the price-movements of any other product so that they could be observed as in a vacuum.

To assess the validity of this statement it may be useful to analyse the effect on commodity prices of a change in wages when any single commodity is chosen as *numéraire* and then compare the results with those obtaining when the standard commodity is used as the unit of measurement.

As shown in the appendix to this chapter, the impact on the price of commodity i of a change in w can be analysed in terms of what may be called the 'dated capital–labour'[17] ratio of commodity i (as compared with that of the *numéraire*). This ratio will be indicated as

$$K^i = \frac{\sum\limits_s \left(\sum\limits_h p_h a_{hs}\right) a^{si}}{\sum\limits_s n_s a^{si}} \tag{16}$$

where with a^{si} we denote the elements of the matrix $[I - (1 + r)A]^{-1}$, which already appears in (10) above and is associated with the 'dating' process. The numerator of (16) is thus the dated value of the means of production directly and indirectly required to produce a unit of commodity i, while the denominator is the dated quantity of labour directly and indirectly required to produce a unit of the same commodity i.

It is clear that K^i is a function of w, both on account of the fact that the value of the means of production depends on prices and of the fact that the dating process implies the rate of profit. With the assumption here made that A is a non-negative and indecomposable matrix, the strong version of the Perron–Frobenius theorems holds (Pasinetti (66), pp. 267ff.). A unique value of r and of the price vector p is thus associated with each value of w, implying that both the numerator and the denominator are single-valued functions of w. K^i is therefore uniquely determined once w is given.

Using the letter u for the commodity chosen as unit of measurement, the direction of change in the price of commodity i may then be expressed, as proved in the appendix to this chapter, by

$$\text{sign}\left\{\frac{dp_i}{dw}\right\} = \text{sign }\{K^u - K^i\} \tag{17}$$

On account of what has been said above, no ambiguity may arise as to the sign of the difference $(K^u - K^i)$ since this difference is a single-valued function of w. Equation (17) means that a change in w will lead to a change, in the same direction, in the price of commodity i if the proportion of the dated value of the means of production to the dated quantity of labour for commodity i is lower than the same proportion for the *numéraire*, i.e. if commodity i exhibits a lower 'overall capital intensity' than the *numéraire*; and vice versa.[18] The direction of change of p_i in the neighbourhood of any particular level of w can therefore be clearly predicted.

However, as both dated capital–labour ratios appearing in (17) depend on w, the sign of the derivative and thus the direction of change of p_i with respect to changes in w cannot be determined once and for all. It depends, instead, on the specific value of w considered for the calculation of the derivative. The 'overall capital intensity' of commodity i may, in other words, be greater than that of the *numéraire* commodity at some value of w and smaller at other values, implying that the sign of dp_i/dw may be positive, nil, or negative, according to the situation with respect to which changes in distribution are considered.[19]

Considering now the price of commodity i in terms of the unit of measurement u, it is clear that, due to the invariance (by definition of *numéraire*) of p_u with respect to w, we have

$$\text{sign}\left\{\frac{d\left(\frac{p_i}{p_u}\right)}{dw}\right\} = \text{sign}\left\{\frac{dp_i}{dw}\right\} \tag{18}$$

We can say, therefore, that (17) supports Sraffa's proposition that ((86), p. 12) '[t]he key to the movement of relative prices consequent upon a change in the wage lies in the inequality of the proportions in which labour and means of production are employed in the various industries', where the 'proportions' mentioned by Sraffa are to be read as 'dated' proportions.[20]

Comparison between equation (17) above, referring to the Sraffian price model, and equation (9) of Chapter 2, which refers to the Ricardian price model, shows that the explanation of price movements given in the two models has a basic common feature. In both cases the point of reference for the definition of the direction of change in the price of any commodity i is represented by the circumstances of production of the commodity chosen as *numéraire* – *whatever this may be*. The analytical difference between the results obtained in the two instances (dated capital-labour ratios in Sraffa as opposed to current, physical capital-labour ratios in Ricardo) obviously stems from the different structure of the two models – a variety of circulating-capital goods in in the Sraffian model, a single type of fixed capital in the Ricardian framework. The appendix to this chapter shows in particular that this difference is not to be attributed to the different nature of the means of production assumed in the two models, but rather to the different number of these means considered in the two analytical frameworks.

A direct implication of the results obtaining in the two models should, however, be stressed. In the Ricardian model, as shown by equation (9) of Chapter 2, the sign of the price change associated with a change in wages is defined only on the basis of strictly technological parameters, i.e. independently of distribution. In the Sraffian model, on the contrary, as it has been pointed out with reference to equation (17), the sign of price changes depends both on technology and on distribution. Whereas in the former case, 'switches' in the direction of price movements cannot occur, in the latter these cannot be ruled out.

In order to evaluate the consequences for the problem of the choice of the standard commodity as *numéraire* of the system, it is sufficient to insert in equation (17) the dated capital-labour ratio of the standard commodity K^{sc} in place of K^u. As shown in the appendix, this ratio for the standard commodity is

$$K^{sc} = \frac{1}{R} \tag{19}$$

which coincides with the current capital-labour ratio defined in (13). Equation (17) thus becomes:

$$\text{sign}\left\{\frac{dp_i}{dw}\right\} = \text{sign}\left\{\frac{1}{R} - K^i\right\} \tag{20}$$

We may then conclude that the use of the standard commodity as *numéraire* of the system helps to trace the origin of price movements to the 'peculiarities of production' of the commodities that are being compared with the standard commodity itself. Changes in w affect, in other words, only the dated capital-labour ratio of the commodities being measured and not that of the standard commodity; in all other cases, changes in w affect, instead, *both* the dated capital-labour ratio of the commodities being measured *and* that of the unit of measurement.

In (17) and (20) the problem is considered of the effect of a change in w on the price of the commodity i in terms of the *numéraire* (any commodity u, or the standard commodity, respectively). When, on the other hand, we consider the relative price of commodity i in terms of commodity j, neither of which plays the role of *numéraire*, the study of the consequences of a change in w on this relative price clearly requires the joint consideration of the separate effects on the prices of both commodities measured in terms of the same *numéraire*. With a procedure analogous to that indicated in (18), we have:

$$\text{sign}\left\{\frac{d\left(\frac{p_i}{p_j}\right)}{dw}\right\} = \text{sign}\left\{p_j\frac{dp_i}{dw} - p_i\frac{dp_j}{dw}\right\} \tag{21}$$

Repeated recourse to (17) (or to (19)) makes it possible to establish whether the two separate effects on p_i and p_j go in the same direction, thus partially offsetting each other in the net result on p_i/p_j, or instead in the opposite direction, thus exerting a combined influence in the direction of change of p_i/p_j.

Also in this case the use of the standard commodity as *numéraire* of the system would help to clarify the origin of the price movements ensuing from changes in distribution.

3.9 The notion of invariance *per se* of the standard commodity

The role of the standard commodity just discussed appears to be strictly linked to the independence of the dated capital-labour ratio from w, which obtains only when the standard commodity is the unit of measurement. While the standard ratio R is independent of distribution, whether or not the standard commodity is the unit of measurement, the dated capital-labour ratio K^{sc} (as well as the current capital-labour ratio k_{sc}) is equal to the inverse of the standard ratio − and is thus independent of distribution − only when the standard commodity is the *numéraire*.

This analytical property carries, however, no implication for the notion of what may perhaps be termed the 'invariance *per se*' of the standard commodity. This notion, which has been widely accepted in the literature, calls in our opinion for some discussion aiming at clarifying Sraffa's idea of the 'balanced industry' on the basis of which the standard commodity is defined. Even at the cost of a somewhat lengthy description, it seems necessary to consider in detail Sraffa's construction.

Abstracting from the question of 'dating', it may be recalled that Sraffa's discussion of the effects of a change in distribution on the prices of commodities is centred around the concept of 'the inequality of the proportions in which labour and means of production are employed in the various industries'.

Let us suppose, with Sraffa ((86), p. 12), that, '[s]tarting from a situation in which the whole of the national income goes to labour' (and commodity prices are defined accordingly), wages are reduced so that a positive rate of profit arises. According to Sraffa, this circumstance — except for the case of equality of capital–labour ratios in all industries — implies that *at the initial prices* some industries would have a deficit (cost exceeding price) and some would have a surplus (price exceeding cost). If we let the initial situation be described by

$$p_0 = p_0 A + n w_0 \tag{22}$$

the situation obtaining after the assumed change in distribution is

$$p_0 \neq (1 + r_1) p_0 A + n w_1 \tag{23}$$

where $w_1 < w_0$. Expression (23) means that industries with a 'sufficiently low proportion of labour to means of production will have a deficit, while industries with a sufficiently high proportion would have a surplus, on their payment for wages and profits' (Sraffa (86), p. 13). This implies, in Sraffa's ((86), p. 13) words, that

> [t]here would be a 'critical proportion' of labour to means of production which marked the watershed between 'deficit' and 'surplus' industries. An industry which employed that particular 'proportion' would show an even balance — the proceeds of the wage-reduction would provide exactly what was required for the payment of profits at the general rate.

If there was, then, 'an industry which employed labour and means of production in that precise [critical] proportion' (Sraffa (86), p. 16) and if it were true that 'the same [critical] proportion *recurs* in all the successive layers of the industry's aggregate means of production without limit', it could be said that

> [t]he commodity produced by such an industry would be under no necessity, arising from the conditions of production of the industry itself, either to rise or to fall in value relative to any other commodity when wages rose or fell; for, as we have seen, a necessity of this sort can originate only from a potential deficit or surplus

and an industry operating under the conditions described would *ipso facto* be in balance.

Although individual commodities are unlikely to possess the requisites of the 'balanced' commodity, such requisites can be met in an appropriately constructed composite commodity — the standard commodity.

Sraffa's construction of the standard — *qua* balanced — commodity seems to imply the idea that such a commodity is invariant *per se* with respect to changes in distribution, in the specific sense of being under no necessity of changing in price when distribution changes independently of its choice as *numéraire*.

The whole argument seems to rest on the idea that it is possible to define the notion of deficit and surplus industries (and thus the notion of balanced industry) *without the prior definition of the relation between wages and the rate of profit* (Sraffa (86), p. 13): '[N]othing is assumed . . . as to what rate of profits corresponds to what wage reduction; all that is required . . . is that there should be a uniform wage and a uniform rate of profits throughout the system.'

It appears instead that the definition of deficit and surplus industries requires the prior knowledge of the inverse relation between *w* and *r*; for, without this prior knowledge, it seems impossible to make any type of calculation about the compensation effect between 'the proceeds of the wage-reduction and what [is] required for the payment of profits at the general rate'. (The fact that the initial situation considered is one in which the profit rate is nil is no exception to this rule.) This, in turn, requires that *a numéraire* be chosen. As shown in Chapter 2, it is precisely this choice that makes it possible to derive the *w–r* relation for the price model, implying, for the commodity used as unit of measurement, that changes in the wage rate are, by definition, exactly compensated by changes in the opposite direction in the rate of profit. The need for a change in the price of this commodity is thus, by definition, ruled out.

It is clear that these properties of the *numéraire* are totally independent of the 'circumstances of production' of the commodity chosen as standard of value. They are not associated with the idea that the invariance of the *numéraire* depends on its somehow representing a 'social average'. In other words, they remain unaltered even if the function of unit of measurement were to be assigned to a commodity constituting one of the two 'extremes' considered by Ricardo.[21] The analysis carried out in the preceding section shows, in effect, that all one needs in order to define the direction of price changes consequent upon changes in distribution is a knowledge of the 'circumstances of production' of each commodity as compared with those of the *numéraire – whatever this may be*. The balanced industry thus turns out to be that which produces the commodity which happens to be chosen as *numéraire* of the system.

Sraffa's argument in chapter 3 of *Production of Commodities* appears to be based on the choice of the net national product as *numéraire* of the system. This choice is explicitly made by Sraffa in his preceding chapter and is carried over in the discussion of the role of the 'proportions of labour to means of production' in the study of price movements. The opening sentence of chapter 3 is in effect (Sraffa (86), p. 12):

> We proceed to give the wage (*w*) successive values ranging from 1 to 0: these now represent fractions of the national income (cp. §§10 and 12)

where Sraffa's reference to his sections 10 and 12 makes it clear that the assumption is made that both the 'total annual labour of society' and the net national income are taken as equal to one.

With this choice of *numéraire* and with the consideration of *w* as an exogenous variable, Sraffa's price model is complete, and his reasoning in chapter 3 is thus based on a fully specified *w–r* relation. It is only with reference to this relation that the proceeds of a wage reduction can be weighed against the increased payment of profits and the specification made of deficit and surplus industries *at the initial prices*.

It may be noted, furthermore, that the particular choice of *numéraire* (the net national product) made by Sraffa implies the coincidence of the balanced industry with the industry exhibiting a capital–labour ratio equal to the 'social average' – a circumstance which, as we have already stressed, does not apply in general.

We may then conclude that the standard commodity, which is constructed by Sraffa with the aim of representing a balanced commodity *per se*, acquires this property only inasmuch as it is chosen as *numéraire* of the system. The peculiarities of production ('recurrence' of the same proportion of labour to the value of the means of production in all its successive layers) confer to the standard commodity, *qua numéraire*, specific analytical properties which help, in particular, to identify the origin of changes in relative prices consequent upon changes in distribution. This fact, however, has no implication for the notion of the invariance *per se* of the standard commodity.

3.10 The existence of the standard commodity in the Ricardian model with fixed capital

We can now tackle the question concerning the possibility of a significant use of the standard commodity in the study of the crucial issue,
raised by Ricardo, of the relation between diminishing returns in
agricultural and capital accumulation. To this end we must examine
the problem of the existence of the standard commodity for the
Ricardian model with fixed capital, i.e. the model with reference
to which (in Chapter 2) the relation between technology and the
profit rate has been analysed. It is sufficient from this point of view
to show the equivalence of the Ricardian price model to the Sraffian
joint production model in which the output of each industry consists
of commodities and of machines a year older than the ones entering
the means of production at the beginning of the year (Sraffa (86),
part 2, esp. ch. 10).

In Chapter 2, the price equations (3) of the Ricardian model express
the assumption that commodities are produced by means of labour
(i.e. the commodities entering the wage basket) and of fixed capital.
With the hypothesis there adopted that no wear and tear of machines
takes place, the only component of the cost of production connected
with the use of machines is 'the annual charge to be paid for interest'
(Sraffa (86), p. 64) — no depreciation charge having to be allowed
for. In this case the above-mentioned price equations (3), formulated
in terms of single-product industries, can be easily transformed into
a price system expressing the assumption of joint production. From
this point of view, machines can now be regarded 'as part of the annual
intake of a process, on the same footing as such means of production
(e.g. raw materials) as are entirely used up' in the productive process;
but are, at the same time, to be considered as a 'portion of the annual
joint product of the industry' (Sraffa (86), p. 63).

The 'transformation' of the price model (3) into a joint production
price system is particularly simple. With the assumption that no wear
and tear takes place, the machines appearing as part of the annual
output are exactly the same as the machines entering the annual intake
of the process both from the point of view of their productive efficiency and from that of their value.

The price system (3) of Chapter 2 can thus be rewritten as follows:

$$p_1 + p_m n_1 k_1 = (1 + r)n_1 (w + p_m k_1)$$
$$p_2 + p_m n_2 k_2 = (1 + r)n_2 (w + p_m k_2)$$
$$\vdots \qquad\qquad \vdots \qquad\qquad \vdots$$
$$p_m + p_m n_m k_m = (1 + r)n_m (w + p_m k_m)$$

$$(24)$$

When depreciation of machines is taken into account, the transformation of the single production model into the corresponding joint production system requires the prior definition of the specific assumption chosen to allow for the process of wear and tear. Two especially simple types of assumptions can be made:

(i) That depreciation implies a progressive loss of efficiency of machines and that this loss can be expressed in terms of a reduction in the physical quantity of the existing fixed capital – the measure of such a reduction being a constant percentage of the existing stock of capital goods. In this case the price of machines remains the same throughout the physical life of machines, and is therefore unaffected by the process of wear and tear, which manifests itself only in terms of reduced availability of machines (hypothesis of 'radioactive decay');

(ii) That the physical life of machines is given and finite, and that the process of wear and tear does not affect their efficiency, which remains unaltered until the end of their physical life when machines suddenly, so to speak, 'disappear'. In this case, the process of depreciation only affects the value of machines, whose price progressively diminishes as the machines grow older (hypothesis of 'sudden death of machines').

The introduction of the first type of assumption in the price model would produce a transformed price system analogous to that defined by (24), while the adoption of the second type of assumption would require a different presentation of the joint production model; for in the first case the only difference with (24) would be that the quantity of machines considered as part of the joint product would be a constant fraction $(1 - \sigma)$ of the quantity considered as input, where σ is obviously the rate of 'radioactive decay'. In the second case, on the contrary, the transformation of a single-product model like (3) – where machines appear only in the cost side of the equations for the annual charge for interest and depreciation – into a joint-product model requires that separate sets of equations for each successive 'age' of the machines be explicitly formulated for each of the m commodities produced in the system.

This is in effect the approach followed by Sraffa. After defining the set of equations 'for the separate processes which correspond to the successive ages of the machine' (Sraffa (86), p. 65), he combines these equations in a single expression that, with reference to the Ricardian price model, would be

$$p_i = (1 + r)n_i w + p_m n_i k_i \frac{r(1 + r)^t}{(1 + r)^t - 1} \qquad (25)$$

It is clear that, when depreciation is ruled out, i.e. when there is no limit to the physical life of machines and t thus tends to infinity, (25) coincides with the equations in (3) of Chapter 2.

We may then conclude that all the properties of the Sraffian joint production model, for the case of fixed capital, apply to the Ricardian price model discussed in Chapter 2. The most relevant property in the present context relates to the existence – stated by Sraffa ((86), pp. 72-3) and explicitly proved by Schefold (78) – of the standard commodity for the model with fixed capital. It is therefore legitimate to raise the problem of the role of the standard commodity for the solution of Ricardo's fundamental problem of the relation between diminishing returns in agriculture and the rate of profit.

3.11 The standard commodity and the requisites of Ricardo's invariable measure of value

We are now in a position to draw a comparison between the properties of Sraffa's standard commodity and the requisites of Ricardo's invariable measure of value, in order to explore the possibility of using the Sraffian *numéraire* for the solution of the problems that had prompted Ricardo's search for the invariable standard of measurement. As we have seen in section 3.2 above, the two requisites indicated by Ricardo are: (i) that the commodity to be used as the measuring-rod should at all times require for its production the same quantity of labour; and (ii) that this commodity should be such as to make the prices of the other commodities (measured in terms of this unit) invariant to changes in distribution.

We shall start discussing the problems connected with the second requisite, which, in Ricardo's mind, should have performed the role of establishing a direct connection between decreasing returns and the rate of profit, to the exclusion of the disturbing effects of changes in distribution working through changes in prices.

With reference to this question, it must be immediately stressed that, as we maintained in section 3.3, the problem of changes in distribution cannot be envisaged in Ricardo's framework of natural equilibrium analysis independently of changes in technology, i.e. of the difficulty of production of agricultural goods. From this point of view, the standard commodity which is defined for a given technology represents an analytical tool lying outside Ricardo's main scheme of reference.

If, nevertheless, one should want to consider in Ricardo the Sraffian problem of changes in distribution due to changes in *real* wages – technology being given – the natural-equilibrium framework of analysis would have to be dropped. Assuming, however, for the sake of the comparison to be made, that it were legitimate to pursue this line of reasoning, let us consider what function would be performed by the standard commodity in this different non-natural-equilibrium Ricardian context. Reference to Ricardo's corn model may help to clarify the issue.

As is well known, the corn model has the following two analytical properties: (i) as the labour theory of value holds true, prices are independent of distribution; and (ii) as in the corn-producing sector both input and output consist of the same commodity, the rate of profit can be determined as a ratio between quantities of corn without reference to prices.

Ricardo's search for an invariable standard of value aims at restoring, for the *general case* (as distinct from the special case in which the labour theory of value holds), property (i) of the corn model. Had Ricardo's effort in this direction been successful, the relation between the rate of profit and diminishing returns would have appeared as straightforward as in the corn model, i.e. not disturbed by changes in distribution working through prices.

Given the impossibility of finding a solution along these lines, Sraffa chooses a different approach. Since the dependence of prices on distribution must in general be recognized, he does not attempt to restore the validity of property (i) of the corn model, but goes back to property (ii). The standard system thus represents a generalized version of the corn model;[22] here too the rate of profit is determined as a ratio between quantities of the same (composite) commodity without reference to prices. (The warning given above on the matter of the relation in the standard system between the independence of the rate of profit from prices and the role of the 'institutional rules' for the definition of the price system does not touch upon the difference of approach here underlined.)

It may be thus said in conclusion that the standard commodity as *numéraire* in this non-natural-equilibrium Ricardian context would perform an analytical function wholly different from that envisaged by Ricardo for his invariable measure of value.

It may be added incidentally that, while the use of the standard commodity as *numéraire* makes the solution of the distributive variables prior to that of prices, had Ricardo's search for an invariable standard of value been successful his approach would have made the determination of prices prior to that of the rate of profit – a somehow different instance of the 'aggregative approach'.

If we revert now to the problems connected with the first requisite indicated by Ricardo for the invariable standard of value, an interpretative strain of opposite sign may be said to occur. While it was so far the crucial Ricardian assumption of a fixed real wage that had to give way, it is now the equally crucial Sraffian hypothesis of a given technology that must be dropped.

In fact, when we come to the first requisite, it is clear that the constancy of the quantity of labour necessary at all times and places to produce the measuring-rod is a meaningful requirement in Ricardo's framework only inasmuch as the technology of other commodities (namely, agricultural goods) is assumed to undergo a process of change through time. Thus, as agricultural goods must necessarily be included among the 'basic' commodities, the problem must be faced of a change in the technology of the standard system – a problem clearly lying outside Sraffa's original framework of analysis. This technological change, which is expressed in the model of Chapter 2 in terms of a continuous increase in the labour input in the agricultural sector (n_1), implies the existence of an infinite set of standard commodities, each one of them corresponding to each of the infinite values of n_1. If the standard commodity were then chosen as *numéraire* of the Ricardian system, it would clearly *not* fulfill the first requisite indicated by Ricardo.[23]

If in spite of this one should intend to pursue this line of reasoning in Ricardo's analytical scheme, the implications of such a choice should be carefully considered, with regard to both the rate of profit and to the prices of commodities. With reference to the rate of profit, no problem would seem to arise. As in the Ricardian theory the wages of labour do not participate in the division of the net product,[24] the rate of profit turns out to coincide with the Sraffian maximum rate of profit, i.e. with the standard ratio R. The same inverse relation between r and n_1 would thus be determined both in the actual system (see the appendix to Chapter 2) and in the standard system – the only difference being one of methodological type (simultaneous approach in the first case, aggregative approach in the second).

With reference to prices, instead, the use of a 'variable' *numéraire* would seem to raise relevant difficulties as to the possibility of significant comparisons through time. The prices of commodities would be measured in terms of a *numéraire* whose conditions of production would continuously change. It would then be impossible to analyse without ambiguity the behaviour of prices through time due to the absence of a common base of reference. To overcome this difficulty, it would be necessary to possess a sequence of transformation factors making it possible to pass from one standard commodity (appropriate to a particular period of time) to another (appropriate to a different period of time) – a sort of price index (e.g. base 1960) for standard commodities. This would mean, however, that the standard commodity would be abandoned as *numéraire*, in the sense that the prices of each period of time would not be measured in terms of the standard commodity appropriate to the technology of that period but in terms of a standard commodity referring to the technology of the base period.

It may be said, by way of conclusion, that the attempt to use the standard commodity in the Ricardian framework does not appear to be fruitful. Sraffa's *numéraire* does not seem to represent, in other words, an analytical tool capable of resolving the issues from which Ricardo's search for the invariable measure had originated.

The difficulties can be substantially traced back to the circumstance that the standard commodity and the invariable measure of value move on different logical planes – the study of distribution for a given technology, and the analysis of changes in distribution caused by changes in technology, respectively. It has been the aim of this chapter to show that the transposition of an analytical tool conceived within one type of logical framework to the other is by no means automatic.

Appendix   Changes in distribution and relative prices

The case of a generic *numéraire*

In line with the approach followed in section 3.8, the analysis in

Sraffa's context of the effects on relative prices of a change in distribution will be first considered in the case that the unit of measurement is one of the commodities produced in the system — the commodity u.

The price equations of Sraffa's model

$$p = (1 + r)pA + nw \tag{A.1}$$

can be conveniently rewritten as

$$p[I - (1 + r)A] = nw \tag{A.2}$$

Differentiating (A.2) with respect to w, we obtain:

$$\frac{dp}{dw} [I - (1 + r)A] - \frac{dr}{dw} pA = n \tag{A.3}$$

Rearranging terms and assuming $r < R$,. as required for the matrix $[I - (1 + r)A]^{-1}$ to exist and to be non-negative, we arrive at the set of equations defining the effect of a change in w on the prices of commodities:

$$\frac{dp}{dw} = \left[n + \frac{dr}{dw} pA \right] [I - (1 + r)A]^{-1} \tag{A.4}$$

The derivative of r with respect to w can be determined considering the *numéraire* commodity, the absolute price of which, by definition, remains unchanged when distribution changes. We have, then:

$$\frac{dp_u}{dw} = \sum_{s=1}^{m} \left[n_s + \frac{dr}{dw} \sum_{h=1}^{m} p_h a_{hs} \right] a^{su} = 0 \tag{A.5}$$

where the a^{ij}s are the elements of the inverse matrix $[I - (1 + r)A]^{-1}$, which are all positive (Perron–Frobenius theorems). Solving (A.5) for dr/dw, we obtain:

$$\frac{dr}{dw} = - \frac{\sum\limits_{s} n_s a^{su}}{\sum\limits_{s} \left(\sum\limits_{h} p_h a_{hs} \right) a^{su}} \tag{A.6}$$

Recalling the definition of dated capital-labour ratio given in the text with reference to (16), it is clear that

$$\frac{dr}{dw} = - \frac{1}{K^u} \tag{A.7}$$

Substituting (A.7) in (A.4), and considering the effect of a change in w on the price of commodity i, we have:

$$\frac{dp_i}{dw} = \sum_{s} \left[n_s - \frac{1}{K^u} \sum_{h} p_h a_{hs} \right] a^{si} \tag{A.8}$$

Rearranging terms, we can write:

$$\frac{dp_i}{dw} = \frac{\sum\limits_{s} n_s a^{si}}{K^u}[K^u - K^i] \tag{A.9}$$

Since $\sum n_s a^{si}$ and K^u are both positive, we can conclude that

$$\text{sign}\left\{\frac{dp_i}{dw}\right\} = \text{sign}\{K^u - K^i\} \tag{A.10}$$

The case of the standard commodity

To evaluate the effect on prices of a change in w when the standard commodity is chosen as *numéraire*, it is sufficient to insert in (A.10) — in place of K^u — the value of the dated capital–labour ratio for the standard commodity. By definition, this ratio is equal to

$$K^{sc} = \frac{pA[I-(1+r)A]^{-1}Q^*}{n[I-(1+r)A]^{-1}Q^*} \tag{A.11}$$

where the numerator is the dated value of the means of production required to produce the net standard product, $Q^* = [I - A]x^*$, and the denominator represents the dated quantity of labour needed to obtain the same net standard product.

As the standard net product Q^* is proportional to the gross standard product x^*, (A.11) can be rewritten as

$$K^{sc} = \frac{pA[I-(1+r)A]^{-1}x^*}{n[I-(1+r)A]^{-1}x^*} \tag{A.12}$$

Taking the series expansion of $[I - (1 + r)A]^{-1}$, and recalling the definition of the standard system given in section 3.5 of this chapter, we have

$$[I-(1+r)A]^{-1}x^* = [I+(1+r)A+(1+r)^2A^2 + \ldots]x^*$$

$$= \left[1 + \left(\frac{1+r}{1+R}\right) + \left(\frac{1+r}{1+R}\right)^2 + \ldots\right]x^* = \left(\frac{1+R}{R-r}\right)x^* \tag{A.13}$$

Substituting (A.13) in (A.12) and taking account of (13) and (14) of the text, we obtain

$$K^{sc} = \frac{pAx^*}{nx^*} = k_{sc} = \frac{1}{R} \tag{A.14}$$

Equation (A.10) thus becomes

$$\text{sign}\left\{\frac{dp_i}{dw}\right\} = \text{sign}\left\{\frac{1}{R} - K^i\right\} \tag{A.15}$$

A comparison with the results of the Ricardian price model

In the appendix to Chapter 2 (pp. 51-3) we considered the problem of determining the effects on prices of changes in w with reference to the Ricardian price model analysed in that chapter. As (A.26) of that appendix shows, the conclusion was reached that the sign of the price change depends on the difference between the physical capital-labour ratio of the commodity chosen as standard of value and that of the commodity i.

When this result is compared with that of (A.10) of this appendix, differences of two kinds emerge between the Sraffian and the Ricardian models. First, Sraffa's capital-labour ratio is a ratio of the value of the means of production to the quantity of labour, whereas Ricardo's capital-labour ratio is defined as the quantity of machines employed per unit of labour. Second, in Sraffa's context price movements depend on *dated* capital-labour ratios, whereas in the Ricardian model they depend on *current* capital-labour ratios.

Both these differences are to be attributed to the different structure of the two models (i.e. to the different assumptions regarding the production of commodities in the two contexts). They do not depend on the different nature of the means of production used in the two models — fixed versus circulating capital — but rather on the different *number* of the means of production considered, one as opposed to a variety.

This statement can be verified assuming that in the Sraffian system (A.1) the means of production consist of a single commodity — the mth commodity. Denoting with a_{mi} the quantity of commodity m required to produce a unit of commodity i, the price of the *numéraire* commodity can be written as

$$p_u = (1 + r)p_m a_{mu} + n_u w \qquad (A.16)$$

Solving (A.16) for p_m and substituting in the equation expressing the price of commodity i, we obtain:

$$p_i = \frac{a_{mi}}{a_{mu}} (p_u - n_u w) + n_i w \qquad (A.17)$$

Differentiating now with respect to w, and recalling that, by definition of *numéraire*, $dp_u/dw = 0$, we have:

$$\frac{dp_i}{dw} = -\frac{a_{mi}}{a_{mu}} n_u + n_i \qquad (A.18)$$

The sign of the effect of a change in w on the price of commodity i

can therefore be expressed as follows:

$$\text{sign}\left\{\frac{dp_i}{dw}\right\} = \text{sign}\left\{-\frac{a_{mi}}{a_{mu}}\,n_u + n_i\right\} = \text{sign}\left\{\frac{a_{mu}}{n_u} - \frac{a_{mi}}{n_i}\right\} \quad (A.19)$$

where a_{mu}/n_u and a_{mi}/n_i are the ratios of the physical quantity of the circulating capital m to the quantity of labour required to produce one unit respectively of commodity u and commodity i. The direction of price change thus turns out to depend on the difference between current, physical 'capital-labour' ratios.

Part II
Growth and distribution

4 Pasinetti's formulation of the Ricardian system

4.1 Introductory remarks

The analysis carried out in Chapter 2 has enabled us to define a fundamental relation – the 'profit equation' – between the labour input of the agricultural sector and the general rate of profit. This relation – although inherently dynamic in nature in that it implies the direction of movement of the economy – cannot, however, account for the process through which the rate of profit gradually falls and the economic system moves from the progressive to the stationary state. To that end, the equations of the price system must be considered in the framework of a truly dynamic model incorporating the essential hypotheses of Ricardo's reasoning as regards aggregate expenditure, capital accumulation and population growth. It is only with reference to such a model that the movement of the economy through time can be fully specified.

The versions of the dynamic Ricardian model examined in the following chapters take as their starting-point Pasinetti's (64) analytical formulation of the Ricardian system. As already pointed out in Chapter 1, there are two basic reasons for this choice. On the one hand, Pasinetti's contribution represents, in our opinion, the best example of that type of analysis of Ricardo's thought which is conceived in a 'constructive' rather than in a 'critical' light – the distinguishing feature of this method being the attempt to set out in explicit analytical terms the fundamental assumptions required to 'eliminate the ambiguities' of Ricardo's theory. On the other hand, a careful examination of Pasinetti's work makes it possible to bring out certain limitations of his approach from the dynamic point of view and consequently the need to cast Ricardo's thinking in a framework of analysis in which the interaction between capital accumulation and population adjustment is fully taken account of.

4.2 The concept of 'point natural equilibrium' used by Pasinetti

Pasinetti's mathematical formulation of the Ricardian system is centred on the definition of individual positions of *moving equilibrium* in a two-commodity economic system and on the proof that, with diminishing returns, all these equilibrium situations are unstable except that of the stationary state.

The notion of equilibrium used by Pasinetti goes back to the terminology introduced by Frisch (25) in a paper dealing with some methodological issues of economic dynamics. Frisch suggests that in the study of the time paths of the economic unknowns it may be helpful to introduce the concept of 'natural equilibrium', which presupposes the prior definition of the 'normal' values of one or more key variables (constant or changing through time). The natural equilibrium can be of two types: *stationary* or *moving*.

Stationary equilibrium is defined as that situation (stationary state) in which there is no inherent tendency towards change, and, therefore, both the structure and the scale of the economy remain unaltered over time.

The concept of moving equilibrium, on the contrary, refers to a specific stage of the evolution of the system, i.e. to the position of the economy at a given moment of time, the structure and/or the scale of the system being subject to potential changes. From the analytical point of view this equilibrium position is defined as the solution – with respect to a specific subset of variables (e.g. output, consumption, investment, income distribution) – of a system of equations in which the 'dynamic forms' (lagged values, for instance) of these same variables, as well as the current and lagged values of the other variables (e.g. fixed capital, the labour force), are taken as given parameters.[1] The unknowns are therefore *single 'natural equilibrium' values* of the variables at a particular time *t* and not the same variables as *functions of time*, as would happen in the solution of a dynamic model. The resulting system is thus *static*[2] rather than dynamic.

The procedure for the determination of an equilibrium position can be applied to any one of the infinite points – taken in isolation – of the evolution of the system, provided the right values of the variables being treated as parameters are known and inserted into the system of equations. The natural equilibrium values may therefore be considered, according to Frisch, 'functions of time'. Hence the expression of 'moving equilibrium'.[3]

Strictly speaking, however, it seems improper and perhaps potentially misleading to consider the equilibrium values of the variables (thus calculated) as 'functions of time'. These values are actually instantaneous solutions referring to a single point of time, which is characterized by a specific set of values of the parameters.

The static nature of moving equilibrium becomes even more apparent if we consider that the idea of a functional link between the equilibrium solutions of two successive moments of time is completely extraneous to the notion of moving equilibrium. This notion is, therefore, not equivalent to the modern one of *dynamic equilibrium*.[4] A moving equilibrium does not describe the paths of the relevant magnitudes through time but confines itself to identifying, case by case, a single position – i.e. a single point on the time path of the system.[5] The seemingly dynamic implication of the expression used by Frisch should not therefore be the source of any confusion.

Pasinetti borrows Frisch's notion of moving equilibrium to define what may be called his *point natural equilibrium* of the Ricardian system. The central role assigned by Pasinetti to this concept implies that all the features and limitations of the moving equilibrium are carried over to his analytical formulation of Ricardo's theory.

The way in which Pasinetti considers the two fundamental 'dynamic mechanisms' of the Ricardian theory confirms the methodological characteristics of his approach. In fact, the dynamic mechanisms – (i) population adjustment, and (ii) capital accumulation – are taken into account for the sole purpose of showing that all positions of point natural equilibrium different from the stationary state are unstable. Furthermore, these mechanisms are examined in isolation (so to speak), i.e. each one independently of the other. The interaction between them is substantially disregarded, as it is considered only with reference to the properties of the stationary state.

The analysis thus falls short of permitting the definition of the time path of the variables of the Ricardian system. This aim can be attained solely through the use of a truly dynamic model, incorporating as integral parts the two dynamic mechanisms and their interaction, and thus capable of establishing a link between successive moments of time.

It should be clear that the methodological limitations just pointed out of Pasinetti's approach relate to his *use* of the concept of natural equilibrium and not to the *concept* itself. As we have shown in Part I, this notion plays a central role in Ricardo's analytical construction as regards both the theory of value and distribution, and the theory of distribution and growth.

4.3 The hypotheses of the model

In his formulation of the Ricardian model Pasinetti starts from the following hypotheses which simplify, but reflect faithfully, the essential logical structure of Ricardo's thought portraying in particular the corn model:[6]

(a) Two sectors are considered: the agricultural one (which produces a wage-good, corn) and the industrial one (which produces a luxury good, gold); the period of production is the same and equal to a year in both sectors.

(b) Capital consists only of corn which is advanced as wages to the workers at the beginning of each productive cycle; fixed capital is not considered.

(c) The amount of land available is given; its characteristics (fertility of the various lots and suitability for intensive cultivation) are considered as known.

(d) The labour employed in the two productive sectors is homogeneous, and the wage rate is the same in the whole system.

(e) The technical conditions of production in the agricultural sector are described by the twice differentiable function:

$$X_1 = f(N_1) \tag{1}$$

where X_1 represents the physical amount of corn produced in a year and N_1 the number of workers employed in the agricultural sector. The agricultural production function has the following properties:[7]

- Production of corn is an increasing function of agricultural employment: $f'(N_1) > 0$
- Given the natural or subsistence wage rate in terms of corn, $\bar{x}$, production is initially profitable – that is, the first worker employed on the most fertile land produces more than is necessary to support himself: $f(0) > \bar{x}$
- Production shows diminishing returns: $f''(N_1) < 0$

$f'(N_1)$, which is the product of labour employed in the less favourable conditions, is the inverse of the n_1 defined in Chapter 2 as the labour input in the production of a unit of corn.

(f) The production function of the industrial sector is linear (constant returns to scale):

$$X_2 = \beta N_2 \tag{2}$$

where X_2 indicates the physical quantity of gold produced in a year,

N_2 the number of workers employed, and β (a positive constant) the physical quantity of gold produced by a labourer in a year. β is clearly equal to the inverse of the n_2 defined in Chapter 2 as the labour input of gold.

(g) Gold, the production of which requires 'the same amount of labour at all times and places', is taken as the (invariable) standard of value. The unit of measurement is the quantity of gold produced by the labour of one worker in one year. In the absence of fixed capital and on the assumption that the productive processes last the same time, the labour theory of value holds true: relative prices are equal to the ratios of the labour inputs of the various commodities and absolute prices coincide with the respective direct labour inputs (i.e. the inverse of the productivities of labour in the 'less favourable' conditions):

$$p_1 = \frac{1}{f'(N_1)} \tag{3}$$

$$p_2 = \frac{1}{\beta} \tag{4}$$

This definition of prices clearly coincides with that given in (7) of Chapter 2.

(h) There are three social classes — landowners, capitalists and workers. Landowners use all their income to buy luxury goods (gold). Workers consume all their income, which, in real terms, consists of corn. Both these classes therefore have a zero propensity to save. Capitalists, on the contrary, allocate all their income (profits) to capital accumulation. Their propensity to save is accordingly equal to unity.

It should be added here that, if we postulate that the real wage is fixed at the natural (subsistence) level and that the initial wages fund is given, we must also assume that the supply of labour is adequate.

4.4 Distribution of output and Say's law

The distribution of output between the various categories of income recipients — landowners, capitalists and workers — may be expressed by means of the following equations:

$$R = f(N_1) - N_1 f'(N_1) \tag{5}$$

$$W_1 = x N_1 \tag{6}$$

$$P_1 = f(N_1) - R - W_1 = N_1 [f'(N_1) - x] \tag{7}$$

$$W_2 = xN_2 \tag{8}$$

$$p_2 P_2 = p_2 X_2 - p_1 W_2 = N_2 (p_2 \beta - p_1 x) \tag{9}$$

where: R = rent in terms of corn, W_1 = total wages in the agricultural sector in terms of corn, x = market wage in terms of corn, W_2 = total wages in the industrial sector in terms of corn, P_1 = profits in the agricultural sector in terms of corn, and P_2 = profits in the industrial sector in terms of gold.

Equation (5) reflects Ricardo's definition of rent as a *surplus*, i.e. a net gain for the owners of the most fertile lands as compared with the owners of 'marginal' land (the land which yields no rent). Equations (6) and (8) express the wages fund in the agricultural and the industrial sectors, respectively, whereas equations (7) and (9) define profits in the two sectors. In the agricultural sector it is possible to express profits in physical terms, thanks to the homogeneity of the variables. In the industrial sector, on the contrary, profits have to be expressed in value terms because production consists of the luxury good (gold) while circulating capital is represented by the wage-good (corn).

Explicit form can now be given to the behaviour assumptions stated above and their implications with respect to aggregate demand can be considered. As will be recalled, workers use all their income in consuming corn and landowners in buying gold, while capitalists (as an 'abstract' class of economic agents) devote all their profits to accumulation. In analytical terms, we therefore have:

$$p_1 R = p_2 X_2 \tag{10}$$

$$p_1 (W_1 + W_2) + p_1 P_1 + p_2 P_2 = p_1 X_1 \tag{10a}$$

The first of these relations expresses the assumption that landowners' income absorbs the entire production of corn. The second shows that the incomes from labour and capital completely absorb the production of corn. (Since there is no fixed capital, profit-earners demand only corn.)

The composition of expenditure is thus specified. Its absolute level (in line with Say's law, accepted by Ricardo)[8] coincides with the total amount of the incomes earned in the economy. In the formulation of the complete model it is therefore sufficient to include only equation (10), since (10a) can be readily obtained from equations (5)–(9) defining the distributive shares. (The same would obviously apply if (10a) were inserted in the model instead of (10).)

4.5 Natural and market equilibrium

If we add to the set of equations (1)–(10) the definitions respectively of total employment, total wages and wages fund:

$$N = N_1 + N_2 \tag{11}$$

$$W = W_1 + W_2 \tag{12}$$

$$K = W \tag{13}$$

where K indicates the circulating capital (corn) advanced to workers as wages, we obtain a system of thirteen equations in fifteen unknowns $(X_1, X_2, N_1, N_2, N, p_1, p_2, R, W_1, W_2, W, x, P_1, P_2, K)$. Two more equations are thus required to complete the model.

As the equations of the model imply $K = xN$ (a relation which expresses the 'wages-fund theory'), it will be seen that any two of these three fundamental variables must be regarded as given if the solution of the model is to be determined. If we are to comply, however, with the logic of the Ricardian theory, capital must in any case be considered as a datum, because the dimensions of the productive process cannot be fixed independently of the amount of capital available to support the labourers that are to be employed in the economy in the period taken into consideration. The alternative thus turns out to be between assuming as given the wage rate *or* the population – the other one of the two variables being determined by the equation defining the wages fund.

If we assume then that wages are at the natural (subsistence) level, we add to the set of equations (1)–(13) the following relations:

$$K = \bar{K} \tag{14}$$

$$x = \bar{x} \tag{15}$$

The model thus obtained defines a situation of *point natural equilibrium*.

If, on the other hand, instead of (15), we assume

$$N = \bar{N} \tag{15a}$$

the resulting model defines a situation of *point market equilibrium*, i.e. a situation in which the wage rate clearing the labour market (*market wage*) – demand being represented by the wages fund and supply being given – will in general diverge from the *natural wage*.

As we mentioned in Chapter 1, the concept of natural equilibrium plays a fundamental role in Ricardo's analysis, in the sense that it represents a sort of centre of gravity towards which market positions ultimately tend to converge. The problem is considered by Pasinetti in the context of the approach above specified in terms of the stability of single positions of natural equilibrium. The question is examined from two points of view: (i) of the convergence of the market wage to the natural wage; and (ii) of the process of capital accumulation.

From the first point of view, Pasinetti shows that, assuming the existence of a Malthusian population response, there is a tendency on the part of the system to resume the natural equilibrium position whenever the market results diverge from the natural values. This is obtained through the joint consideration of the population response and of the wage-adjustment mechanism based on the wages-fund theory. In Pasinetti's context population is assumed to be constant when the market wage is equal to the natural one ($x = \bar{x}$), to increase when $x > \bar{x}$, and to fall when $x < \bar{x}$. As we have said, the model implies, on the other hand, $\bar{K} = xN$ whence $dx/dN < 0$, which means that market wages decline when population increases, and vice versa. The joint operation of these two mechanisms ensures that market equilibrium tends to converge to the natural equilibrium (Pasinetti (64), pp. 85–6).

The working of the population-adjustment mechanism is, however, conditioned by the hypothesis that no accumulation of capital is taking place. If this hypothesis is discarded, we cannot avoid taking into account, in addition to the conditions determining the supply of labour, those affecting the demand for it, which depend precisely on accumulation. But in that case the joint analysis of the two 'dynamic mechanisms', if set in its correct perspective, would become more complex than the pure and simple study of the Malthusian response to which we have referred above.

From the second point of view, it should be noted that the presence of a positive rate of profit, given the assumption that capitalists invest all their income, implies in the Ricardian theory an active process of capital accumulation. The problem of the process of economic growth is considered by Pasinetti in terms of the study of the direction of change of the variables as a consequence of an increase in K starting from a predefined position of natural equilibrium (a type of problem which can be meaningfully raised only with reference to positions of natural equilibrium different from the stationary state). The results obtained show that all the derivatives of the variables considered are positive except that of the price of gold (which is nil) and that of the profit rate (which is negative).

The analysis is, however, carried out on the basis of a *ceteris paribus* assumption symmetric to that conditioning, as we have seen, the study of the population adjustment, i.e. the hypothesis that 'the demographic mechanism has already fully worked through'. An assumption of this kind reflects, according to Pasinetti, Ricardo's approach to the problem (Pasinetti (64), p. 87):

> Ricardo . . . investigates the properties of his system at a very particular stage of the whole movement, which he considers the relevant one. Most of his analysis is carried on *as if* the demographic mechanism has already fully worked through, while the capital accumulation process has not yet been completed.

In other words, Pasinetti assumes that through the working of market forces the natural wage rate 'has been permanently achieved' ((64), p. 88) – a state of affairs which, according to his own definition, implies that population is constant.

This hypothesis, however, does not seem to be consistent with the working of the model. A contradiction arises in effect with the results obtained by Pasinetti: the first derivative actually shows, contrary to the assumption stated, that employment (population) tends to grow, at the fixed natural wage rate, as a consequence of capital accumulation.

This circumstance – in itself quite correct – shows that in Pasinetti's model the definition of the natural wage, as that wage at which population remains constant, is acceptable (i.e. non-contradictory) only if capital accumulation does not take place (stationary-state equilibrium). A different approach then becomes necessary if the phenomena taking place during the process of capital accumulation are to be adequately treated. The assumption that the natural wage rate has been permanently achieved does not justify the exclusion from the analysis of the supply side of the labour market. The consideration of the growing demand for labour, as a consequence of accumulation, must therefore be accompanied by the joint study of the problems relating to the supply of labour. As we have mentioned in Chapter 1, a new definition of the concept of natural wage is required in this context. The argument will be developed in the following chapter.

The need for a logical connection between the two dynamic mechanisms emerges very clearly from the above discussion. Pasinetti ((64), p. 87) is fully aware of such a need when he writes that the differential equation defining the time derivative of the stock of capital should be considered jointly with that defining the time derivative of the total labour force. However, he confines himself to pointing out that these differential equations have stationary solutions, at which the two dynamic mechanisms cease to operate, and to proving (in his appendix) that 'the system necessarily converges towards them' (Pasinetti (64), p. 87), so that:

> When the situation they represent is attained . . . [t]he wage-rate is at its natural level (no longer disturbed by capital accumulation) and the rate of profit has fallen to zero. The system has reached a stable equilibrium − the Ricardian equilibrium of the stationary state.

The immediate implication of this approach is that the effects of investment on the scale of the economic process are ignored. Capital accumulation is taken into account only to prove the instability of equilibrium positions different from the stationary state and does not belong, therefore, to the core of Pasinetti's analysis.

The consideration of the two dynamic mechanisms in a systematic way would imply building the argument not in terms of stability of single positions of point natural equilibrium, but rather in terms of the modern concept of 'dynamic' equilibrium, which corresponds in Ricardo to the notion of the natural equilibrium path discussed in Chapter 1. The importance from a methodological point of view of such a change in perspective has been aptly stressed by Domar (22) with his emphasis upon the 'dual' effect of investment (on productive capacity and income generation). This is precisely the approach followed in the present work and pursued in the next chapters through the analysis of some dynamic formulations of the Ricardian system.

4.6 The behaviour of distributive shares in the process of capital accumulation

Pasinetti's formulation of the Ricardian system makes it possible to examine in some detail the question of the behaviour of distributive shares in the course of the process of growth. The problem is touched upon only marginally by Pasinetti ((64), p. 89), who concentrates instead on the analysis of the response of the aggregate amount of profits to capital accumulation.

A general solution for the issue of the behaviour of distributive shares in a two-sector Ricardian model cannot be attained. A range of indeterminacy appears that cannot be filled in with the generic assumption of the existence of diminishing returns.[9] The behaviour of distributive shares depends on the evolution of the structure of the system (expressed by means of an appropriate employment ratio), which can be defined solely in the context of an exact determination of the growth path of the economy, given specified technological assumptions.

This statement can be easily proved on the basis of the definitions of the three distributive shares. Given the choice of *numéraire* (equation (4) of this chapter), it is easy to show that the value of the production of corn is equal to total employment in the economy, and that of the production of gold is equal to employment in the same industrial sector. From equations (2) and (4) we have immediately:

$$p_2 X_2 = N_2 \tag{16}$$

On the other hand, by definition:

$$p_1 X_1 = p_1 R + p_1 W_1 + p_1 P_1 \tag{17}$$

Substituting (6), (7) and (10) in (17), we have:

$$p_1 X_1 = p_2 X_2 + p_1 N_1 f'(N_1) \tag{18}$$

Taking account of (3) and (16), we then obtain:

$$p_1 X_1 = N_1 + N_2 = N \tag{19}$$

National income (value of total production of the two sectors) is therefore:

$$p_1 X_1 + p_2 X_2 = N + N_2 \tag{20}$$

Distributive shares in natural equilibrium are accordingly:

$$\rho = \frac{p_1 R}{p_1 X_1 + p_2 X_2} = \frac{N_2}{N + N_2} \tag{21}$$

$$\eta = \frac{p_1 W}{p_1 X_1 + p_2 X_2} = p_1 \bar{x} \frac{N}{N + N_2} \tag{22}$$

$$\pi = \frac{p_1 P_1 + p_2 P_2}{p_1 X_1 + p_2 X_2} = (1 - p_1 \bar{x}) \frac{N}{N + N_2} \tag{23}$$

where ρ indicates the share of rent, η that of wages, and π that of profits.

In order to examine the behaviour of the three distributive shares in the process of growth, we must now examine the sign of the derivatives of ρ, η and π with respect to capital. The derivatives are:

$$\frac{d\rho}{dK} = \frac{N N_2}{(N + N_2)^2} \left(\frac{1}{N_2} \frac{dN_2}{dK} - \frac{1}{N} \frac{dN}{dK} \right) \tag{24}$$

$$\frac{d\eta}{dK} = \frac{N\bar{x}\frac{dp_1}{dK}(N+N_2) - \bar{x}p_1 NN_2\left(\frac{1}{N_2}\frac{dN_2}{dK} - \frac{1}{N}\frac{dN}{dK}\right)}{(N+N_2)^2} \tag{25}$$

$$\frac{d\pi}{dK} = \frac{-N\bar{x}\frac{dp_1}{dK}(N+N_2) - \left[(1-\bar{x}p_1)NN_2\left(\frac{1}{N_2}\frac{dN_2}{dK} - \frac{1}{N}\frac{dN}{dK}\right)\right]}{(N+N_2)^2} \tag{26}$$

As can be easily realized from these expressions, the evolution of the distributive shares can be determined solely if the productive structure of the system, expressed in terms of the relative weights of employment in the two sectors, remains unchanged in the course of the process of growth.[10] If the rate of growth of employment is the same in both sectors, so that the relative weights of employment in agriculture and industry do not change, the share of rent remains constant, that of wages increases, and that of profits diminishes.

If, vice versa, the structure of employment changes in the course of the process of capital accumulation, the behaviour of distributive shares is not fully determinate. In this case, if employment in the industrial sector increases more rapidly than in the agricultural sector, the share of rent increases, that of wages is indeterminate, while that of profits diminishes. If, on the contrary, the situation occurs in which agriculture expands more rapidly than industry, it appears that the share of rent falls, that of wages increases, while the behaviour of the share of profits is indeterminate.

This last result would seem at odds with Ricardo's idea of the ultimate reduction of total profits connected with the assumption of diminishing returns in agriculture (Ricardo (67), p. 17, and (68), p. 123). A more careful scrutiny of equation (26) shows, however, that no such contradiction arises. The indeterminacy of the evolution of π depends on the fact that, assuming that the agricultural sector grows more rapidly than the industrial one, the two terms in the numerator of (26) are of opposite sign. It should be observed, however, that as the process of capital accumulation goes on the expression $(1 - \bar{x}p_1)$, i.e. profit per worker in terms of value,[11] tends to zero. The first term, always negative, assumes therefore a predominant influence and (26) thus becomes negative.

The indeterminancy of π on the specific hypothesis just considered must therefore be qualified in the sense that, although an increase in the share of profits during certain phases of the growth process is possible, π ultimately tends to diminish. This result may be said to reflect Ricardo's opinion about the behaviour of total profits.

The specific case, which could be labelled 'strongly Ricardian', of a monotonic increase of the share of rent and of a corresponding monotonic decrease of the share of profits can only occur when the model generates a situation in which industrial employment grows faster than agricultural employment.

It can be said in conclusion that the hypothesis of diminishing returns in agriculture is not sufficient to determine in general the behaviour over time of distributive shares in the context of a two-sector Ricardian model. This circumstance, however, as we pointed out in Chapter 2, does not represent a major hindrance for the comprehension of the basic theme of Ricardo's theoretical investigation. Ricardo's concern for the progressive slowing down of the process of capital accumulation can find a full-fledged analytical expression in terms of the behaviour of the general rate of profit — rather than of the share of profits — in presence of diminishing returns in the production of the subsistence of the labourers.

The problem concerning the determination of the rate of profit and the link between that rate and the technological conditions of the agricultural sector have already been dealt with in Chapter 2; those concerning the dynamics of the rate of profit — in equilibrium and in disequilibrium — are the object of the analysis carried out in the following chapters.

5 A one-sector Ricardian model

5.1 Introductory remarks

The study of Pasinetti's formulation of the Ricardian system has shown that an adequate interpretation of Ricardo's growth theory requires that the dynamic mechanisms of capital accumulation and population adjustment become an integral part of the analysis. This means that the model to be considered must be truly dynamic and that the interpretation must be carried out with the use of the characteristic tools of dynamic analysis. The present chapter and the following ones, in a 'constructive' rather than in a 'critical' spirit, aim precisely at this end.

As we have mentioned in Chapter 1, the Ricardian growth model represented here may be interpreted as an attempt to carry a stage further the logic of Baumol's suggestion ((5), p. 8) with respect to the substantial similarity between classical dynamics and Harrod's approach to economic growth.

In formulating the model, it is convenient to proceed by successive approximations. We start in this chapter from the single-sector model (agriculture), and move on in the following to the two-sector model (agriculture and industry), finally considering in the appendix to Chapter 6 some problems relating to the three-sector model (corn, gold and machines). The preliminary examination of the one-sector dynamic model allows us to bring out more directly certain fundamental relations between the key variables of the model and their growth rates. The main results attained in this simplified framework remain valid in the two-sector model.

With reference to the methodological approach to growth problems set out in the opening chapter, and in particular to the distinction between *equilibrium* and *disequilibrium paths*, the analysis is carried out in two phases. In the first the conditions of equilibrium growth are stated and the time paths of the relevant variables are described. In the second attention is concentrated on the dynamic behaviour of the system when there are departures from the equilibrium path. The study of the sources of disequilibrium and of the reaction mechanisms — with the formulation of behaviour hypotheses of the economic agents valid both in equilibrium and disequilibrium conditions — represents the link from one type of analysis to the other.

5.2 The equilibrium model

The fundamental hypotheses of the Ricardian theory have already been set out in detail in the previous chapter with reference to a two-sector model. They need to be modified here only as regards those aspects depending on the assumption of a single commodity.

Using the symbols already introduced, with the suffix t to indicate time, and denoting by a dot above the letter the derivative of a variable with respect to time (which is regarded as a continuous variable), the equilibrium model can be described by the following equations:

$$X_t = f(N_t)$$

Production function of the agricultural sector (fundamental importance is attached to property (1d) regarding diminishing returns) (1)

$$f(0) = 0 \tag{1a}$$

$$f'(N_t) > 0 \tag{1b}$$

$$f'(0) > \bar{x} \tag{1c}$$

$$f''(N_t) < 0 \tag{1d}$$

$$R_t = f(N_t) - N_t f'(N_t) \qquad \text{Rent} \tag{2}$$

$$W_t = K_t$$

Wages fund (K_t representing the circulating capital advanced as wages to the workers) (3)

$$P_t = N_t [f'(N_t) - \bar{x}] \qquad \text{Profits} \tag{4}$$

$$\dot{K}_t = P_t$$

Investment (on the hypothesis that the capitalists' propensity to save is unity) (5)

$$N_t = \frac{W_t}{\bar{x}} \qquad\qquad \text{Demand for labour} \quad (6)$$

Two characteristics of this model should be stressed: (a) the hypothesis that the wage rate is permanently at the *natural* level, and (b) the condition that growth is not constrained by the supply of labour. The implications of these assumptions will be discussed in section 5.4 below. Specific reference will be made to the need for a definition of the natural wage consistent with the concept of natural equilibrium in growth (a definition which is also valid in the particular case of the stationary state).

5.3 The relation between the rates of growth of income and capital

In order to examine the dynamic properties of the simple Ricardian model just presented, we now define the rates of growth of income and capital and examine the relation between them. The rate of growth of capital (which we shall denote as G_k) can be easily determined from equations (3)-(6). It is equal to

$$G_k = \frac{\dot{K}_t}{K_t} = \frac{f'(N_t)}{\bar{x}} - 1 \qquad (7)$$

and obviously coincides, on account of equation (5), with the rate of profit r_t – this being a typical property of the models which assume a 'classical' saving function.

Given the assumptions about the production function, the rate of growth of capital steadily diminishes over time and falls to zero when the marginal productivity of labour becomes equal to the natural wage. Profits disappear and the economy reaches the stationary-state position.

The rate of growth of income (which we shall denote as G_x) can be obtained from equations (1), (2), (3) and (6) as follows:

$$G_x = \frac{\dot{X}_t}{X_t} = \frac{f'(N_t)\dot{N}_t}{X_t} = \frac{f'(N_t)\dfrac{\dot{K}_t}{\bar{x}}}{X_t}$$

$$= \frac{N_t f'(N_t)\dfrac{\dot{K}_t}{K_t}}{X_t} = \frac{P_t + W_t}{P_t + W_t + R_t} \cdot G_k \qquad (8)$$

The rate of growth of income is therefore equal to the product of the rate of growth of capital and the income share of profits plus wages. Because of diminishing returns, this share is less than unity; the rate of growth of income is consequently less than that of capital.

One might be tempted to interpret the relation expressed by (8) as a consequence of the fact that the part of total product absorbed by rent represents a 'loss' for subsequent productive cycles, i.e. a diversion of resources away from the process of accumulation that reduces the possibility of increasing the scale of production. In other words, remembering that in this model the rate of growth of capital is equal to the rate of profit, one might be induced to interpret equation (8) as being a definition of the rate of income growth as the rate of profit applied only to the share of profits plus wages in each period, which represents the circulating capital (wages fund) of the subsequent period.

This interpretation, however, would not be correct. Let us assume for a moment – contrary to Ricardo's hypotheses, but in line with certain observations put forward by Malthus on rent[1] – that land-owners reinvest all their income: that is to say, rent is thus assimilated to profits as regards its utilization. Equation (5) would then be substituted in the model by

$$\dot{K}_t = P_t + R_t \tag{5a}$$

The result achieved as regards the relation between the rates of growth of capital and income would, however, not be changed in any way: G_x would still be equal to G_k times the share of profits plus wages in income.

The different assumption about the behaviour of landowners would only affect the levels of the growth rates and hence the rate of expansion of the economy. Capital accumulation would, in fact, be defined as:

$$G_k = \frac{f(N_t)/N_t - \bar{x}}{\bar{x}} \tag{7a}$$

which is clearly greater than the corresponding growth rate defined by equation (7) because, with the hypothesis of diminishing returns, the average product of labour is always greater than the marginal product. Given the relative share of profits plus wages, the rate of growth of income would also be greater than the one obtained when investment is defined by (5).

It is therefore the *presence* of rent – and not its utilization for consumption or for investment – which is responsible for the divergence between the rates of growth of capital and income. As we have seen, and as will be further shown in Section 5.5 below, the way rent is expended does not affect the properties of the model but only the rate of expansion of the economic system and its stationary-state position.

Since the presence of rent is the direct outcome of diminishing returns, it is to this latter factor that the result expressed by equation (8) must be attributed. The link between this result and the assumption of diminishing returns may be usefully clarified with the consideration of two implications of (8): (a) the fact that the rate of growth of income is lower than that of capital; and (b) the fact that the relation between the two rates is determined by the share of profits plus wages in the sense that, the greater that share, the less will be the divergence between the two rates. Reference to the 'modern' tools of analysis will make these points clear.

As regards the first aspect, note that the production function of the model belongs to the class of homogeneous functions of degree less than one in which increases in the amount of the factor employed — we may here regard the variable factor as being indifferently circulating capital or labour — are accompanied by less than proportionate increases in the amount of product. The rate of growth of income is therefore necessarily lower than that of the variable factor.

As regards the second aspect, it can be easily realized from our previous remarks that the divergence between the rate of growth of income and that of capital increases with the intensity of diminishing returns, of which rent is the outstanding manifestation. This fact can be made clearer in analytical terms by means of the generalization of Euler's theorem for homogeneous functions of any degree[2] which makes it possible to show that the share of profits plus wages coincides with the degree of homogeneity of the production function. Recalling now that in the Ricardian theory of distribution the joint income of capitalists and labourers is explained on the basis of a 'marginal productivity principle',[3] it may be said that the absolute value of profits plus wages is equal to the product of the number of workers employed, N_t, times the corresponding marginal productivity, $f'(N_t)$. Then, taking account of the already-mentioned generalization of Euler's theorem, we can write:

$$N_t f'(N_t) = \mu X_t \tag{9}$$

where μ represents the degree of homogeneity of the production function $X_t = f(N_t)$. It is obvious that μ also expresses the share of profits plus wages in income.

These considerations therefore confirm the view that the result expressed by equation (8) must be interpreted as a direct consequence of the technological hypotheses, which have a specific impact on the distribution of income in the Ricardian model.

The result reached above as regards the relation between the rates of growth of income and capital may be taken as a generalization of a fundamental property of growth models – the coincidence of these two rates. Diminishing returns in agriculture explain the difference which, from this point of view, emerges between the Ricardian model and current growth models. Since the latter do not consider land as a scarce factor, rent does not appear among the distributive shares, and the two rates coincide. Equation (8) emphasizes that this is a particular case, valid solely in the absence of rent.

It is worth underlining, moreover, the analogy between this result and the conclusions reached in von Neumann's model (63), notoriously of classical inspiration. In the latter – with hypotheses identical to the Ricardian ones (subsistence wage, supply of labour always adequate for the needs of growth, total reinvestment of profits and consumption of all labour income), but with the assumption of constant returns – the rate of increase in production is equal to that of capital, which coincides in turn with the rate of profit.

A further remark should be made. The divergence between the two rates of growth of income and capital depends on the behaviour through time of the share of rent. If that share is constant, the relation between the two rates of growth is also constant; if, on the contrary, that share is variable, the relation also changes. In particular, if the share of rent increases, the divergence between the rates of growth of income and capital tends to become greater. From this point of view, the study of the behaviour of distributive shares assumes specific importance.

5.4 Full employment as a necessary condition of equilibrium growth

In the presentation of the model in section 5.2, we mentioned the condition that the availability of manpower should not represent an obstacle to the expansion of the system determined by capital accumulation. This condition can be met both in a situation of permanent surplus of supply over demand at the natural wage level and in a situation of permanent equilibrium between demand and supply of labour at the same natural wage. In Kaldor's words ((43), p. 180):

> The rate of accumulation of capital . . . determines [in the Ricardian system] the rate of increase in the employment of labour . . . without enquiring very closely where this additional labour comes from. The model is consistent with the assumption that there is an unlimited labour reserve, say, in the form of surplus population in an under-developed country (the assumption favoured by Marx), or with assuming that the rate of increase in population is itself governed by the rate of growth in the demand for labour (the assumption favoured by Ricardo).

Both these assumptions have been considered in recent growth models. The main strand of growth theory is linked with the second of these hypotheses, since full employment is one of the essential conditions of equilibrium growth. The models incorporating such a hypothesis are usually known as *golden age* models (Robinson (72), p. 99), precisely because of the difficulty of realizing in practice the conditions posed in the theoretical construction. The first of the above hypotheses is associated, on the other hand, with what are usually called *bastard golden age* models (Kahn (41)), in which the necessary existence of a reaction mechanism of the economy to a situation of permanent unemployment is denied and steady-state growth is considered compatible with high and ever increasing levels of unemployment.

The problems posed by these alternative approaches must, in our opinion, be resolved by a clear stand in favour of the explicit inclusion of full employment among the conditions of balanced growth; for it seems very unrealistic to adopt the hypothesis of the existence of significant and even increasing levels of unemployment without this fact having any impact on the pace of growth of income through variations in wage levels, consumption patterns, and so on.[4]

This choice appears particularly appropriate in the Ricardian context, where considerable difficulties would be encountered with the Marxian assumption of a 'reserve army' so large as to satisfy the employment requirements up to the stationary state.

Even abstracting from the question of the origin of the means of subsistence of the 'reserve army', it is in fact hard to conceive — in the logical framework of the Ricardian theory — of a persistent state of extensive unemployment without the wage rate being affected. A contradiction appears to exist, in other words, between the hypothesis of the reserve army and the wage–population-adjustment process which, as we have already seen in Chapter 4, is so deeply rooted in the Ricardian system. Acceptance of the Marxian approach would then necessarily imply the refusal of the Malthusian mechanism, contrary to the evidence of Ricardo's analytical construction. It should be further recalled here that the assumption of an unlimited supply of labour seems to be better suited to depicting a typical feature of underdeveloped countries[5] rather than the situation of the early nineteenth-century English economy, whose deep transformations (industrial revolution) Ricardo could directly observe[6] and whose long-term prospects he meant to analyse.

The Ricardian one-sector model of section 5.2 must then be supplemented with the condition that demand and supply of labour be equal. Assuming that the system considered starts out from an initial situation of full employment, this condition may be expressed in terms of an equality between the rates of change of the demand and the supply of labour. Since equations (5) and (6) show that the demand for labour expands (at constant wages) at the same rate as capital, the equilibrium condition can be written as:

$$\frac{\dot{N}_t}{N_t} = \frac{\dot{K}_t}{K_t} = \frac{f'(N_t)}{\bar{x}} - 1 = n_t \tag{10}$$

where n_t indicates the rate of growth of the labour force in period t. On account of equation (5), this condition may also be expressed as an equality between the rate of growth of the labour force and the rate of profit:

$$r_t = n_t \tag{10a}$$

Equations (1)-(6) and (10) define, therefore, what may be called a Ricardo-type (and, more generally, a classical-type) *golden age growth model*. The path generated by this model is what we have defined the *natural equilibrium path* of the Ricardian growth model. As we have seen, this path is characterized, because of diminishing returns, by rates of growth of capital and population always decreasing over time and permanently greater than the rate of increase of national product.

The conclusion arrived at offers a clear hint of the way in which the notion of the *natural wage* should be redefined.

Contrary to the idea implicit in the definition of the *Principles*, but in accordance with that of the *Essay on Profits*, a constant wage rate at the natural level is in fact compatible with a situation in which the labour force is growing. The natural wage must then be defined as the one at which the labour force expands at exactly the same

113

rate as capital, i.e. the wages fund. It is clear that, with this definition, wages can remain at the natural level only on condition that demand and supply of labour are in equilibrium, i.e. only if a situation of permanent full employment is maintained.

We may say in conclusion that, while the definition of natural wages given in the *Principles* is compatible only with the stationary-state situation, the definition adopted here, in line with the *Essay on Profits*, is consistent with the progressive phase of the economy as well as with the situation of stationarity.

5.5 Equilibrium growth with the production function N_t^α

To illustrate the equilibrium path identified by the conditions mentioned in the previous sections, we can choose a specific form for the production function. We will for convenience examine the case of a particularly simple function which makes it easy to determine the equilibrium solution of the model, the distributive shares, and hence the relationship between the rates of growth of income and capital.

Let us consider the production function:

$$X_t = N_t^\alpha \tag{11}$$

with $0 < \alpha < 1$.[7] As the first derivative is always positive, while the second derivative is always negative, the conditions for diminishing returns are satisfied.

The rate of growth of capital, defined in general by (7), becomes:[8]

$$G_k = \frac{\alpha N_t^{(\alpha-1)}}{\bar{x}} - 1 \tag{12}$$

Given equations (3) and (6), the stationary state value of capital can be now obtained setting G_k equal to zero:

$$\bar{K} = \alpha^{\left(-\frac{1}{\alpha-1}\right)} \bar{x}^{\left(\frac{\alpha}{\alpha-1}\right)} \tag{13}$$

The stationary-state value of population, determined in the same way, is:

$$\bar{N} = \left(\frac{\bar{x}}{\alpha}\right)^{\frac{1}{\alpha-1}} \tag{14}$$

Turning now to the distributive shares, from equations (3), (4) and (11) we can determine the absolute value of profits plus wages:

$$P_t + W_t = N_t[\alpha N_t^{(\alpha-1)} - \bar{x}] + \bar{x}N_t = \alpha N_t^{\alpha} \qquad (15)$$

The corresponding share in total income is therefore constant over time and equal to α.

The rate of growth of income, always smaller than that of capital, is thus equal to α times G_k, and the relationship between these two rates remains constant over time.

It is clear that the constancy of the share of profits plus wages obviously implies the constancy of the share of rent, which assumes the value of $(1 - \alpha)$. It can easily be shown that the share of wages, equal to $\bar{x}N_t^{(1-\alpha)}$, is always increasing up to the point at which it reaches the stationary-state value, while that of profits, equal to $\alpha - \bar{x}N_t^{(1-\alpha)}$, is always diminishing.

Examining the problems connected with the hypothesis of diminishing returns, we observed in section 5.3 that the ultimate allocation of rent to investment rather than to consumption would affect not only the rate of growth of the economy but also the stationary-state values of the variables. We can now revert to this subject in relation to the particular technological hypothesis formulated here.

The rate of accumulation, when investment is equal to the sum of profits plus rent, already defined in general by equation (7a), is now

$$G_k = \frac{N_t^{(\alpha-1)}}{\bar{x}} - 1 \qquad (12a)$$

The stationary-state value of capital, obtained by putting investment equal to zero, is now equal to

$$\bar{K} = \bar{x}^{\left(\frac{\alpha}{\alpha-1}\right)} \qquad (13a)$$

which is clearly greater than the corresponding value defined by (13). Similarly, the stationary-state value of population is

$$\bar{N} = \bar{x}^{\left(\frac{1}{\alpha-1}\right)} \qquad (14a)$$

which is equally greater than the corresponding value indicated by (14).

The rate of accumulation being higher and the stationary-state values greater, the whole equilibrium path in this new hypothesis of land-owners' behaviour would clearly be above the one followed by the economic system on the hypothesis that rent is allocated to consumption.[9]

5.6 Disequilibrium mechanisms

Having thus defined the equilibrium conditions of the one-sector Ricardian model, both in general and on a particular assumption as regards the production function, we shall now deal with the problems of the disequilibrium dynamics of the model, in line with the methodological approach stated at the beginning of the book and referred to in the first section of the present chapter.

It should be said at the outset that, since the model of section 5.2 is strictly an equilibrium model, the treatment of disequilibrium situations requires a restatement of some equations. More general hypotheses have to be introduced in order to make it possible for the model to express the behaviour of economic agents both in equilibrium and in disequilibrium conditions.

The problem then arises as to what types of disequilibrium situations are compatible with the logic of the Ricardian theoretical framework.

In principle, three classes of disequilibrium phenomena could be conceived of in the one-sector Ricardian model. The first, concerning the labour market, could take the form either of a divergence between the market and the natural wage rate, or of a difference between the actual and the equilibrium supply of labour. The second, relating to the commodity market, would consist of a failure of aggregate demand to coincide with aggregate supply. The third, dealing with productive capacity, could be expressed in terms of a discrepancy between actual and desired capital.

It is argued here that only the first class of disequilibrium situations appears to be compatible with the Ricardian logical scheme. In the following sections two alternative formulations of the adjustment mechanism in the labour market are examined and their consistency with the Ricardian theory is discussed in detail. In the rest of this section we consider the difficulties that would arise if the attempt were made to fit into the Ricardian context the last two classes of disequilibrium situations.

With reference to the possibility of general overproduction, it should be stressed that Ricardo substantially identified the act of saving with the decision to invest.[10] This implies the automatic fulfilment of Say's law, thereby excluding the possibility of a general glut. This circumstance, which is particularly evident in the case of the extreme classical saving function incorporated in the model of section 5.2, is not modified by the formulation of more general hypotheses about the saving behaviour of the social classes, considered in Chapter 7.

Problems of overproduction could arise only if money as an asset were explicitly considered and the possibility of hoarding thereby taken into account. This, however, would require dealing with problems of uncertainty and expectations about the future and would imply admitting the possibility of unsold stocks of commodities (corn in this model) — a whole set of issues that appear to be far removed from Ricardo's thinking.

As regards the last class of disequilibrium situations, i.e. those which might derive from a divergence between actual and desired productive capacity, it would seem hard to conceive of these problems in a model in which capital consists only of advances to workers. However, even if fixed capital were introduced into the model, the consideration of this disequilibrium hypothesis would require the existence of an investment function, independent of saving, capable of expressing entrepreneurial reactions to a difference between actual and desired capacity. But, as we have just recalled, this would clearly clash with Ricardo's view that saving is automatically invested.

5.7 The wages–population interaction mechanism: the wages-fund theory

In the model describing the conditions of balanced growth, the hypothesis was made that the supply of labour expands over time at the same rate as the corresponding demand (represented by the available stock of circulating capital), in such a way as to allow wages to remain stable at the natural level, which is taken as given among the initial conditions of the model.

In order to move now to a disequilibrium analysis of the labour market, we must suppose that demand and supply of labour are no longer equal at the level of the natural wage. We shall assume that this will arise because of an initial divergence between the *actual* supply of manpower and the amount of labour required to keep the wage rate at the natural level (the *equilibrium* supply of labour).

We might be tempted, incidentally, to identify the source of disequilibrium directly in a divergence of the going wage rate from the natural rate, attributing this divergence, for example, to an imperfect transparence of the labour market, i.e. to incomplete knowledge of market conditions. Such an approach would, however, be incompatible with the Ricardian theory and with the model presented here.

Indeed if, by mistake, the market wage rate should depart from

117

the natural level, while the initial conditions in the labour market (N_t/K_t) make it possible for the market to be cleared at the natural wage, a situation would arise either of unused capital or of unemployed labour. The first alternative would be clearly alien to the spirit of the Ricardian theory (in particular, it would come up against the fundamental hypothesis regarding the behaviour of capitalists). The second, on the contrary, can be taken into consideration but only on condition that its scope and *modus operandi* be adequately defined, as will be done below in the context of a specific assumption about the working of the labour market.

If, instead, we attribute the cause of disequilibrium to a divergence between the *actual* and the *equilibrium* supply of labour, no problems of consistency with the logic of the Ricardian model arise and it becomes possible at the same time to stress the crucial role of the labour-market equilibrium condition. Obviously, a disequilibrium hypothesis of this kind leads us back to the question of a departure of the actual wage rate from its natural level. It stands out at once, however, that the situation now considered is very different from the preceding one: a divergence between the actual and natural wage rate is now the consequence and not the source of disequilibrium.

In accordance with the Ricardian theory, we shall suppose that the effects of a disequilibrium situation reflect themselves not only on the labour market (i.e. on wages and/or employment) but also on the rate of change of population. This set of phenomena is indicated here as the *wage–population interaction mechanism*.

Two formulations of this interaction mechanism will be considered here. The first, based on the wages-fund theory and on the Malthusian theory of population, is examined in the present and in the following section. The second – considered'in sections 5.10 and 5.11 – retains the Malthusian principle, but assumes instead an incomplete downward flexibility of the market wage rate.

In the first formulation centred on the wages-fund theory, the labour market is in a permanent state of full employment. The flexibility of the market wage rate ensures the continuous balance between the demand and supply of labour, both of these being determined at all times independently of each other – the former related to capital accumulation, the latter to population growth.

In the equilibrium model, the theory of the wages fund has been used to define – given the level of the natural wage – the rate of population growth, n_t, required for the system to move along the natural equilibrium path. In the present context we assume instead that, in a specific period, the supply of labour is given and that it diverges from its equilibrium value; the wages-fund theory then performs the task of determining that particular *market* wage rate, different from the *natural* one, corresponding to full employment of the available labour force.

We further assume that a divergence between the market and the natural wage rate leads to a situation in which the rate of growth of the supply of labour differs from the equilibrium one (equal to the rate of growth of capital). Nor could it be otherwise in the present model, since the equilibrium growth of population obtains only if the wage rate is constant at the natural level. The specific hypothesis adopted here of the population-adjustment mechanism follows the Malthusian approach, which forms an integral and fundamental part of Ricardo's theory.[11] However, while the original formulation is cast in terms of absolute population levels, the present formulation — in line with the new interpretation of the concept of the natural wage in a dynamic context — refers to the rate of change of population.

The demographic mechanism described by Ricardo in the *Principles* is based, as we have said, on a definition of the natural wage as that level of wages at which population is constant. An increase in wages above the subsistence level is thought to lead to a population expansion; movements of opposite sign are supposed to occur when the market wage falls below the natural wage. The reasoning is clearly carried out in terms of absolute levels of population.

The interpretation of the natural wage rate given here involves a more general formulation of the demographic mechanism, a formulation which may be valid both in the case of population growth and in the case in which population is constant. Given that, in the present Ricardian model, the natural wage is the one at which the supply of labour grows at the same rate as the demand for it, the demographic mechanism is presented here in terms of adjustment of the rate of change of population. If, as a result of labour shortage in relation to its equilibrium value, wages rise above the natural level, the rate of population growth increases; and vice versa if wages are below the natural level.

5.8 Disequilibrium dynamics on the hypothesis of the wages-fund theory

The disequilibrium model based on the wages-fund adjustment mechanism is set out below in full for convenience of reference:

$$X_t = f(N_t) = N_t^\alpha \qquad \text{Production function with diminishing returns} \qquad (16)$$

$$R_t = f(N_t) - N_t f'(N_t) \qquad \text{Rent} \qquad (17)$$

$$W_t = K_t \qquad \text{Wages fund} \qquad (18)$$

$$P_t = N_t[f'(N_t) - x_t] \qquad \text{Profits} \qquad (19)$$

$$\dot{K}_t = P_t \qquad \text{Investment} \qquad (20)$$

$$N_t^D = \frac{W_t}{x_t} \qquad \text{Demand for labour} \qquad (21)$$

$$\frac{\dot{N}_t^S}{N_t^S} = n_t + \gamma(x_t - \bar{x}) \qquad \text{Labour supply} \qquad (22)$$

$$n_t = \frac{f'(N_t)}{\bar{x}} - 1 \qquad \text{Equilibrium rate of growth of the labour supply} \qquad (23)$$

$$N_t^D = N_t^S = N \qquad \text{Equilibrium conditions in the labour market} \qquad (24)$$

N_t^D and N_t^S represent respectively the demand and supply of labour at time t. For the sake of clarity, these variables are kept distinguished from the level of employment N_t, particularly in view of subsequent comparison between the model being examined here and the one incorporating a different wage–population mechanism, presented in the following sections.

In the set of relations describing the wage–population mechanism, equation (21) expresses the theory of the wages fund. Equation (22) defines the rate of change of the supply of labour in the simplified hypothesis that there are no time lags and that the demographic response is directly proportional to the difference between the market and the natural wage (the parameter γ, which is always positive on the Malthusian hypothesis adopted, denotes the intensity of that response). Equation (24), lastly, specifies the equilibrium condition of full employment in the labour market.

The distinguishing feature of the model, as compared with the equilibrium one analysed in the initial sections of this chapter, is represented by its more general formulation. In fact, it describes a whole set of growth paths, the natural equilibrium path being only one among them.

This feature stems essentially from the combination of: (a) the hypothesis (which substitutes that of a fixed wage rate at the natural level) that the cost of labour is determined by the interaction of demand and supply; and (b) the type of assumptions underlying the behaviour equations, which are now capable of expressing the path of the corresponding variables both in equilibrium and in disequilibrium conditions.

The time path of the economy described by the model has been determined with the help of the computer for the case in which the value of α in the production function (16) is equal to 0.75. We set out below the results in terms of the variables x_t (market wage) and N_t (employment) from which the behaviour of the other unknowns can easily be deduced.

As is clear from Figure 2, starting from an initial divergence between the market and the natural wage due to a departure of the supply of labour from its equilibrium value, the market rate tends to approach asymptotically the natural wage level following a path which gradually brings it (the market rate) closer to the natural rate. The speed of adjustment depends on the value of the reaction parameter γ. The higher the value of γ, the sooner convergence takes place.

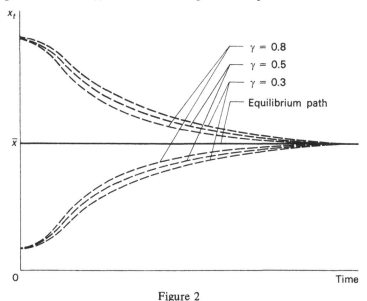

Figure 2

The behaviour of employment in a disequilibrium situation – as can be seen in Figure 3 – also shows a tendency to approach asymptotically the equilibrium path with a gradual reduction of the initial

121

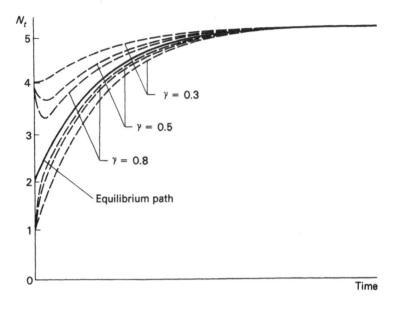

Figure 3

divergence. However, unlike the case of the wage rate, the path is not always monotonic. If the initial supply of labour exceeds the equilibrium value and if the parameter γ assumes appropriate values, employment presents, to start with, a drop in absolute terms, which is all the more accentuated, the more intense the population response, i.e. the greater the value of γ. If, on the contrary, the initial supply of labour is lower than the equilibrium value, the level of employment is always increasing, and the influence of γ, as in the preceding case, manifests itself in the speed of adjustment to the equilibrium path.[12] This apparent asymmetry should, however, be qualified in the sense that both the absolute and the percentage distance between the actual and the equilibrium path of employment tend, in both cases, to become smaller.

The rationale of the adjustment process portrayed in Figures 2 and 3 is obviously to be traced back to the interaction of the two mechanisms described in the preceding section. The initial disequilibrium in the labour market affects population growth via the market wage rate; changes in the supply of labour, in turn, reduce the initial divergence between the market and the natural wage. The process continues until the natural equilibrium path is attained.

Dealing finally with the problem of distributive shares, it should be observed that the distribution of output between profits plus wages on the one hand, and rent on the other, is identical to that of the equilibrium model. The fact that the economy does not move along the equilibrium path does not, in other words, influence the distribution of the product between these two shares – which, as we have seen in section 5.5, depends solely on technology.

The problem of distribution within the share of profits plus wages is more complex. With the particular production function used in the model under examination, the share of wages and that of profits are respectively equal to:

$$\frac{W_t}{X_t} = x_t N_t^{(1-\alpha)} \tag{25}$$

$$\frac{P_t}{X_t} = \alpha - x_t N_t^{(1-\alpha)} \tag{26}$$

Owing to the presence of terms of opposite sign[13] in the derivatives of (25) and (26) with respect to time, no clear-cut results can be reached in general about the behaviour of the above-mentioned shares. Computer simulation for the specific case here considered supplies, however, the following results:

(a) when there is an initial excess supply of labour, the share of wages is increasing – its path is characterized by an initial value lower than the equilibrium one and by the fact that it intersects the equilibrium path, gradually attaining thereafter the stationary-state value;

(b) when, on the contrary, there is an initial shortage of labour, the actual path of the share of wages starts above the equilibrium one, decreases and intersects the latter, then changes direction and increases asymptotically towards the stationary-state value.

The share of profits obviously moves in opposite directions in the two cases considered.

Hence an important difference emerges in the model between the disequilibrium behaviour of such variables as income, capital, employment and the market wage rate, and the time paths of the distributive shares of profits and wages. For the former group of variables the divergence of the actual from the equilibrium path is always of the same sign, this being determined by the type of the initial disequilibrium; for the latter, on the contrary, this does not happen. This fact would seem to suggest a greater complexity of the problems regarding the dynamics of distributive shares.

5.9 The possibility of unemployment in the Ricardian theory

Ricardo's *Principles* do not contain an explicit enunciation of the wages-fund theory, and indeed the rigid formulation of this theory is attributed, for example by Schumpeter ((79), pp. 810–21) and Baumol ((5), p. 18), not to Ricardo but to post-Ricardian economists such as McCulloch ((51), part III, ch. 2, section 1) and J. S. Mill ((59), ch. 9). It is significant in this respect that Marshall, with his profound knowledge of Ricardo, does not mention his name but indicates only that of J. S. Mill in the appendix of his *Principles* ((54), pp. 677–82) devoted to the wages-fund theory.

The question may therefore be raised of the possibility of unemployment in the Ricardian theoretical framework.

Ricardo's explicit acceptance of Say's law[14] might give rise to the belief that the result of full employment is implicit in his analytical model, and hence to the conclusion that Ricardo adhered to a strict version of the wages-fund theory. In fact, as has been emphasized by Garegnani (29), the implications of Say's law for Ricardo are quite different from those which it has for the neoclassics.

These economists assume, on the one hand, that saving and investment decisions are kept in equilibrium through the working of a specific adjustment mechanism (the rate of interest) and, on the other hand, that the demand for the 'productive factors' is elastic to changes in relative prices. They accordingly deduce from Say's law an inherent tendency towards a situation of permanent full employment.

In Ricardo, on the contrary, the act of saving coincides with the decision to invest whatever the rate of profit and hence the rate of interest.[15] Say's law is therefore automatically verified without there being necessarily implications as regards full employment, as Ricardo's passages dealing with the question of 'excess population' confirm ((68), pp. 56–7).

Full employment of labour, in Ricardo's theoretical framework, can occur only under particular circumstances, and does not constitute, therefore, a general and necessary feature of the model. Specific hypotheses are in fact required for full employment to obtain regarding: (a) the working of the labour market (i.e. validity of the wages-fund theory), when only circulating capital is considered; and (b) when fixed capital is explicitly taken into account, the nature of technology (i.e. flexibility of the capital–labour ratio). If these conditions are not fulfilled, Say's law does not involve full employment. Specific attention must therefore be devoted to the possibility that these two conditions may not be met.

(a) When only circulating capital is considered, the plausibility of a hypothesis about the functioning of the labour market different from the wages-fund theory (and thus compatible with departures from full employment) can be traced back to the fact that, in Ricardo's theoretical model, there appears to be a firm belief that the market wage rate is not completely flexible in the downward direction. More specifically, this means that the notion of the natural wage implies that the corresponding level of consumption is considered as customary or normal. This represents, so to speak, a 'brake' to significant reductions of the market wage below the natural level. Institutional factors may, in other words, prevent a full adjustment of wages below this level.

Garegnani's reasoning, if placed in the context of a model with no fixed capital, seems to rely precisely on the hypothesis of a partial downward rigidity of the wage rate when there is unemployment. In fact, Garegnani links the possibility of the recovery of full employment to an acceleration of the rate of capital accumulation and to a reduction of the rate of increase in population, both of these being determined by a drop in wages, rather than to the mechanical and immediate operation of the wages-fund doctrine.

The hypothesis of bargaining power examined in the following section represents an attempt to supply a possible explanation of a wage-adjustment mechanism insufficient to clear the labour market.

It should be noted that the recovery of full employment might be realized even on the hypothesis of absolute wage rigidity downwards provided that the demographic mechanism is formulated in a slightly different way. Equation (22) states that a reduction in the rate of population increase below the equilibrium rate may take place only when the market wage is lower than the natural one; if we now assume that the wage rate is rigid at this level, it is clear that the demographic mechanism would cease to operate and the presence of unemployment would have no effect on the rate of accumulation. When there is unemployment, however, the ratio of people employed to total population is reduced below its full-employment value. A divergence would arise therefore between the *actual* and what may be called the *subsistence* (or natural) *per capita income*; the role of driving-force of the demographic mechanism could be attributed to this divergence. In this case unemployment would tend to be gradually eliminated as a consequence of the reduction in the rate of population increase.

(b) When fixed capital is considered, the possibility of unemployment can arise – even assuming complete wage flexibility – from technological reasons.

If technology involves a fixed ratio of machines to labour, the demand for labour at a certain level of accumulation may happen to be lower than the supply, and the number of persons employed would therefore be independent of the wage rate. Garegnani's reference ((29), p. 341 n) to Ricardo's chapter 'On machinery' confirms that in this context the possibility of unemployment is linked to the assumed fixity of the ratio of machines to labour determined by technology.

(In this case, given the independence of demand for labour from wages, it is not clear through what mechanism a reduction in wages below subsistence would take place, thus leading to the recovery of full employment through the speeding up of the accumulation process and the slowing down of the demographic expansion.)

5.10 The wage–population interaction mechanism: the bargaining-power hypothesis

Going back now to the assumption that there is no fixed capital, as we have stated at the beginning of this chapter when the basic Ricardian one-sector model was presented, we shall now examine a specific hypothesis about the labour market which is compatible with situations of less than full employment. This hypothesis refers to the case – mentioned in the preceding section – of limited downward flexibility of wages, depending on institutional factors which may inhibit the full working of the competitive mechanism of the labour market on which the type of wage–population interaction considered in sections 5.7 and 5.8 was based.

This new hypothesis reflects, in other words, a situation of the labour market in which two institutionally organized parties, both of them in a substantially monopolistic position, confront each other. The term 'bargaining-power hypothesis' will be used to identify this case. A situation of the same type could also arise because of the existence of external constraints, for example of a legislative nature, to the full operation of market forces.

The essential feature of the bargaining-power hypothesis concerns the behaviour of the market wage rate. In particular, it is here assumed that when the supply of labour exceeds the demand, labour unions successfully resist the reduction of wages that would make possible the absorption of the complete supply of labour. Conversely, when the labour supply is less than the demand, it is assumed that the workers' organizations are in a position to reap the full benefits from the situation, driving up wages to the maximum level compatible with the demand for labour (which also in this case is represented by the amount of circulating capital available at the beginning of the period).

The asymmetry thus introduced reflects the assumption of a different degree of market power of the two social parties, which may find a place in the Ricardian framework as a consequence of the fact that an incomplete utilization of (circulating) capital cannot be conceived of, as mentioned in section 5.6 above. In other words, contrary to what happens when the wage–population interaction mechanism is based on the wages-fund theory, the present hypothesis is compatible with less than full employment of the available labour force – the existing capital being, however, fully utilized also in this case.

To describe the time path of the economy in the present context we maintain unchanged the assumption as regards the supply of labour specified by equation (22), which excludes a direct influence of unemployment on population growth. On the other hand, as regards the demand for labour, we assume that entrepreneurs, given the available wages fund, make their decisions for the current period supposing that the wage rate of the previous period will remain unchanged. We assume, in other words, that the demand for labour is determined by the relation between the amount of capital available (wages fund) and the market wage in the previous period. Such a behaviour may be qualified as being 'myopic', in the sense that entrepreneurs, at the time they formulate their demand for labour, are incapable of foreseeing the new equilibrium situation and the corresponding market-clearing wage rate.

Lastly, as regards the mechanism for determining the market wage and the related level of unemployment, the bargaining-power hypothesis can be clarified (and easily distinguished from the competitive-type hypothesis implicit in the wages-fund theory) by reference to Figure 4, which shows total product net of rent and the wages fund as functions of the level of employment.

If we suppose that the system has moved along the equilibrium path up to the point in time considered and that the available circulating capital (wages fund) at that time is represented by OK_0, the demand for labour – on the previous hypothesis regarding the behaviour of entrepreneurs – is equal to ON^D independently of supply.

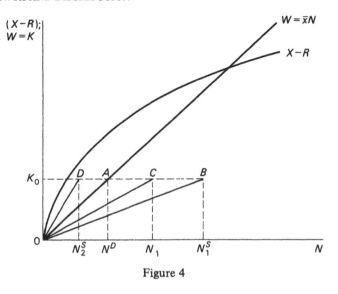

Figure 4

If the supply of labour, for whatever reason, does not coincide with demand and is, for example, equal to $ON_1^S > ON^D$, according to the wages-fund theory the market wage rate would have to fall until it became equal to the slope of OB. We shall, however, assume that the market wage rate settles somewhere in between the slopes of OA and OB, because of the unions' power to resist, to some extent, the tendency of wages to fall as a result of market conditions. The intensity of the drop in wage below the previous level would depend on the bargaining power of the workers' organizations, as well as on the set of institutional factors which can influence the process of price formation in the labour market.

The new market wage having been determined in this way (and being equal, for example, to the slope of OC), the level of employment is given by the number of workers ON_1 who can be employed with the capital available.

If, on the contrary, the supply of labour is lower than demand and equal, for example, to ON_2^S, we shall assume that the new wage level is determined according to the wages-fund theory, and hence corresponds to the slope of OD. The impossibility, which we have already emphasized, of assuming less than full utilization of the available capital prevents wages from being fixed at a level in between the slopes of OD and OA. If that were to happen, the limited supply of manpower would not exhaust the existing wages fund.

5.11 Disequilibrium dynamics with the bargaining-power hypothesis

As we have done before for the hypothesis of the wages-fund theory, we set out below, for convenience of reference, the equations which constitute the complete one-sector Ricardian model when the wage-population interaction mechanism is represented by the bargaining-power hypothesis:

$$X_t = f(N_t) = N_t^\alpha \qquad \text{Production function with diminishing returns} \tag{27}$$

$$R_t = f(N_t) - N_t f'(N_t) \qquad \text{Rent} \tag{28}$$

$$W_t = K_t \qquad \text{Wages fund} \tag{29}$$

$$P_t = N_t [f'(N_t) - x_t] \qquad \text{Profits} \tag{30}$$

$$\dot{K}_t = P_t \qquad \text{Investment} \tag{31}$$

$$N_t^D = \frac{K_t}{x_{t-1}} \qquad \text{Demand for labour on the hypothesis of capitalists' myopia} \tag{32}$$

$$\frac{\dot{x}_t}{x_t} = \begin{cases} -\theta \left(1 - \dfrac{N_t^D}{N_t^S}\right) & \text{if } N_t^D \leqslant N_t^S \\[3mm] \dfrac{\dot{K}_t}{K_t} - \dfrac{\dot{N}_t^S}{N_t^S} & \text{if } N_t^D > N_t^S \end{cases} \qquad \text{Determination of market wage} \tag{33}$$

$$N_t = \begin{cases} \dfrac{K_t}{x_t} & \text{if } N_t^D \leqslant N_t^S \\[3mm] N_t^S & \text{if } N_t^D > N_t^S \end{cases} \qquad \text{Employment} \tag{34}$$

$$\frac{\dot{N}_t^S}{N_t^S} = n_t + \gamma(x_t - \bar{x}) \qquad \text{Labour supply} \tag{35}$$

The symbols used coincide with those of the model examined in section 5.8. The parameter θ which appears in equation (33) measures the influence of the labour unions' bargaining power on the determination of wages. It is assumed that this parameter is positive and less than unity. It should be observed that when $\theta = 1$ the wage rate determined on the basis of the first 'branch' of (33) does not — as mentioned in the discussion of Figure 4 — diverge from the one determined on the basis of a strict application of the wages-fund theory. In this case, the percentage change of wages would coincide, obviously with opposite sign, with the 'potential rate of unemployment' expressed by $(1 - N_t^D/N_t^S)$ and the change in wages would therefore exactly offset this potential disequilibrium in the labour market, thus allowing full employment to be maintained.

As regards the set of equations describing the wage–population mechanism here considered, equation (32) defines the demand for labour on the hypothesis of capitalists' myopia. Equation (33), on the other hand, sets out in analytical terms the assumed asymmetry in the determination of the market wage; it defines in fact the percentage rate of change of wages: (a) as a function of the potential rate of unemployment, when the demand for labour is lower than supply; and (b) as a direct application of the wages-fund theory, when demand is instead greater than supply. Lastly, equation (34) expresses the level of employment corresponding to the two cases envisaged in equation (33).

With reference to the distinction between the structure of the disequilibrium model now being examined and the equilibrium model of section 5.2, it is clear that the considerations already made in section 5.8 as regards the model incorporating the wages-fund adjustment hypothesis apply also in the present case. Here, too, the more general formulation of the hypotheses makes it possible to analyse both the equilibrium path and the many possible disequilibrium paths.

There is, however, a substantial difference between the model based on the bargaining-power hypothesis and the wages-fund model and, *a fortiori*, between the former and the equilibrium model – the possibility of unemployment of labour. This is expressed in analytical terms by the absence of the equilibrium condition in the labour market and is matched by the presence of a different mechanism for the determination of the market wage.

The behaviour of the economy described by the model has been determined – as already done for the case considered in section 5.8 – by numerical simulation, assuming for α in the production function (27) the same value of 0.75. This behaviour is illustrated in Figures 5 to 10 with reference to the key variables represented by the level of employment (N_t), the market wage rate (x_t), and the ratio between demand and supply of labour (N_t^D/N_t^S).

For the reader's convenience, the disequilibrium paths associated with an initial surplus of labour with respect to the equilibrium level are distinguished (Figures 5, 6 and 7) from those associated with an

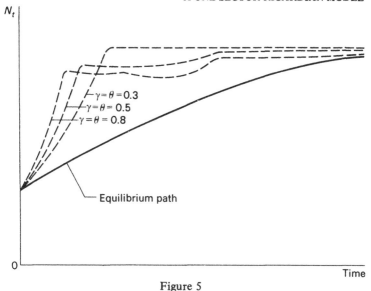

N_t

$\gamma = \theta = 0.3$
$\gamma = \theta = 0.5$
$\gamma = \theta = 0.8$

Equilibrium path

0

Time

Figure 5

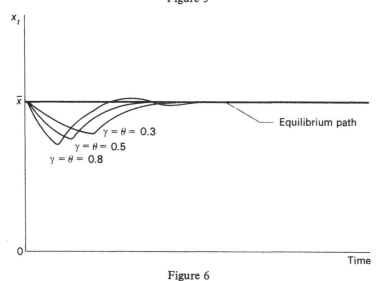

x_t

$\bar{x}$

Equilibrium path

$\gamma = \theta = 0.3$
$\gamma = \theta = 0.5$
$\gamma = \theta = 0.8$

0

Time

Figure 6

initial shortage of manpower (Figures 8, 9 and 10). In each of the diagrams three curves are shown, each one corresponding to a different combination of values of the reaction parameters γ and θ; this makes it possible to appreciate the influence of these parameters on the disequilibrium paths.

131

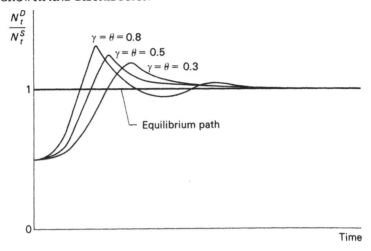

Figure 7

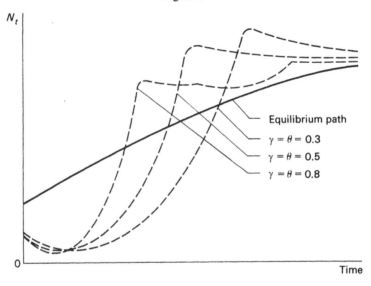

Figure 8

We shall refrain from going into detailed comments on the numerical results obtained and confine ourselves to some remarks on the more general aspects of the time paths of the variables. These aspects focus on what appears to be, beyond the limitations of a numerical analysis, the basic property of the economy portrayed by the model.

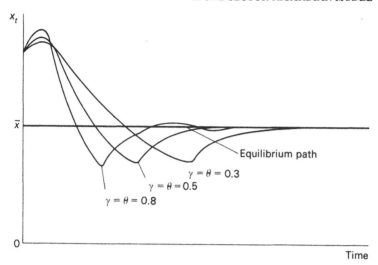

Figure 9

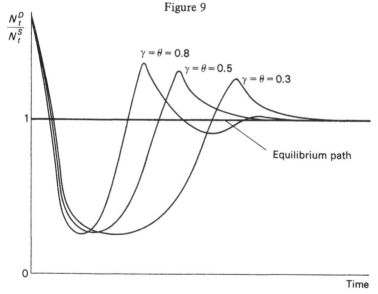

Figure 10

Notwithstanding the presence of irregularities and interruptions in the paths, the movement of the variables is of a cyclical nature, unlike what happens in the model previously examined. The irregularities and the interruptions are clearly due to the assumed asymmetry of the mechanism for the determination of the wage rate.

133

The magnitude of the fluctuations exhibited by the model obviously depends on the value of the reaction parameters. From the numerical tests carried out, a predominant influence of θ with respect to γ seems to emerge, thus pointing out the crucial role of the wage-adjustment mechanism (equation (33)).

Oscillations tend, however, to peter out. The convergent nature of the movement is explained by the stabilizing role of the wage-population mechanism, even when imperfections in the labour market are taken into account.

Considering, finally, the behaviour of distributive shares, the results are similar to those reached with the wages-fund hypothesis. The share of rent and the share of profits plus wages remain constant over time and show, therefore, no departure from their respective equilibrium values of $(1 - \alpha)$ and α.

The distribution within the share of profits plus wages is, in this case too, a more complex matter which cannot be solved in analytical terms on the basis of the derivatives with respect to time of equations (25) and (26). Numerical computation seems to indicate, however, that, whatever the source of the initial disequilibrium (excess or shortage of labour), the share of wages – and, of course, symmetrically, that of profits – fluctuates around the equilibrium path, with oscillations that tend to flatten out gradually through time. Also in this case, the influence of θ with respect to γ appears to be largely predominant.

6 A two-sector Ricardian model

6.1 General remarks

We turn now from the analysis of the agricultural one-sector Ricardian model to the study of the corresponding two-sector model (agriculture and industry). As in the previous chapter, the analysis is in two parts. The first defines the balanced growth path (equilibrium dynamics); the second considers problems in the causes of disequilibrium, possible responses and resulting time paths (disequilibrium dynamics).

The notion of structure of employment (defined as the ratio between employment in industry and in the whole economy) plays here a central role in the study of the equilibrium dynamics, in that it makes it possible to establish the relation between variables (such as production and capital accumulation) referring to the two sectors of the economy. It is obvious that this aspect takes on particular importance when, as in the Ricardian model, the assumption is made of diminishing returns in one sector and constant returns in the other.

The definition of the conditions for balanced growth enables the results obtained in the one-sector model to be generalized to the two-sector one, with particular reference to the relation between the growth rates of income and capital. The fundamental role of diminishing returns in agriculture in Ricardo's theory emerges therefore in full evidence also in the context of a model no longer confined to the sole consideration of the agricultural sector.

The problems in disequilibrium analysis examined in the second part of the chapter deal with situations of structural imbalance. The choice of concentrating on the issue of structural imbalance flows directly from the basic feature of the equilibrium analysis, hingeing, as we have noted, precisely on the concept of the structure of employment. Disequilibrium situations of the type taken into consideration

·imply, in this model, different sectoral profit rates and affect accordingly the process of accumulation in the two sectors. By means of the explicit formulation of a reaction mechanism, as simple as it is intuitively acceptable, we are in a position to highlight the corrective role played by the hypothesis of competition, so deeply embedded in Ricardo's theory, i.e. of the 'readiness [of capitalists] to move their capital towards the most profitable sectors of the economy' (Pasinetti (64), p. 85).

6.2 The equilibrium model

The two-sector model outlined in this chapter is based on Pasinetti's analytical formulation of the Ricardian system illustrated in Chapter 4. It departs from Pasinetti's contribution only in the direction of filling in the gaps in the dynamic aspects of the model indicated earlier.

Using the notation of the previous chapter and recalling in particular that the suffixes 1 and 2 refer respectively to the agricultural sector which produces wage-goods (corn) and to the industrial sector which produces luxury goods (gold), the model may be described by the following relations:

Agricultural sector

$$X_{1t} = f(N_{1t})$$

Production function with diminishing returns (1)

$$R_t = f(N_{1t}) - N_{1t}f'(N_{1t})$$

Rent in terms of corn (2)

$$P_{1t} = N_{1t}[f'(N_{1t}) - \bar{x}]$$

Profits in terms of corn (3)

$$p_{1t} = \frac{1}{f'(N_{1t})}$$

Price of wage-goods (4)

Industrial sector

$$X_{2t} = \beta N_{2t}$$

Production function with constant returns (5)

$$p_{2t}P_{2t} = p_{2t}X_{2t} - p_{1t}N_{2t}\bar{x}$$

Profits in value terms (6)

$$p_{2t} = \frac{1}{\beta}$$

Price of luxury goods (7)

Macroeconomic relations

$$N_t = N_{1t} + N_{2t}$$

Employment (8)

$$W_t = K_t \qquad \text{Wages fund} \qquad (9)$$

$$N_t = \frac{W_t}{\bar{x}} \qquad \text{Demand for labour} \qquad (10)$$

$$P_t = p_{1t}N_t\,[f'(N_{1t}) - \bar{x}] \qquad \text{Total profits in value terms} \qquad (11)$$

$$p_{2t}X_{2t} = p_{1t}R_t \qquad \text{Demand for luxury goods} \qquad (12)$$

$$p_{1t}\dot{K}_t = P_t \qquad \text{Total investment} \qquad (13)$$

Briefly recapitulating the salient aspects of the model to help in understanding subsequent reasoning, note that, while in the agricultural sector incomes received by categories participating in production can be expressed without the use of prices because of the homogeneity between input and output, this cannot be done for the industrial sector. This difference emerges clearly if we compare equations (3) and (6), which define profits in the two sectors.

Absolute prices in equations (4) and (7) comply with the labour theory of value when this is supplemented with the hypothesis that the unit of measurement is represented by the quantity of gold produced by the labour of one worker in one year.

The demand for industrial goods and the expenditure behaviour of rentiers are jointly defined by equation (12), which closes the model from the point of view of equality between aggregate demand and supply (Say's law). Despite the highly simplified nature of the consumption behaviour of the social classes implied by (12), this equation plays a crucial role in the model as it establishes the basic link between variables belonging to the two sectors and thus determines the distribution of employment between agriculture and industry. From a formal viewpoint, equation (12) must be clearly specified in value terms because rent R_t (defined in (2) in terms of corn) is not homogeneous with respect to the output of the industrial sector X_{2t} (consisting of luxury goods).

Total profits, obtained as the sum of profits in value terms separately earned in the two sectors, are defined in (11) so as to bring out the fundamental impórtance, for the economy as a whole, of (diminishing) labour productivity in agriculture.

In the two-commodity model under consideration there is no fixed capital (machines), but only circulating capital (corn). None the less, in equation (13), which states that profits are entirely reinvested, the capital stock (wages fund) needs to be expressed in value terms since total profits are likewise defined.

We assume, lastly, also that the two-sector system satisfies the condition that the supply of labour does not place any constraint on the growth of the economy.

6.3 The growth rate of capital

As with the one-sector model, the study of the behaviour of the system over time begins with an analysis of the properties of the equilibrium path. In this connection, the first point to deal with is the definition of the growth rates of capital in the two productive sectors, separately considered, and in the economy as a whole.

To this end it is useful to introduce a new variable expressing the sectoral structure of employment, thus enabling us to interpret the dynamics of the system in terms of the evolution of its structure. Let λ_t be the ratio of employment in the industrial sector to total employment in period t. The levels of employment in the two sectors can be now defined as follows:

$$N_{1t} = (1 - \lambda_t)N_t \tag{14}$$

$$N_{2t} = \lambda_t N_t \tag{15}$$

Given the existence of a uniform wage rate, the sectoral distribution of capital coincides with that of employment:

$$K_{1t} = (1 - \lambda_t)K_t \tag{16}$$

$$K_{2t} = \lambda_t K_t \tag{17}$$

Taking the logarithmic derivatives of (16) and (17), the rates of capital accumulation in the two sectors are defined as:

$$G_{k1} = \frac{\dot{K}_{1t}}{K_{1t}} = G_k - \frac{\dot{\lambda}_t}{(1 - \lambda_t)} \tag{18}$$

$$G_{k2} = \frac{\dot{K}_{2t}}{K_{2t}} = G_k + \frac{\dot{\lambda}_t}{\lambda_t} \tag{19}$$

From equations (10), (11) and (13), G_k, the growth rate of capital for the economy as a whole, turns out to be:

$$G_k = \frac{\dot{K}_t}{K_t} = \frac{P_t}{p_{1t}K_t} = \left[\frac{f'(N_{1t})}{\bar{x}} - 1\right] \tag{20}$$

Some comments can be usefully made at this point. (i) With the assumption made on capitalists' saving behaviour, the growth rate of capital is equal to the general profit rate (calculated as the ratio of total profits to total capital in value terms). The latter obviously coincides – along the natural equilibrium growth path – with the profit rates earned in each of the two sectors. (ii) The rate of accumulation for the economy as a whole is the same as in the one-sector model,[1] provided that we now substitute agricultural for total employment, so that in both instances G_k is defined with reference to labour productivity in agriculture. It is therefore the agricultural profit rate which determines, in both cases, the pace and the limits of the accumulation process. (iii) As is clearly shown by (20), the employment structure has only an indirect influence, through N_{1t}, on the aggregate rate of growth of capital, whereas the sectoral rates of accumulation explicitly depend, as (18) and (19) prove, on the rate of change of λ_t.

These properties have an important implication for the problem of equality between the profit rate and the accumulation rate in equilibrium growth. As we have just mentioned, these rates are equal at the *aggregate* level. At the *sectoral* level, on the contrary, the rates of accumulation may diverge from the profit rate – obviously unique, when conditions of natural equilibrium growth obtain. As (18) and (19) show, this happens whenever changes in the structure of employment take place on the equilibrium path. The conditions for this result to obtain depend both on the form of diminishing returns in agriculture and on the saving behaviour of economic agents. In section 6.5 we will show that, with the assumption adopted in the present model, changes in λ_t occur only if the elasticity of agricultural output with respect to the labour input varies (in time) with the level of employment. It will also be shown in Chapter 7 (section 7.7) that a different set of hypotheses as regards the saving behaviour of the social classes entails changes in λ_t even though the above-mentioned elasticity is constant.

6.4 The growth rate of production in value terms

We now move to the definition of the growth rates of output for each of the two sectors and for the economy as a whole in value terms (it is obvious that due to the presence of heterogeneous outputs total production cannot be expressed in physical terms). These growth rates will be subsequently decomposed into separate rates of change of prices and physical quantities.

As we have seen in Chapter 4 (section 4.7), in the Ricardian model represented by the set of equations (1)–(13) the value of output of the agricultural sector coincides with total employment, while the value of output of the industrial sector equals industrial employment. Therefore, denoting as Y_{1t} and Y_{2t} the values of output in the two sectors (to distinguish them from X_{1t} and X_{2t}, which refer to output in physical terms), we have:

$$Y_{1t} = p_{1t}X_{1t} = N_t \qquad (21)$$

$$Y_{2t} = p_{2t}X_{2t} = N_{2t} \qquad (22)$$

On account of (15), national income (total value of the output of the two sectors) is thus equal to:

$$Y_t = Y_{1t} + Y_{2t} = (1 + \lambda_t)N_t \qquad (23)$$

As for the sectoral distribution of capital in (16) and (17), so the sectoral structure of output in value terms can be expressed with reference to the parameter λ_t. From (21)–(23), it immediately follows that:

$$\frac{Y_{1t}}{Y_t} = \frac{N_t}{(1 + \lambda_t)N_t} = \frac{1}{(1 + \lambda_t)} \qquad (24)$$

$$\frac{Y_{2t}}{Y_t} = \frac{\lambda_t N_t}{(1 + \lambda_t)N_t} = \frac{\lambda_t}{(1 + \lambda_t)} \qquad (25)$$

An important aspect of the equilibrium dynamics of the two-sector model can be established from the comparison between (14) and (24) on the one hand, and between (15) and (25) on the other. Since $1/(1 + \lambda_t) > (1 - \lambda_t)$,[2] the relative weight of the agricultural sector is clearly greater when reckoned in terms of value of output than when measured in employment terms. The opposite obviously holds true for the industrial sector. Moreover, (24) and (25) show that the percentage weight of agriculture in national income always exceeds that of industry, independently of the sectoral distribution of employment, i.e. whatever the value of λ_t.

These two (apparently surprising) results stem directly from the assumption made about the structure of the model, the behaviour of the social classes and the technology of production. These assumptions have, in fact, an immediate bearing on equations (21) and (22), which supply the basis for an intuitive understanding of those results. With regard to the first of them (the greater relative importance of agriculture with respect to industry when comparison is made in terms of value of output rather than in employment terms), let us observe that, while N_{1t} workers are employed in agriculture, the value of output is N_t (obviously greater than N_{1t}); the ratio of output value to employment is accordingly greater than one. This ratio is, on the contrary, equal to one in the industrial sector, output value and workers employed both being equal to N_{2t}.

With regard to the second of the above-mentioned results, it is sufficient to recall that rent is only a part of the agricultural output and yet absorbs – in value terms – the whole industrial output. The value of agricultural output thus necessarily exceeds that of industrial output by an amount equal to the sum of profits and wages in agriculture. With the assumptions made, the very existence of the industrial sector is indeed conditioned by the presence of rent, i.e. by diminishing returns in agriculture. This means that a two-sector model incorporating the typically Ricardian behaviour assumptions of the social classes that did assume constant returns to scale throughout could not even be thought of.

From (21)-(23) and taking into account (9), (10) and (15), we can easily derive the growth rates of the value of output in the two sectors and in the economy as a whole:

$$G_{y1} = \frac{\dot{Y}_{1t}}{Y_{1t}} = \frac{\dot{N}_t}{N_t} = \frac{\dot{K}_t}{K_t} = G_k \qquad (26)$$

$$G_{y2} = \frac{\dot{Y}_{2t}}{Y_{2t}} = \frac{\dot{N}_{2t}}{N_{2t}} = \frac{\dot{N}_t}{N_t} + \frac{\dot{\lambda}_t}{\lambda_t} = G_k + \frac{\dot{\lambda}_t}{\lambda_t} \qquad (27)$$

$$G_y = \frac{\dot{Y}_t}{Y_t} = \frac{\dot{N}_t}{N_t} + \frac{\dot{\lambda}_t}{(1+\lambda_t)} = G_k + \frac{\dot{\lambda}_t}{(1+\lambda_t)} \qquad (28)$$

Note that (28) can also be obtained as a weighted average of the sectoral growth rates (26) and (27), the weights being equal to the percentage share of the output value of the two sectors in the total. Note, furthermore, that the rate of change of output value in agriculture – defined in (26) with reference to total employment – can also be expressed using (14) in terms of changes in employment in that sector:

$$G_{y1} = \frac{\dot{N}_t}{N_t} = \frac{\dot{N}_{1t}}{N_{1t}} + \frac{\dot{\lambda}_t}{(1-\lambda_t)} \qquad (26a)$$

6.5 Employment structure, distributive shares and technology

An explanation of these results on growth rates requires some preliminary remarks on the relations between employment structure, distributive shares and technical assumptions.

Let us first of all consider the question of the distribution of output in the sole agricultural sector. To this end let ρ_{1t} be the ratio of rent to agricultural output, in physical and in value terms:

$$\rho_{1t} = \frac{p_{1t}R_t}{p_{1t}X_{1t}} \tag{29}$$

Recalling that – from (12) – the value of rent is equal to the value of output in the industrial sector, and that – from (21) and (22) – the value of output in industry and in agriculture are respectively equal to N_{2t} and N_t, we obtain, taking account of (15):

$$\rho_{1t} = \frac{N_{2t}}{N_t} = \lambda_t \tag{30}$$

The ratio of industrial employment to total employment λ_t is thus equal to the share of rent in agricultural output, while the share of profits and wages, always in the agricultural sector, is equal to $(1 - \lambda_t)$.

Dealing now with the problem of distributive shares for the economy as a whole, let us observe that, still in connection with (12), $\lambda_t/(1 + \lambda_t)$ – which, according to (25), is the ratio of output value in the industrial sector to national income – represents the rent share. It is then clear that $1/(1 + \lambda_t)$ is the share of profits plus wages.

The close connection between diminishing returns and rent is thus seen to imply an equally close connection between diminishing returns and the employment structure. The parameter λ_t, introduced to facilitate the analysis of the dynamics of the two-sector model, depends in effect on the particular technological hypothesis which specifies the behaviour of the marginal product of labour under diminishing returns.

The relation between λ_t and the elasticity α_t of agricultural output with respect to labour applied in production can be usefully explored at this stage. Given

$$\alpha_t = \frac{N_{1t}f'(N_{1t})}{f(N_{1t})}$$

where α_t is a function of time through N_{1t}, from the definition of rent in equation (2), and considering (30) as well, we have $\rho_{1t} = \lambda_t = 1 - \alpha_t$. It clearly follows that the percentage share of agricultural employment in the total is equal to the elasticity of the production function of that sector. This proves the proposition made in section 6.3 above that, if this elasticity is constant, so is the sectoral structure of employment.[3]

Let us lastly point out a particular property of the equilibrium path. Since corn production is entirely absorbed by profits plus wages (Say's law), the general profit rate can be defined both by (20) and by:

$$r_t = \frac{P_t}{p_{1t}K_t} = \frac{p_{1t}X_{1t} - p_{1t}\bar{x}N_t}{p_{1t}K_t} = \frac{f(N_{1t})}{\bar{x}N_t} - 1 \tag{20a}$$

Comparing (20) with (20a), we see that in the equilibrium path:

$$\frac{f(N_{1t})}{N_t} = f'(N_{1t}) \tag{20b}$$

where the left-hand side may be called the '*per capita* agricultural output' – the agricultural product per worker employed in the economy as a whole. This means that the necessary condition for capital accumulation to continue – implicit in (20) – can also be expressed in terms of the existence of a positive surplus of the '*per capita* agricultural output' above the natural wage rate.

6.6 The growth rate of output at constant prices

The growth rates of output value can be split into rates of change of physical quantities and of prices – the interest in this breakdown obviously being connected with the possibility of defining, also for a two-sector model, the growth rate of national income in real terms, i.e. on the basis of an assessment of changes in production at constant prices.

Incidentally, observe that this problem is of a general significance going beyond the specific context of the Ricardian model analysed here. In reality, two-sector growth models[4] are generally based on a set of assumptions which imply that relative prices remain unchanged on the equilibrium growth path. If there is a difference in the rate of increase of money and real income, this is then to be attributed to a change in the price level. When such a change in absolute prices is excluded, the growth rate of national income in real terms necessarily coincides with that of national income in value terms (i.e. at current prices).

This obviously does not occur in the Ricardian model. The assumptions about the sectoral production functions, together with the definition of absolute prices ensuing from the labour theory of value, determine a progressive increase in the price of corn as opposed to the constancy of the price of gold. Hence the growth rate of national income at current prices differs from that of national income at constant prices.

Taking the logarithmic derivative of the production function (1) and recalling that, with a constant wage rate, employment and capital are proportional, the rate of change of agricultural physical output is:

$$G_{x1} = \frac{\dot{X}_{1t}}{X_{1t}} = \frac{f'(N_{1t})\dot{N}_{1t}}{X_{1t}} = \frac{N_{1t}f'(N_{1t})}{X_{1t}} \cdot \frac{\dot{N}_{1t}}{N_{1t}}$$

$$= \frac{P_{1t} + W_{1t}}{X_{1t}} \cdot \frac{\dot{K}_{1t}}{K_{1t}} = (1 - \lambda_t)G_{k1} \tag{31}$$

This result is identical to that obtained in (8) of Chapter 5 where, in the context of a one-sector (agricultural) model, the relation between growth rates of output and capital was defined. Note that, using (18), which defines the growth rate of capital in agriculture in terms of the aggregate rate of accumulation, (31) becomes:

$$G_{x1} = [(1 - \lambda_t)G_k] - \dot{\lambda}_t \tag{31a}$$

The rates of change of physical output in industry G_{x2} and of prices in the two sectors (respectively G_{p1} and G_{p2}) may be easily deduced from (26)-(28) and (31a):

$$G_{x2} = \frac{\dot{X}_{2t}}{X_{2t}} = G_{y2} = G_k + \frac{\dot{\lambda}_t}{\lambda_t} \tag{32}$$

$$G_{p1} = \frac{\dot{p}_{1t}}{p_{1t}} = G_{y1} - G_{x1} = \lambda_t G_k + \dot{\lambda}_t \tag{33}$$

$$G_{p2} = \frac{\dot{p}_{2t}}{p_{2t}} = G_{y2} - G_{x2} = 0 \tag{34}$$

To define the rate of increase in national income at constant prices deflated figures must be calculated with reference either to a fixed or to a moving base. Also for the purpose of an easier analytical exposition we choose here the second alternative, adopting as a moving base the preceding period. Real income is thus calculated evaluating current output of both sectors at the prices of the preceding period.[5]

The rate of change of real income between two successive *finite* time periods is therefore

$$G_x = \frac{(p_{1t}X_{1t+1} + p_{2t}X_{2t+1}) - (p_{1t}X_{1t} + p_{2t}X_{2t})}{p_{1t}X_{1t} + p_{2t}X_{2t}}$$

$$= \frac{p_{1t}\Delta X_{1t} + p_{2t}\Delta X_{2t}}{p_{1t}X_{1t} + p_{2t}X_{2t}} \tag{35}$$

where ΔX_{1t} and ΔX_{2t} indicate the absolute difference between quantities produced in $t + 1$ and in t in the two sectors respectively. Reverting to *infinitesimal* time, we can substitute for the finite differences of (35) the corresponding differentials. Recalling the definitions (24) and (25), we obtain:

$$G_x = \frac{p_{1t}\dot{X}_{1t} + p_{2t}\dot{X}_{2t}}{p_{1t}X_{1t} + p_{2t}X_{2t}} = \frac{p_{1t}\dot{X}_{1t}}{p_{1t}X_{1t}} \cdot \frac{p_{1t}X_{1t}}{p_{1t}X_{1t} + p_{2t}X_{2t}}$$

$$+ \frac{p_{2t}\dot{X}_{2t}}{p_{2t}X_{2t}} \cdot \frac{p_{2t}X_{2t}}{p_{1t}X_{1t} + p_{2t}X_{2t}}$$

$$= G_{x1}\frac{1}{1 + \lambda_t} + G_{x2}\frac{\lambda_t}{1 + \lambda_t} \tag{36}$$

The income change in real terms is therefore defined as the weighted average of changes in quantities produced in the two sectors, with weights equal to the percentage share of output in each sector. Owing to the lack of homogeneity, these weights are clearly calculated with reference to (sectoral and aggregate) output values. Substituting in (36) the definitions of the two growth rates of physical output in the two sectors given in (31) and (32), we obtain:

$$G_x = \frac{1}{1 + \lambda_t} G_k \tag{37}$$

where $1/(1 + \lambda_t)$ represents, as we have pointed out, the share of profits plus wages in total income.

The result expressed by equation (37) is a relevant one: it shows that the relation between the growth rate of real national income and that of capital obtained in (8) of Chapter 5, in the context of a one-sector model, is valid also in the two-sector model. In both cases the ratio between these growth rates is represented by the share of profits plus wages. Under the assumption of diminishing returns, this share is less than one: the growth rate of real income is accordingly smaller than that of capital. As we have already argued in Chapter 5, this result is due solely to the presence of rent; it is therefore the direct consequence of diminishing returns in agriculture and it does not depend in any way on rentiers' consumption behaviour.

The explicit consideration of a constant-returns industrial sector does not alter the structural characteristics of the growth process of the 'Ricardian economy'. This fact, which could not be readily guessed on *a priori* grounds, reasserts the crucial importance of the assumption of diminishing returns in agriculture.

Extension to the case in which a variety of luxury goods is produced under constant returns to scale and consumed solely by rentiers would not modify these conclusions. Equation (12) of the model would in this case be substituted by

$$p_{1t}R_t = \sum_{i=2}^{m-1} p_{it}X_{it} \tag{12a}$$

where the index $i(i = 2, 3, \ldots, m - 1)$ refers to luxury goods produced under constant returns. The circumstance that the model does not make it possible to determine the physical quantity produced of each of the luxury goods does not, as shown by Pasinetti ((64), pp. 90-2), affect the full determinacy of macroeconomic equilibrium.

We can lastly define the rate of change of the average price level G_p (obviously also the average price level is expressed in terms of the *numéraire* of the system defined with (7)):

$$G_p = G_y - G_x = \frac{\lambda_t}{1 + \lambda_t} G_k + \frac{\dot{\lambda}_t}{1 + \lambda_t}$$

$$= \frac{1}{1 + \lambda_t} (\lambda_t G_k + \dot{\lambda}_t) \tag{38}$$

Note that this result, on account of (33) and (34), coincides with the weighted average of the rates of change of prices in the two sectors (the weights being equal to those used in (36) to determine G_x).

The apparent divergence between (8) of Chapter 5 and (28) of this chapter, referring to the relation between the growth rate of income in value terms and that of capital, flows, therefore, from the role of prices in the two-sector model and disappears, as we have seen in (37), when the rate of growth of income in real terms is considered.

6.7 Equilibrium growth with full employment

As for the one-sector model, and for the same reasons, the definition of the situation of dynamic equilibrium can be completed by specifying the conditions that must be satisfied by the supply of labour over time. As we have seen, if wages are to remain constant at the natural level, it is essential that — starting from a position of equilibrium in the labour market — the supply of manpower grows at the same rate as the demand for it. Since the latter increases (at the constant natural wage) at the same rate as capital, the equilibrium condition — which is identical with that expressed by (10) of Chapter 5 — becomes

$$n_t = \frac{\dot{N_t}}{N_t} = G_k \qquad (39)$$

where n_t denotes the equilibrium growth rate for the labour force and obviously coincides, by the very definition of the rate of accumulation, with the general rate of profit.

The equilibrium dynamics of the two-sector Ricardian model are thus fully described. The time path of all the variables considered in the model can be expressed in terms of the rates of change defined above and of the sectoral structure of employment.

6.8 Final considerations on the equilibrium dynamics of the two-sector Ricardian model

In concluding the analysis of equilibrium dynamics, it may be stressed that the results obtained as regards the fundamental macroeconomic relations characterizing the equilibrium path in the two-sector model coincide with those for the one-sector model examined in Chapter 5. It may then suffice to emphasize and briefly comment on certain aspects that are peculiar to the two-sector model.

The most important aspect is that the sectoral structure of the economy (both in terms of employment and output) and its growth behaviour are determined by the technical conditions of the agricultural sector — a circumstance which flows from the assumption that agricultural rent absorbs the whole output of the industrial sector. Two basic reasons for this may be mentioned. (i) Since the existence of the industrial sector depends on the presence of rent, the structure of the system is clearly determined by the size of rent itself and hence by the relevance of diminishing returns. (ii) The relative dynamics of the two sectors, i.e. the movement of λ_t over time, depends on the behaviour of the share of rent in total income. If the rent share is constant, the structure remains unchanged. If, on the contrary, this share is growing, the relative importance of the industrial sector increases, and vice versa. Given the connection between rent and the technological conditions of the agricultural sector, the development of the productive structure must be attributed to the specific characteristics of diminishing returns and hence to the intensity (constant, growing or decreasing) with which they occur in the course of growth.

Another aspect to be mentioned concerns the relation between the productive structure and the process of accumulation in the two sectors. If the production structure remains unchanged, the sectoral accumulation rates coincide with the respective profit rates, which are always equal in equilibrium. The accumulation process in each of these sectors is then wholly sustained from profits arising in each of them – a case which could be defined as one of 'self-financing' of sectoral capital formulation.

On the contrary, if the production structure varies during the accumulation process, there will be a divergence between the sectoral accumulation rates and the sectoral profit rates (note that sectoral profit rates always coincide in equilibrium). This divergence necessarily implies a transfer of profits from the less dynamic to the more rapidly expanding sector. This transfer may take the form *either* of a direct entrepreneurial engagement in the other sector by capitalists with resources to invest over and above growth needs in the original sector, *or* of the grant of loans at an interest rate equal to the general profit rate. In both cases the 'self-financing' of sectoral capital accumulation would no longer occur.

Note finally that the fundamental importance of the agricultural sector is confirmed by the fact that the technical conditions of production in the industrial sector (constant returns) have no influence on growth rates and profit rates. Indeed, these rates are independent of the productivity level of the labour employed in industry, which is relevant only for the determination of the position (not of the form) of the equilibrium growth path, i.e. of the scale of production and hence of the stationary-state position which represents the terminal level of that path.

6.9 Equilibrium growth with $X_{1t} = N_{1t}^{\alpha}$

As for the one-sector model, we shall work out the equilibrium growth path identified by the conditions set up above giving an explicit form to the agricultural production function. We assume again that agricultural technology can be expressed by

$$X_{1t} = N_{1t}^{\alpha} \qquad (40)$$

a function which, α being a positive constant less than one, satisfies the Ricardian assumption of diminishing returns.

As we have seen in sections 6.5 and 6.8, the sectoral structure of employment λ_t is equal to $(1 - \alpha)$, and is thus constant. We have therefore:

$$G_k = G_y = \frac{\alpha N_{1f}^{\alpha-1}}{\bar{x}} - 1 \tag{41}$$

$$G_x = \frac{1}{2-\alpha} G_k \tag{42}$$

$$G_p = \frac{1-\alpha}{2-\alpha} G_k \tag{43}$$

It also follows that, on account of (18), (19), (26) and (27), the sectoral accumulation rates and the sectoral growth rates of the value of output coincide with G_k. From (31a), (32) and (33), we finally have:

$$G_{x1} = \alpha G_k \tag{44}$$

$$G_{x2} = G_k \tag{45}$$

$$G_{p1} = (1-\alpha) G_k \tag{46}$$

The stationary-state values can be easily determined setting G_k in (41) equal to zero:

$$\bar{K} = \left(\frac{\bar{x}}{\alpha}\right)^{\frac{\alpha}{\alpha-1}} \tag{47}$$

$$\bar{N}_1 = \left(\frac{\bar{x}}{\alpha}\right)^{\frac{1}{\alpha-1}} \tag{48}$$

$$\bar{N}_2 = \frac{1-\alpha}{\alpha} \cdot \left(\frac{\bar{x}}{\alpha}\right)^{\frac{1}{\alpha-1}} \tag{49}$$

$$\bar{N} = \frac{1}{\alpha} \cdot \left(\frac{\bar{x}}{\alpha}\right)^{\left(\frac{1}{\alpha-1}\right)} \tag{50}$$

$$\bar{X}_1 = \left(\frac{\bar{x}}{\alpha}\right)^{\frac{\alpha}{\alpha-1}} \tag{51}$$

$$\bar{X}_2 = \beta \cdot \frac{1-\alpha}{\alpha} \left(\frac{\bar{x}}{\alpha}\right)^{\frac{1}{\alpha-1}} \tag{52}$$

$$\bar{p}_1 = \frac{1}{\bar{x}} \tag{53}$$

$$\bar{p}_2 = \frac{1}{\beta} \tag{54}$$

$$\bar{Y} = \frac{2 \overset{\bullet}{-} \alpha}{\alpha} \cdot \left(\frac{\bar{x}}{\alpha}\right)^{\frac{1}{\alpha-1}} \tag{55}$$

First, from the results listed it emerges that the growth rates are independent of the technical conditions of production in the industrial sector. The parameter β, which expresses the productivity of labour in industry, is relevant only in determining the stationary-state value of industrial production and the corresponding price. This confirms the crucial importance of the agricultural sector, expressed by the presence of α, in the definition of the macro growth rates and of the stationary-state values of all the variables except prices.

Second, note the coincidence — expressed by (47) and (51) — between the stationary-state values of the capital stock and agricultural production. This coincidence obviously flows from the assumption that capital consists solely of advances to the workers and from the other assumption that rent, entirely devoted to the purchase of luxury goods, does not absorb any portion of agricultural produce.

Third, the price of corn assumes in the stationary state, as shown by (53), a value equal to the inverse of the natural wage rate. This clearly reflects the circumstance that profits are wiped out when the labour productivity in the less favourable conditions equals the natural wage.

We have already shown in Chapter 4 (section 4.7) that the movement of distributive shares along the equilibrium growth path depends on the dynamics of the sectoral structure of employment, in the sense that their behaviour is fully determined only in the particular case in which employment grows at the same rate in both sectors. This occurs precisely on the technological assumptions examined here. The distributive shares of workers, capitalists and rentiers are as follows:

$$\frac{p_{1t} W_t}{Y_t} = \frac{p_{1t}\bar{x}}{2 - \alpha} \tag{56}$$

$$\frac{P_t}{Y_t} = \frac{1 - p_{1t}\bar{x}}{2 - \alpha} \tag{57}$$

$$\frac{p_{1t}R_t}{Y_t} = \frac{1-\alpha}{2-\alpha} \tag{58}$$

The constant level of the rent share – and hence of the share of profits plus wages – flows directly from the assumed constancy of α. As regards the separate shares of profits and wages, it is clear that the continuous increase in p_1 determines on the one hand the progressive fall of the share of profits, and on the other the gradual increase in the share of wages.

6.10 Disequilibrium mechanisms

Having thus completed the analysis of equilibrium growth for the two-sector Ricardian model, we now consider problems in disequilibrium dynamics, as we have already done – in line with our methodological approach – for the one-sector model.

A distinction must be drawn in the two-sector model between *macroeconomic* sources of disequilibrium which affect only aggregative relations, and *sectoral* sources of disequilibrium, whose essential manifestations concern the interrelations between the two sectors.

As regards the first type of disequilibrium sources – which, as already discussed in Chapter 5 (section 5.6) may occur in the labour market or take the form of a divergence between aggregate demand and supply or between actual and desired productive capacity – the arguments put forward in that connection retain full validity. Also for the two-sector model the conclusion then holds that only disequilibria in the labour market are compatible with the Ricardian logical scheme.

As regards the second type of disequilibrium sources, it appears at once that the counterpart of a macroeconomic disequilibrium in the labour market is represented by a disequilibrium in the sectoral structure of employment λ_t. The analysis of this source of imbalance is obviously interesting because the equilibrium dynamics of the two-sector model were formulated with specific reference to the notion of employment structure. Indeed, the assumption of a departure of λ_t from its equilibrium value is particularly fruitful, as will be seen below, in that it gives rise to disequilibrium phenomena in such fundamental variables as relative prices and sectoral rates of profit. The entire process of capital accumulation is thereby affected.

While this origin of disequilibrium seems substantially compatible with the logic of the Ricardian model,[6] other sources of initial sectoral disequilibrium seem to involve unacceptable departures from the spirit of Ricardo's theoretical construction. This would occur, for instance, if we were to assume the disequilibrium adjustment process to be occasioned by: (i) a divergence of commodity prices from their respective equilibrium values; (ii) a difference in sectoral profit rates; and (iii) the existence of two different wage levels.

(i) If we were to consider disequilibrium as originating in a divergence of prices from their equilibrium values due, for example, to imperfect information on demand and supply conditions in one or both sectors, a difficulty would arise — the failure of aggregate demand to coincide with supply. In fact, if we suppose that prices are exogenously given and are different from their equilibrium values, it is clear that only by accident could the sectoral distribution of the labour force be such as to satisfy the macroeconomic condition posed by (12). As nothing could then guarantee, in general, equality between the value of rent and that of gold production, the consequent departure from Say's law would give rise to a situation incompatible with Ricardian theory.

(ii) If we were to identify the source of disequilibrium in a divergence of the profit rates earned in the two sectors, we would run into the same type of problem. For a divergence in sectoral profit rates to arise, we should suppose a departure of prices from their respective equilibrium values and we would thus be back to the already-mentioned question of Say's law.

(iii) Finally, if we were to assume the existence of a wage differential between the two sectors, this would involve dropping the assumption of a unified labour market, i.e. the assumption that labour can move freely from one sector to another. As will be recalled, Ricardo ((68), p. 11) solved the problem of non-homogeneous labour by considering skilled manpower as a multiple of unskilled labour — the multiplying factor, determined by the market, being relatively stable over time. For the non-homogeneity of labour to justify a sectoral wage differential, one would therefore have to assume not only that all the workers of one sector were more skilful as compared with those of the other sector, but also that they could not be employed in the other. These conditions would imply, however, a splitting of the labour market into separate components, contrary to the Ricardian idea of its substantial unity.

In the following section we present a disequilibrium model formulated so as to allow a joint examination both of macroeconomic disequilibria in the labour market and of sectoral disequilibria in the employment structure.

The first type of disequilibria, considered in isolation, and assuming a constant equilibrium employment structure, gives rise to results in the two-sector model identical to those of the one-sector model; for, as we have mentioned, the productive conditions of the industrial sector do not influence the growth rates of the variables, which are all defined in terms of the rate of growth of capital for the economy as a whole and of the rate of change of the employment structure. Therefore, since the employment structure remains constant through time with the assumption made regarding production conditions in agriculture, the growth rates in the two-sector model coincide — given the same level of agricultural employment — with those defined in Chapter 5 for the Ricardian one-sector model.

We may conclude that macroeconomic disequilibrium at the aggregate level of employment, unaccompanied by a change in the employment structure, produces in the two-sector model types of growth paths identical to those obtained, for the corresponding cases, in the one-sector model. Also the disequilibrium behaviour of the system is therefore unaffected by the presence of an industrial sector, the impact of which is confined to influencing the position of the time paths and not their form. The analysis carried out in the remaining part of the chapter will thus concentrate on the second type of disequilibrium, i.e. that due to an imbalance in the employment structure.

It should be noted that the conclusion just reached about the effects of a macroeconomic disequilibrium strictly depends on the assumed constancy of the sectoral structure of employment. If the latter changes over time — as would occur with an agricultural production function different from (40) and characterized, instead, by a variable elasticity of output with respect to the labour input — macroeconomic disequilibria would involve, in general, sectoral disequilibria in employment as well.

6.11 An analysis of sectoral employment disequilibria

The essential characteristic of the sectoral disequilibria examined here is the divergence of the employment structure from its equilibrium value. Whether this is accompanied or not by a macroeconomic disequilibrium affecting the whole labour force is irrelevant for formulating the disequilibrium assumption. In other words, the initial situation can be either of 'pure' structural disequilibrium with a total labour supply equal to the equilibrium amount, or a combination of both phenomena.

In the discussion here of the disequilibrium source, we shall refer to the latter case and consider, in particular, a situation where the initial employment in one of the two sectors is in equilibrium, while that of the other sector is different from the corresponding equilibrium value. The analytical model presented in the following sections is, instead, formulated in general terms, and can therefore take account of both situations envisaged.

Let us, then, suppose that the initial situation is characterized by a level of agricultural employment equal to, and of industrial employment greater than, the respective equilibrium values. Let us also suppose that the initial value of capital is the equilibrium one. According to the wages-fund theory, the market wage of labour is lower than the natural wage. The physical output of agriculture is then equal to, and that of industry is greater than, the respective equilibrium values. This means that if we wish to maintain the assumption of equality between aggregate demand and supply (Say's law), we must suppose an appropriate change in relative prices.

In what follows, we assume – in line with Ricardo's idea that gold can be taken to be an invariable measure of value – that the adjustment is realized exclusively through modifications in the absolute price of corn.[7] This means that for the agricultural sector we must distinguish between the *equilibrium price*, which is defined by equation (4) as the inverse of the marginal product of labour, and the *market price*, which is determined by the condition that aggregate demand and supply be equal given the assumed imbalance in the employment structure. Since the validity of Say's law is established in the model by (12) – equality between the value of rent and the value of industrial output – the market price of corn is defined as:

$$p_{1t} = \frac{p_{2t} X_{2t}}{R_t} \tag{59}$$

With the assumption made about the nature of the initial disequilibrium and denoting the equilibrium price as p_{10}^*, we have:

$$p_{10} > p_{10}^* = \frac{1}{f'(N_{10})} \tag{60}$$

It should be recalled in this regard that as opposed to an unchanged rent in terms of corn a greater industrial output is produced with respect to the equilibrium situation. When the price of industrial goods remains stable, this greater output can be absorbed only if a corresponding increase in the purchasing power of rent occurs. This can be realized through an appropriate increase in the market price of corn above the natural level, as shown by (60).

The divergence between the equilibrium and the market price of corn determines a departure from the condition of equality of the sectoral profit rates, and affects, therefore, the accumulation process in the two sectors and in the system as a whole.

The agricultural profit rate – definable here in physical terms and thus independent of the price of corn[8] – is initially equal to

$$r_{10} = \frac{f'(N_{10})}{x_0} - 1 = \frac{1}{p_{10}^* x_0} - 1 \qquad (61)$$

Since, with an aggregate supply of labour exceeding the equilibrium level, the initial market wage is lower than the natural wage, r_{10} is greater than the corresponding equilibrium value.[9]

The industrial profit rate, which (on the contrary) can be defined solely in value terms, is clearly influenced by the prices of the commodities and is initially equal to

$$r_{20} = \frac{p_{20}^* P_{20}}{p_{10} x_0 N_{20}} = \frac{1}{p_{10} x_0} - 1 \qquad (62)$$

It can be proved that, in the case considered, r_{20} is lower than its equilibrium value.[10] Since $p_{10} > p_{10}^*$, it is clear also that $r_{10} > r_{20}$.

It is reasonable to suppose that the divergence between sectoral profit rates must necessarily affect the process of accumulation in both sectors of the economy. With productive resources free to move from one sector to the other, this situation may then be taken to determine a speeding up of the pace of accumulation in the sector with a higher rate of return on capital and a parallel slowing down in the other sector.

A complex reaction mechanism to the sectoral disequilibrium envisaged is thus set in motion. It is a mechanism that – depending on the specific assumptions that can be made about the response of economic agents and thus with different behaviours of the variables over time – may in various ways correct the initial imbalance. It is essentially on a 'competitive' mechanism of equalization of the profit rates of the kind just outlined that Ricardo and, more generally, classical writers seem to have relied.[11]

If the assumption is made that λ_t remains constant along the equilibrium path, the reaction mechanism can be based on the idea that a divergence between r_{1t} and r_{2t} determines a change in λ_t which expresses, on account of equations (14)–(17), the structure both of employment and of accumulation. Sectoral rates of accumulation are thereby modified.

6.12 The disequilibrium model

The whole two-sector model with the disequilibrium mechanism just discussed is reproduced below for convenience:

$$X_{1t} = f(N_{1t}) = N_{1t}^{\alpha} \qquad \text{Agricultural production function} \quad (63)$$

$$R_t = f(N_{1t}) - N_{1t}f'(N_{1t}) \qquad \text{Rent} \quad (64)$$

$$P_{1t} = N_{1t}[f'(N_{1t}) - x_t] \qquad \text{Agricultural profits} \quad (65)$$

$$p_{1t}^* = \frac{1}{f'(N_{1t})} \qquad \text{Equilibrium price of corn} \quad (66)$$

$$X_{2t} = \beta N_{2t} \qquad \text{Industrial production function} \quad (67)$$

$$p_{2t}P_{2t} = p_{2t}X_{2t} - p_{1t}N_{2t}x_t \qquad \text{Industrial profits} \quad (68)$$

$$p_{2t} = \frac{1}{\beta} \qquad \text{Price of gold} \quad (69)$$

$$N_{1t} = (1 - \lambda_t)N_t^D \qquad \text{Agricultural employment} \quad (70)$$

$$N_{2t} = \lambda_t N_t^D \qquad \text{Industrial employment} \quad (71)$$

$$K_t = W_t \qquad \text{Wages fund} \quad (72)$$

$$N_t^D = \frac{W_t}{x_t} \qquad \text{Demand for labour} \quad (73)$$

$$\frac{\dot{N}_t^S}{N_t^S} = n_t + \gamma(x_t - \bar{x}) \qquad \text{Labour supply} \quad (74)$$

$$n_t = \left[\frac{f'(N_{1t})}{\bar{x}} - 1\right] \qquad \text{Equilibrium component of population growth} \quad (75)$$

$$N_t^D = N_t^S \qquad \text{Equilibrium condition in the labour market} \quad (76)$$

$$P_t = p_{1t}P_{1t} + p_{2t}P_{2t} \qquad \text{Total profits} \quad (77)$$

$$p_{1t} = \frac{p_{2t}X_{2t}}{R_t} \qquad \text{Market price of corn} \quad (78)$$

$$p_{1t}\dot{K}_t = P_t \qquad \text{Total investment} \qquad (79)$$

$$r_{1t} = \frac{1}{p_{1t}^{*}x_t} - 1 \qquad \text{Agricultural profit rate} \qquad (80)$$

$$r_{2t} = \frac{1}{p_{1t}x_t} - 1 \qquad \text{Industrial profit rate} \qquad (81)$$

$$\frac{\dot{K}_{1t}}{K_{1t}} = \frac{\dot{K}_t}{K_t} - \frac{\dot{\lambda}_t}{(1-\lambda_t)} \qquad \begin{array}{l}\text{Agricultural accumulation} \\ \text{rate}\end{array} \qquad (82)$$

$$\dot{\lambda}_t = -\delta(r_{1t} - r_{2t})$$

$$= \frac{-\delta}{p_{1t}x_t} \cdot \frac{p_{1t} - p_{1t}^{*}}{p_{1t}^{*}} \qquad \begin{array}{l}\text{Changes in sectoral} \\ \text{structure}\end{array} \qquad (83)$$

The parameters γ and δ in (74) and (83) indicate respectively the intensity of reaction to disequilibria in the labour market and to divergences in sectoral profit rates.

The model (63)–(83) contains: (i) the basic relations of the two-sector model illustrated in section 6.2 above; (ii) the equations (79)–(83) through which the assumed sectoral disequilibrium and the subsequent reaction mechanism are described; and (iii) the equations (72)–(76) incorporating the wage–population adjustment mechanism on the assumption that the wages-fund theory is valid. This last set of equations, which allows macroeconomic disequilibria regarding the sole aggregate labour force to be dealt with, is necessary for a correct specification of the model. In fact, even if we assume that the disequilibrium process is started off by an exclusively sectoral imbalance, we are not authorized to suppose that subsequent macroeconomic disequilibria may be ruled out. As will be seen, they do in fact occur; the hypothesis of a constant natural wage must accordingly be given up.

As regards the sectoral disequilibrium mechanism, note in particular that (82) reproduces (18), which defines the rate of accumulation in the agricultural sector, and that, as shown by (83), the difference between sectoral profit rates can be expressed meaningfully in terms of the percentage deviation of the market price of corn from its equilibrium value. Still in connection with (83), note that the minus sign is justified by the circumstance that λ_t stands for the percentage quantity of capital employed in industry. As the change in λ_t is made to depend upon the difference between the profit rate in agriculture and that in industry, a positive value of this difference must be associated with a reduction in the rate of increase of capital in industry and with a corresponding increase of the percentage amount of capital in agriculture.

The analysis of disequilibrium paths and of the ways in which competition operates in response to divergences in sectoral profit rates can be usefully extended with the consideration of a slightly modified version of the two-sector disequilibrium model, alternative to that including equation (83). In other words the latter can be replaced by

$$\dot{\lambda}_t = -\delta(r_{1,t-1} - r_{2,t-1}) \tag{83a}$$

This relation expresses the assumption of a time lag between the appearance of a difference in sectoral profit rates and the reaction of capitalists in the form of an adjustment in sectoral accumulation rates. An assumption of this kind may be taken to reflect – though only very schematically – the complexity of the decision-making process in which various phases can be distinguished. These range from the occurrence of disequilibrium to its perception by capitalists, from the ensuing decision on the amount of investment to realize to the real manifestation of the effects of the decision taken.

Obviously, other lags could have been considered in the disequilibrium model, for example with reference to the demographic response to divergences of the market from the natural wage. However, in so far as we stick to relatively simple (one or two periods) lag assumptions, significant changes do not occur in the numerical results obtained. For this reason, the introduction of time lags is limited to the case defined with (83a).

6.13 Concluding remarks on disequilibrium paths

The paths of the main variables of the disequilibrium model have been determined, as for the one-sector model, by computer simulation, for the version containing equation (83) – case one – and that containing equation (83a) – case two. The values assigned to the parameters α and β in the production functions (63) and (67) are respectively 0.75 and 1. Several values have been considered for the reaction parameters γ and δ. The paths reproduced in the following diagrams refer to the sole combination of values of $\gamma = 0.8$ and of $\delta = 0.2$. This makes for a quicker reading of the graphs and does not involve a significant loss of information since, in the range of admissible values of the parameters, different combinations of values of γ and δ do not modify the type of results obtained.

The source of disequilibrium considered involves only the employment structure and not aggregate employment. This choice has the advantage of showing how an initial imbalance concerning only the structure of the economy inevitably determines a situation of disequilibrium for the macro variables (aggregate employment and capital) as well. The complex links of interdependence between all variables of the model are thus underlined.

The disequilibrium paths of certain relevant variables (employment structure; market wage; aggregate employment; profit rates in agriculture, in industry, and for the economy as a whole) are shown in the graphs below. With λ_0^* indicating the initial equilibrium value of the employment structure, in each of the graphs two disequilibrium paths — one referring to the case where the initial value of the employment structure is greater than the equilibrium value ($\lambda_0 > \lambda_0^*$), and the other to the opposite case ($\lambda_0 < \lambda_0^*$) — are presented and compared with the natural equilibrium path. The basic features of the behaviour of the economy over time clearly emerge. Before briefly commenting on them, it seems appropriate to stress that the cases considered are in the nature of examples which, no matter how telling, can never constitute a general proof that different types of behaviour can be excluded.

The essential characteristic of case one (see Figures 11-16) is re-

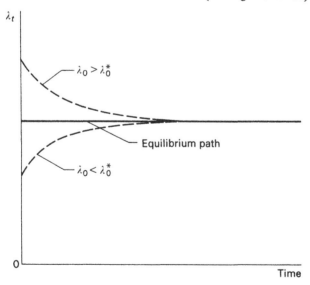

Figure 11

159

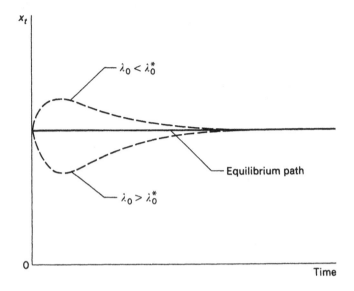

Figure 12

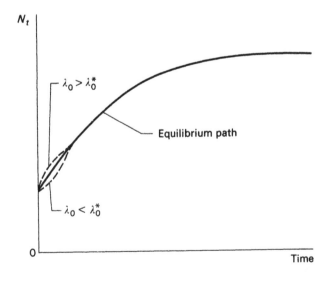

Figure 13

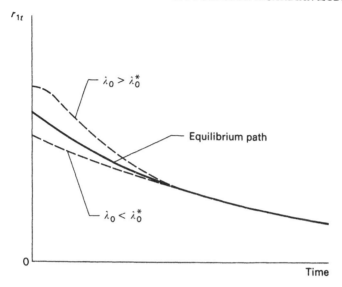

Figure 14

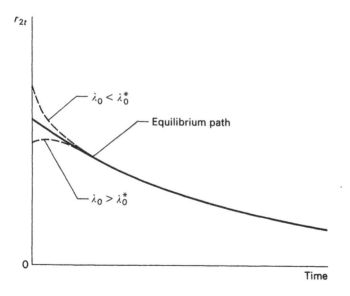

Figure 15

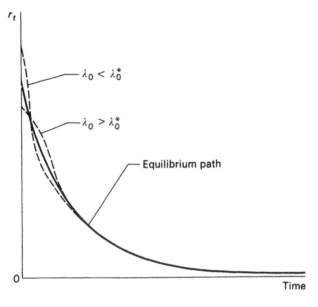

Figure 16

presented by the circumstance that the disequilibrium paths – with the sole exception of the general profit rate – never intersect the corresponding natural equilibrium paths. This means that the position of the disequilibrium paths – above or below the corresponding equilibrium ones – is determined once and for all by the 'sign' of the initial disequilibrium. As just mentioned, the sole exception is the general rate of profit, which – in connection with the behaviour of the market wage, first decreasing and then increasing when $\lambda_0 > \lambda_0^*$, and vice versa when $\lambda_0 < \lambda_0^*$ – intersects (only once) the corresponding equilibrium path, thereafter gradually reverting back towards it.

As regards the behaviour of distributive shares, we may point out that, while in equilibrium the share of rent and that of profit plus wages are constant, this no longer occurs in disequilibrium because of the divergence between the market and the natural price of corn. Also, with respect to the three separate income shares, the position of the disequilibrium paths depends on the 'sign' of the initial imbalance in employment structure. If $\lambda_0 > \lambda_0^*$, the paths of the shares of rent and profits lie below the corresponding equilibrium ones, whereas the opposite occurs for the path of the share of wages; and vice versa if $\lambda_0 < \lambda_0^*$.

The disequilibrium paths of case two, which refers to the model incorporating (83a), are shown in Figures 17–22. The distinguishing feature of case two as compared with case one is clearly represented by the oscillatory nature of the disequilibrium paths, depending on the assumed existence of a time lag in the reaction function of capitalists, i.e. in the adjustment process originating in a divergence of sectoral profit rates. The equilibrium path of the economy is thus attained through fluctuations of decreasing amplitude.

Notwithstanding the already-acknowledged limited validity of numerical examples, this result may be taken to reflect the methodological approach mentioned in Chapter 1, where a significant role was assigned to the existence of reactions to disequilibrium situations. In line with this approach, the existence of damped oscillations can be viewed as a consequence of the fact that economic agents not only react to disequilibrium situations but also that the process of reaction is influenced by the perception of the outcome of earlier reactions. That is, it is assumed that the behaviour of economic agents is based on the rational and critical assessment of individual disequilibrium conditions which may also result from previous 'corrective' decisions, appropriate in direction but not in intensity.

To sum up, one aspect common to both models examined here

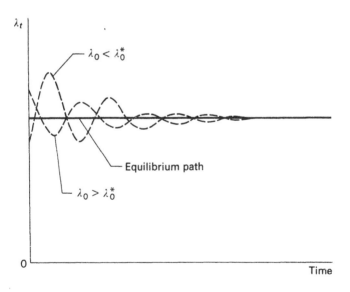

Figure 17

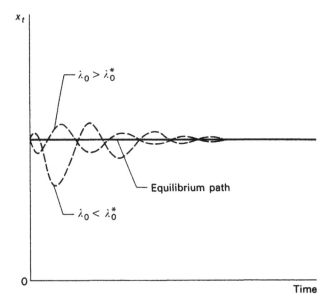

Figure 18

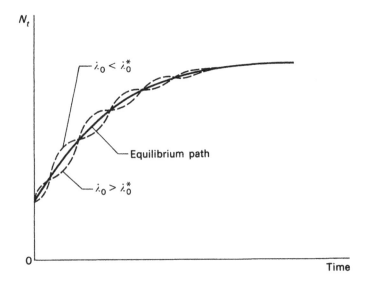

Figure 19

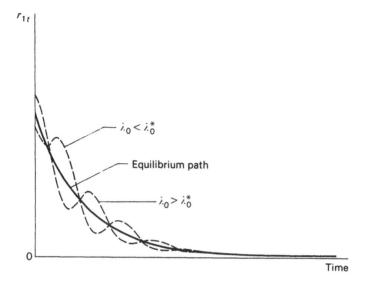

Figure 20

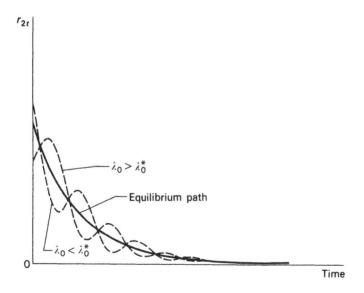

Figure 21

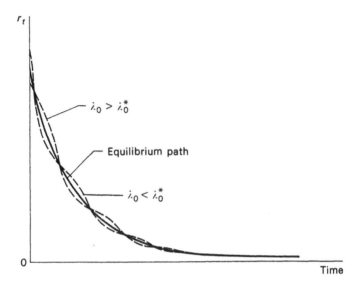

Figure 22

(cases one and two) can be stressed: it concerns the equilibrating role of competition implicit in the Ricardian system. The mobility of capital from one sector to another in response to differences in profit rates makes possible, whatever the reactions of entrepreneurs, the restoration of equilibrium growth, characterized by a uniform rate of profit. When the response is immediate, the return to the equilibrium path is by gradual corrections in the same direction. When, instead, the presence of a time lag in the adjustment mechanism is assumed, the natural equilibrium path is attained, of necessity, through a process of 'trial and error', with decisions which overshoot the target and lead to compensatory adjustments in the opposite direction.

Appendix   The natural equilibrium of a three-sector Ricardian model

Introductory remarks

The aim of this appendix is to take some steps in the direction of removing the limitation of the analysis of the Ricardian dynamic model originating from the exclusion of fixed capital.[12] The natural equilibrium analysis of Chapters 5 and 6 is accordingly extended here to the case of machines, which are supposed to be currently produced and required as an input in production together with labour.

When the study of the Ricardian system is generalized from one- and two-sector models to a three-sector model (corn, gold and machines), the labour theory of value holds only in the particular case of a uniform capital–labour ratio. When no such assumption is made, natural prices must be determined on the basis of a more general theory of value. The existence of non-negative prices and profit rate has already been proved for the general case in Chapter 2. Indeed, the analysis developed here represents an attempt in the direction of a truly dynamic extension of the investigation carried on there. In this attempt the size of the model is reduced from m to three commodities. The $m - 2$ commodities produced under constant returns to scale of the model examined in Chapter 2 are grouped into a single luxury good – gold. As argued by Pasinetti ((64), pp. 90–2), no great loss of generality is thereby involved.

The analysis of the natural equilibrium of a three-sector Ricardian system is carried on in two successive stages:

(i) The problem of the existence of positions of *point natural equilibrium* is first tackled, since Pasinetti's proof cannot be taken to extend automatically to the three-sector model. In fact, the results of Chapters 4 and 6 show that no problem arises as to the full employment of the only type of capital considered in the two-sector model – at the given natural wage, population is assumed to adjust so that full utilization of circulating capital is always attained. The sectoral structure of employment depends accordingly on the consumption behaviour of the social classes, in particular of rentiers. In the three-sector model, instead, if we assume rigidly given sectoral capital–labour ratios, joint full employment of fixed capital (machines) and circulating capital (corn advanced to labour as wages) cannot be taken for granted. It can obtain only if machines and advances to labour are available in a proportion falling in a predefined interval, depending on technological parameters. When this condition is satisfied, joint full employment of fixed and circulating capital requires that an appropriate sectoral distribution of employment be realized. The latter is thus influenced not only by the assumed behaviour of the social classes but also by the availability of fixed and circulating capital. The existence and uniqueness of an economically meaningful point natural equilibrium solution of the three-sector Ricardian system must, therefore, be accurately verified. When this is done, the determination of the stationary-state position is straightforward.

(ii) The second stage of the analysis is represented by the study of the *natural equilibrium path*, which is defined, given the saving behaviour, by the accumulation of fixed and circulating capital. As the determination of the natural path on the basis of the explicit solution of the differential equations (growth rates) of these variables presents considerable difficulties, we have confined ourselves to raising the more general questions of the existence, uniqueness and convergence to the stationary state of the equilibrium paths originating from different initial conditions. This type of analysis represents a preliminary step towards the investigation of the problems of changes in capital–labour ratios, raised by Ricardo in chapter 31 'On machinery' of his *Principles*.

In the study of the natural equilibrium of the three-sector Ricardian model two distinct assumptions are made about the 'organic composition of capital': first, the general case is considered of different sectoral capital–labour ratios, then the special case is made of a uniform proportion of machines to labour. The simplifying role of the labour theory of value can thereby be clearly shown.

The model

The following specific assumptions, in addition to those already stated in Chapters 4 and 6, where the two-sector model was studied, characterize the three-sector Ricardian model:

(a) Labour and machines are required in the production of all commodities. The proportion of fixed capital to labour – denoted here as in Chapter 2 by k_i – is constant over time for each sector. The index i $(= 1, 2, 3)$ refers to, respectively, agriculture (corn), industry (gold), and the machine-producing sector.

(b) Machine production is subject to constant returns to scale.

(c) Machines wear out over time at a constant rate σ (assumption of radioactive decay).

(d) Machines produced at time t are available for productive use only in period $t + 1$.

Denoting as M_t^s the quantity of machines available at time t, M_t the quantity of machines used at time t, X_{3t} the output flow of new machines in period t, n_2 and n_3 the labour inputs of sectors two and three,[13] and maintaining otherwise the notation used in the earlier chapters, the three-sector model can be described by the following relations:

Agricultural sector

$$X_{1t} = f(N_{1t})$$

Production function with diminishing returns (A.1)

$$N_{1t} = \lambda_{1t} N_t$$

Agricultural employment as a percentage of total employment (A.2)

$$M_{1t} = k_1 N_{1t}$$

Quantity of machines used in agriculture (A.3)

$$R_t = f(N_{1t}) - N_{1t} f'(N_{1t})$$

Rent (A.4)

$$P_{1t} = N_{1t}\left[f'(N_{1t}) - \bar{x} - \sigma k_1 \frac{p_{3t}}{p_{1t}} \right]$$

Net profits in terms of corn (A.5)

$$p_{1t} = \frac{1}{f'(N_{1t})} \frac{1 + (r_t + \sigma)n_3(k_1 - k_3)}{1 + (r_t + \sigma)n_3(k_2 - k_3)}$$

Price of corn (A.6)

Industrial sector

$$X_{2t} = \frac{1}{n_2} N_{2t}$$

Production function with constant returns (A.7)

$$N_{2t} = \lambda_{2t} N_t$$

Industrial employment as a percentage of total employment (A.8)

$$M_{2t} = k_2 N_{2t}$$

Quantity of machines used in industry (A.9)

$$p_{2t} P_{2t} = p_{2t} X_{2t} - p_{1t}\bar{x}N_{2t} - p_{3t}\sigma k_2 N_{2t}$$

Net profits in value terms (A.10)

$$p_{2t} = n_2$$

Price of gold (A.11)

Machine sector

$$X_{3t} = \frac{1}{n_3} N_{3t}$$

Production function with constant returns (A.12)

$$N_{3t} = (1 - \lambda_{1t} - \lambda_{2t})N_t$$

Employment in the machine sector as a percentage of total employment (A.13)

$$M_{3t} = k_3 N_{3t}$$

Quantity of machines used in the machine-producing sector (A.14)

$$p_{3t}P_{3t} = p_{3t}X_{3t} - p_{1t}\bar{x}N_{3t} - p_{3t}\sigma k_3 N_{3t}$$

Net profits in value terms (A.15)

$$p_{3t} = \frac{n_3}{1 + (r_t + \sigma)n_3 (k_2 - k_3)}$$

Price of machines (A.16)

Macroeconomic relations

$$W_t = K_t$$

Wages fund (A.17)

$$N_t = \frac{W_t}{\bar{x}}$$

Demand for labour (A.18)

$$p_{2t}X_{2t} = p_{1t}R_t$$

Demand for gold (A.19)

$$P_t = p_{1t}P_{1t} + p_{2t}P_{2t} + p_{3t}P_{3t}$$

Total net profits in value terms (A.20)

$$r_t = \frac{1}{k_3 n_3}\left\{1 - \frac{\bar{x}}{f'(N_{1t})} \cdot [1 + (r_t + \sigma)n_3 (k_1 - k_3)] (1 + r_t)\right\} - \sigma$$

General (net) profit rate (A.21)

$$M_t = M_{1t} + M_{2t} + M_{3t}$$

Aggregate demand for machines (A.22)

$$M_t = M_t^s$$

Condition of full employment of machines (A.23)

$$\dot{M}_t^s = X_{3t} - \sigma M_t^s \qquad \text{Net increase of} \\ \text{machines} \quad (A.24)$$

$$P_t = p_{1t}\dot{K}_t + p_{3t}\dot{M}_t \qquad \text{Capital accumu-} \\ \text{lation} \qquad (A.25)$$

The following remarks may help in clarifying the formulation of the model, which consists of twenty-five equations in the same number of unknowns.

(i) Since by assumption (a) the sectoral capital–labour ratios are constant, the production of every commodity can be expressed as a function of a single variable (labour or machines), the quantity employed of the other 'factor' being determined by the given proportion of machines to labour. Similar to the formulation of the one- and two-sector models, output is here made formally to depend solely on the quantity of the labour input.

(ii) Commodity prices and the profit rate defined in the model represent a sort of 'solution' of a four-equation price-determination system corresponding to (10) (definition of relative prices) and (4a) (choice of *numéraire*) of Chapter 2. The definitions (A.6), (A.11), (A.16) and (A.21) clearly take account of assumption (c) above concerning depreciation of machines. As some straightforward calculation shows, total profits, as defined by (A.20), may be expressed also as

$$P_t = r_t(p_{1t}K_t + p_{3t}M_t) \qquad (A.20a)$$

that is, as the profit charged at the rate r_t on the aggregate value of (fixed and circulating) capital used by the system.

(iii) The process of accumulation is defined by (A.24) and (A.25). Equation (A.25), which states that profits are entirely reinvested, represents the joint demand for additional advances to labour (implying an expansion of the existing wages fund) and for new machines. *Vis-à-vis* this aggregate demand for an increase in 'capital', the model explicitly defines, by equation (A.24), only one of the two components of the additional supply of 'capital' – the supply of new machines. Equation (A.23), however, which establishes a stock equilibrium condition between aggregate demand and supply of (existing) machines for all t, implies that the corresponding flow equilibrium condition

$$\dot{M}_t = \dot{M}_t^s \qquad (A.23a)$$

is equally satisfied for all t. Substituting now in (A.25) the definitions of sectoral profits (A.5), (A.10) and (A.15), then taking account of (A.17), (A.18), (A.19) and (A.24), and using (A.23a), we obtain:

$$\dot{K}_t = X_{1t} - K_t \qquad (A.25a)$$

This may be viewed as an equilibrium condition between demand and supply of additional advances to labour. We can therefore conclude that the model also contains the remaining component of the new supply of 'capital', i.e. circulating capital.

Equations (A.23a) and (A.25a) — both implicitly contained in the model (A.1)-(A.25), as we have just seen — explicitly emphasize the two conditions for balanced growth which must be satisfied in the three-sector model.

The structure of the model

The greater complexity of the three-sector model demands some examination of its structure to help discussion of problems on the definition of point natural equilibrium positions and of the relationship between these positions and the natural equilibrium paths.

If we consider the subset of equations referring to each sector of the economy, we can see that output, machines employed, rent (if present), profits and price in each sector are fully determined on the basis of the labour input and the rate of profit. These variables, in their turn, are determined by the subset of macroeconomic relations (A.17)-(A.25). Furthermore, since aggregate labour employment depends — by (A.17) and (A.18) — on the wages fund, the sectoral employment levels turn out to be a function of the structure variables λ_{1t} and λ_{2t} and of the wages fund.

As also P_t can be expressed in terms of λ_{1t}, λ_{2t} and of the wages fund, the model (A.1)-(A.25) can be reduced, therefore, to a basic subset of six equations in the six variables λ_{1t}, λ_{2t}, r_t, M_t, M_t^s and K_t, which is obtained by performing the required substitutions in the equations (A.19) and (A.21)-(A.25) of the model. For convenience of subsequent reference, this set of six equations can be expressed, respecting the functional interdependences established by the model, in terms of implicit functions:

$$\lambda_{2t} = g_1(\lambda_{1t}, r_t, K_t) \tag{a}$$

$$r_t = g_2(\lambda_{1t}, K_t) \tag{b}$$

$$M_t = g_3(\lambda_{1t}, \lambda_{2t}, K_t) \tag{c}$$

$$M_t = M_t^s \tag{d}$$

$$\dot{M}_t^s = g_4(\lambda_{1t}, \lambda_{2t}, K_t, M_t^s) \tag{e}$$

$$\dot{K}_t = g_5(\lambda_{1t}, K_t) \tag{f}$$

Given K_t and M_t^s, equations (a)-(d) define a point natural equilibrium position with reference to the variables λ_{1t}, λ_{2t}, r_t and M_t, provided that the conditions (to be specified below) for the existence of an economically meaningful solution are satisfied.

Equations (e) and (f) represent a system of differential equations in K_t and M_t^s whose solution — if it exists — describes, given the initial values K_0 and M_0^s, the behaviour of these variables over time, thus defining the dynamics of the three-sector model.

The natural equilibrium with different sectoral capital–labour ratios

Considering first the case of different sectoral capital–labour ratios, assume:

$$k_1 = k_2 > k_3 \tag{A.26}$$

The circumstance that capital–labour ratios are equal in the corn- and gold-producing sectors allows useful analytical simplifications to be made without imposing serious limitations on the generality of the results. The assumption of a greater capital-intensity for corn and gold than for machines will be discussed later.

Let the ratio of machines to labour for the economy as a whole be:

$$k_t = \frac{M_t^s}{N_t} = \bar{x}\frac{M_t^s}{K_t} \tag{A.27}$$

and assume, as before, a constant elasticity production function in agriculture (with the elasticity coefficient α between zero and one), of the type, for example, $f(N_{1t}) = N_{1t}^\alpha$, with $f(0) = 0$.

Assume, lastly, the three-sector model to be 'viable', i.e. the output of machines net of physical wear and tear to be positive. Bearing in mind that, by definition, $n_3 k_3$ is the quantity of machines required to produce a new machine and that, to replace worn-out machines, a quantity $on_3 k_3$ of fixed capital is needed, the condition for the model to be 'viable' is

$$1 - on_3 k_3 > 0 \tag{A.28}$$

The point natural equilibrium position
Referring to the reduced model (a)–(f) above, we have to state in explicit form equations (a)–(d), which, as already mentioned, define the point natural equilibrium position of the three-sector Ricardian model.

Taking account of definitions (A.7), (A.8) and (A.11), the left-hand side of equation (A.19) can be written as:

$$p_{2t}X_{2t} = \lambda_{2t}N_t \tag{A.29}$$

173

Similarly, substituting (A.2) and (A.4) in the right-hand side of (A.19), remembering that (see Chapter 6, section 6.5) with a constant elasticity agricultural production function $R_t = (1 - \alpha)f(N_{1t}) = [(1 - \alpha)/\alpha] N_{1t}f'(N_{1t})$, and considering that on account of (A.26) $p_{1t} = 1/f'(N_{1t})$, we have:

$$p_{1t}R_t = \frac{1-\alpha}{\alpha}\lambda_{1t}N_t \tag{A.30}$$

Equalizing now the right-hand sides of (A.29) and (A.30)

$$\lambda_{2t} = \frac{1-\alpha}{\alpha}\lambda_{1t} \tag{A.31}$$

is obtained. Note that with $k_1 = k_2$ (A.19) can be expressed as a simple relation where the profit rate does not appear.

For equation (A.21) — corresponding to equation (b) of the reduced-form model — no simplification is possible. It therefore remains unchanged.

Lastly, as regards the demand for machines, with appropriate substitutions in (A.22),

$$M_t = [k_1\lambda_{1t} + k_2\lambda_{2t} + k_3 (1 - \lambda_{1t} - \lambda_{2t})] \frac{K_t}{\bar{x}} \tag{A.32}$$

is obtained. Observe that, given the wages fund, the demand for machines is, because of (A.26), higher, the greater the percentage of the labour force employed in agriculture and industry.

The set of equations defining the point natural equilibrium position of the three-sector Ricardian system is then represented by (A.31), (A.21), (A.32) and (A.23).

If the demand for machines as defined by (A.32) is substituted in the equilibrium condition (A.23), and the definition of k_t in (A.27) is taken into account, we have:

$$k_1\lambda_{1t} + k_2\lambda_{2t} + k_3 (1 - \lambda_{1t} - \lambda_{2t}) = k_t \tag{A.33}$$

From equations (A.31) and (A.33) the equilibrium solutions for λ_{1t} and λ_{2t} are then derived:

$$\lambda_{1t} = \alpha\frac{k_t - k_3}{k_1 - k_3} \tag{A.34}$$

$$\lambda_{2t} = (1-\alpha)\frac{k_t - k_3}{k_1 - k_3} \tag{A.35}$$

It is clear — from (A.26) and the assumption $\alpha < 1$ — that λ_{1t} and λ_{2t} are both positive and less than one if the following condition holds:

$$k_3 \leqslant k_t \leqslant k_1 \tag{A.36}$$

Note further that the sum $(\lambda_{1t} + \lambda_{2t})$ – equal to $(k_t - k_3)/(k_1 - k_3)$ – is, on account of (A.36), less than one. The percentage employment in the machine-producing sector – equal to $(k_1 - k_t)/(k_1 - k_3)$ – is therefore equally non-negative and less than unity.

The economic meaning of (A.36) is straightforward. Only if this condition is satisfied is it possible to achieve the full employment of the available quantities of both fixed and circulating capital. For, if $k_t > k_1$, $(\lambda_{1t} + \lambda_{2t})$ would be greater than one, while the percentage employment in the machine-producing sector would be negative. As both these circumstances are clearly not admissible, we could at most set $\lambda_{1t} + \lambda_{2t} = 1$. In view of (A.32) the maximum demand of machines would accordingly be $M_t = k_t(K_t/\bar{x})$, while from (A.27) supply would be $M_t^s = k_3(K_t/\bar{x})$. A situation would ensue where part of the available machines would remain unused. If, instead, $k_t < k_3$, a similar reasoning would show that demand for machines would be $M_t = k_3(K_t/\bar{x})$ and would thus exceed supply. The number of workers for whom the quantity of machines available could provide employment would then be less than the number employable, at the given natural wage, with the available wages fund. Unemployment of a portion of the existing circulating capital would thus result.

Given the solution in λ_{1t} and λ_{2t}, the natural equilibrium value of the profit rate can be determined by (A.21). Obviously it is necessary to verify, in this case too, that the solution is economically meaningful. This obtains if r_t lies between zero and $[(1/n_3k_3) - \sigma]$, this latter value corresponding to a zero labour input in agriculture (see equation (A.21)). A general proof of the existence of a non-negative solution for the Ricardian price model has already been given in the appendix to Chapter 2. The problem is briefly dealt with again with specific reference to (A.21) and is illustrated graphically in Figure 23, following Dorfman, Samuelson and Solow (23), pp. 366–75.

The left-hand side of (A.21) is represented by the 45° line and the right-hand side by the function $h(r_t)$, which, given λ_{1t} and K_t, is an always decreasing function, since $h'(r_t) < 0$. The condition for r_t to lie in the interval indicated above is fulfilled if

$$0 \leqslant h(0) \leqslant \left(\frac{1}{k_3 n_3} - \sigma\right) \tag{A.37}$$

This is, in fact, the case, for

$$h(0) = \frac{1}{k_3 n_3} \left\{ 1 - \frac{\bar{x}}{f'\left(\lambda_{1t} \frac{K_t}{\bar{x}}\right)} [1 + \sigma n_3 (k_1 - k_3)] \right\} - \sigma$$

(A.38)

The condition $h(0) \geqslant 0$ therefore becomes:

$$f'\left(\lambda_{1t} \frac{K_t}{\bar{x}}\right) \geqslant \frac{\bar{x}}{1 - \sigma k_3 n_3} [1 + \sigma n_3 (k_1 - k_3)]$$

(A.39)

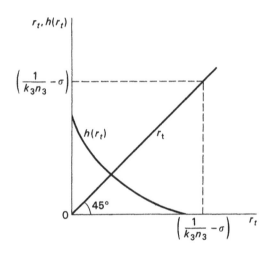

Figure 23

As will be shown, condition (A.39) holds with the equality sign in the stationary state, because the right-hand side represents the constant value of agricultural labour productivity in that situation. Since, with diminishing returns, agricultural labour productivity in the progressive phase of the economy is higher than in the stationary state, (A.39) is always fulfilled.

As can be verified by (A.38), the condition $h(0) \leqslant [(1/k_3 n_3) - \sigma]$ is also always satisfied. We may then conclude that the three-sector Ricardian model has a unique and economically meaningful point natural equilibrium solution.

The stationary-state equilibrium

The stationary state occurs when, profits being nil, the two components of the accumulation process (new machines and additional advances to labour) become zero.[14] Setting $r_t = 0$ in (A.21), we have:

$$f'(N_{1t}) = \bar{x} \frac{1 + \sigma n_3 (k_1 - k_3)}{1 - \sigma k_3 n_3} = \bar{x} \left(1 + \sigma k_1 \frac{n_3}{1 - \sigma k_3 n_3}\right)$$

$$(A.40)$$

Contrary to what happens in the one-sector and the two-sector Ricardian models, agricultural labour productivity in the stationary state is thus greater — due to the assumption of wear and tear of machines — than the natural wage. The analytical condition expressed by (A.40) may be interpreted as follows. The ratio $n_3/(1 - \sigma k_3 n_3)$ represents the quantity of labour required to produce a machine net of its physical wear and tear — $(1 - \sigma k_3 n_3)$ being the net output (always positive on account of (A.28)) of n_3 workers in the machine-producing sector. Moreover, σk_1 is the quantity of machines per worker in agriculture which wears out per unit or time. Consequently, $\sigma k_1 n_3/(1 - \sigma k_3 n_3)$ is the quantity of labour necessary to replace the quantity of machines per worker which 'decay', because of physical depreciation, in the agricultural sector. It follows that the expression in brackets after the second equality sign in (A.40) represents the quantity of total (direct and indirect) labour required in agricultural production per unit of direct labour — in other words, direct labour plus indirect labour associated with the use of k_1 machines. Thus in the stationary state the marginal product of agricultural labour must be equal to the cost (in terms of corn) of that quantity of labour.

The reduction to zero of the rate of growth of the wages fund implies, by (A.25a),

$$f(N_{1t}) = K_t \tag{A.41}$$

Taking account of the definition of elasticity of the agricultural production function and of equations (A.2), (A.18), (A.40) and (A.41), the stationary-state value of λ_{1t} is obtained:

$$\bar{\lambda}_1 = \alpha \frac{1 - \sigma k_3 n_3}{1 + \sigma n_3 (k_1 - k_3)} \tag{A.42}$$

From equation (A.31)

$$\bar{\lambda}_2 = (1 - \alpha) \frac{1 - \sigma k_3 n_3}{1 + \sigma n_3 (k_1 - k_3)} \tag{A.43}$$

is also derived. Since $\bar{\lambda}_1 < \alpha$ and $\bar{\lambda}_2 < (1 - \alpha)$, we have that $\bar{\lambda}_1 + \bar{\lambda}_2 < 1$. The percentage of labour employment in the machine-producing sector is thus also positive.

Given $\bar{\lambda}_1$, the stationary-state value of circulating capital is implicitly defined by (A.41). Assuming $f(N_{1t}) = N_{1t}^{\alpha}$, this value is

$$\bar{K} = \left(\frac{\bar{\lambda}_1}{\bar{x}}\right)^{\frac{\alpha}{1-\alpha}} \tag{A.44}$$

Conditions (A.40) and (A.41) imply that the growth rate of the stock of machines also becomes zero. This means, by (A.23), $X_{3t} = \sigma M_t$, i.e. that the current output of machines must exactly coincide with replacement requirements. On this basis, the stationary-state values of the aggregate capital–labour ratio and of the stock of machines can be determined:

$$\bar{k} = \frac{1}{\sigma n_3}(1 - \bar{\lambda}_1 - \bar{\lambda}_2) = \frac{k_1}{1 + \sigma n_3(k_1 - k_3)} \tag{A.45}$$

$$\bar{M}^s = \bar{k}\frac{\bar{K}}{\bar{x}} \tag{A.46}$$

The natural equilibrium growth

As already mentioned, equations (e) and (f) of the reduced-form model define the natural equilibrium path of the three-sector Ricardian model. The explicit form of these equations is that given by (A.24) and (A.25a). In considering the solution, however, it is useful to express these equations as functions of K_t and k_t rather than as functions of K_t and M_t^s. A link between these two sets of variables is supplied by (A.27). Taking the logarithmic derivatives of this equation, we have:

$$\frac{\dot{k}_t}{k_t} = \frac{\dot{M}_t^s}{M_t^s} - \frac{\dot{K}_t}{K_t} \tag{A.47}$$

Substituting (A.47) in (A.24) and taking account of (A.12), (A.13), (A.34) and (A.35), we obtain:

$$\dot{k}_t = \frac{1}{n_3}\frac{k_1 - k_t}{k_1 - k_3} - \sigma k_t - k_t \frac{\dot{K}_t}{K_t} \tag{A.48}$$

Moreover, (A.25a) can be expressed as

$$\frac{\dot{K}_t}{K_t} = \frac{f\left(\lambda_{1t}\frac{K_t}{\bar{x}}\right) - 1}{K_t} \tag{A.49}$$

For convenience let $\xi_t = \log K_t$, whence $\dot{\xi}_t = \dot{K}_t/K_t$ and $K_t = e^{\xi_t}$. Suppose also, as before, $f(N_{1t}) = N_{1t}^{\alpha}$. Bearing in mind (A.2), (A.18) and (A.34), (A.49) becomes:

$$\dot{\xi}_t = \left(\frac{\alpha}{\bar{x}}\right)^{\alpha}\left(\frac{k_t - k_3}{k_1 - k_3}\right)^{\alpha} \cdot e^{-(1-\alpha)\xi_t} - 1 = \phi_1(\xi_t, k_t) \tag{A.50}$$

Setting, on the other hand, $a = [1 + \sigma n_3(k_1 - k_3)]/[n_3(k_1 - k_3)]$ and remembering the definition of $\bar{k}$ in (A.45), (A.48) can be written as

$$\dot{k}_t = -a(k_t - \bar{k}) - k_t \xi_t = \phi_2(\xi_t, k_t) \qquad (A.51)$$

Equations (A.50) and (A.51) represent the explicit form of the dynamic equations (e) and (f) of the reduced-form model. The dynamic properties of the Ricardian system will now be considered on the basis of (A.50) and (A.51).

We must verify whether the dynamic process described by these equations faithfully reflects Ricardo's idea of an economic system gradually moving from a progressive phase to the stationary state. This requires that we prove: (i) the existence of a unique solution for the system of differential equations (A.50) and (A.51), i.e. the existence of a unique natural equilibrium path for each set of initial conditions; and (ii) the stability of the stationary-state solution, i.e. the convergence of all the natural equilibrium paths to the stationary state.

On the first point, the complexity of the system of differential equations (A.50) and (A.51) – from the viewpoint of the existence and uniqueness of the solution 'in the large' (i.e. for $0 < t < \infty$) – raised problems that it has not been possible to solve. Numerical computer-simulation tests show that, when the constraints on parameters and initial conditions defined below are respected, there is a unique natural equilibrium path for each initial condition. On the second point, a proof of the convergence of the natural path – provided it exists and is unique – to the stationary state is given in the following section.

Convergence of the natural equilibrium path to the stationary state
A theorem by Olech (see Gandolfo (26), p. 425) is used to prove the global stability of the stationary-state equilibrium.

Let the variables be defined in the intervals $\xi^* \leqslant \xi_t \leqslant \xi^{**}$ and $k^* \leqslant k_t \leqslant k_1$ with $k_3 < k^*$, where ξ^* and ξ^{**} are such that $\phi_1(\xi^*, k^*) = 0$ and $\phi_2(\xi^{**}, k_1) = 0$. Note that it is necessary to exclude the value k_3 from the range of admissible values of k_t. The reason is that, when $k_t = k_3$, (A.34) yields $\lambda_{1t} = 0$ and thus, given the assumption $f(0) = 0$, $X_{1t} = 0$. As a consequence, in the following moment of time the aggregate capital–labour ratio as defined by (A.27) would assume an infinite value. To avoid this difficulty, it is sufficient to take as lower limit of the definition interval for k_t any value $k^* < k_3$.

The equation $\phi_1(\xi_t, k_t) = 0$ is the set of points where the rate of change of the wages fund K_t is nil. The partial derivatives of $\phi_1(\xi_t,$

k_t) are:

$$\frac{\partial \phi_1}{\partial \xi_t} = -(1-\alpha)\left(\frac{\alpha}{\bar{x}}\right)^\alpha \left(\frac{k_t - k_3}{k_1 - k_3}\right)^\alpha$$

$$\cdot \; e^{-(1-\alpha)\xi_t} = -(1-\alpha)(1+\phi_1) < 0 \tag{A.52}$$

$$\frac{\partial \phi_1}{\partial k_t} = \frac{\alpha}{k_1 - k_3}\left(\frac{\alpha}{\bar{x}}\right)^\alpha \left(\frac{k_t - k_3}{k_1 - k_3}\right)^{\alpha-1}$$

$$\cdot \; e^{-(1-\alpha)\xi_t} = \frac{\alpha k_t}{k_t - k_3}(1+\phi_1) > 0 \tag{A.53}$$

and thus

$$\left.\frac{\partial \xi_t}{\partial k_t}\right|_{\phi_1=0} = \frac{\alpha}{1-\alpha} \cdot \frac{1}{k_t - k_3} > 0 \tag{A.54}$$

$\phi_1 = 0$ is therefore an ever-increasing function. It is plotted in Figure 24; for all points above the curve we have $\phi_1 < 0$, and vice versa for all points below it. So for values of ξ_t and k_t such that $\phi_1 < 0$, ξ_t (and consequently also the wages fund) diminishes, and vice versa.

The equation $\phi_2(\xi_t, k_t) = 0$ is the set of points where the capital-labour ratio k_t is constant. The partial derivatives are:

$$\frac{\partial \phi_2}{\partial \xi_t} = -k_t \frac{\partial \phi_1}{\partial \xi_t} = (1-\alpha)k_t(1+\phi_1) \tag{A.55}$$

$$\frac{\partial \phi_2}{\partial k_t} = -a - \phi_1 - k_t \frac{\partial \phi_1}{\partial k_t}$$

$$= -a - \phi_1 - \frac{\alpha k_t}{k_t - k_3}(1+\phi_1) \tag{A.56}$$

and thus

$$\left.\frac{\partial \xi_t}{\partial k_t}\right|_{\phi_2=0} = \frac{\alpha}{1-\alpha} \cdot \frac{1}{k_t - k_3} + \frac{a + \phi_1}{(1-\alpha)k_t(1+\phi_1)} \tag{A.57}$$

As regards the sign of this partial derivative, first note that, for the stationary-state values $\xi_t = \bar{\xi}$ and $k_t = \bar{k}$, $\phi_1 = 0$; (A.57) is, therefore, positive at this point. Comparing, moreover, (A.57) with (A.54), always at $\xi_t = \bar{\xi}$ and $k_t = \bar{k}$, it results that the partial derivative defined by (A.57) is greater than that defined by (A.54), so that the curve corresponding to the equation $\phi_2 = 0$ intersects the curve corresponding to the equation $\phi_1 = 0$ from beneath the point indicated.

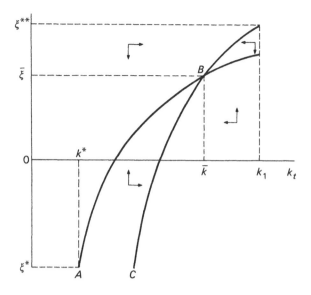

Figure 24

Note further that, for the values of the variables satisfying the equation $\phi_2 = 0$, $\phi_1 > 0$ when $\xi^* \leqslant \xi_t \leqslant \bar{\xi}$ and $k^* \leqslant k_t \leqslant \bar{k}$. The derivative defined by (A.57) is therefore positive in that range and greater than that defined by (A.54). Similarly, when $\bar{\xi} \leqslant \xi_t \leqslant \xi^{**}$ and $\bar{k} \leqslant k_t \leqslant k_1$, $\phi_1 < 0$ with a minimum − for the values of the variables satisfying $\phi_2 = 0$ − equal to $\phi_1(\xi^{**}, k_1)$. The minimum of ϕ_1 over the whole range of admissible values of the variables is, however, at the point (ξ^{**}, k_1). As (A.50) shows, this minimum value of ϕ_1 tends to the value −1 as k^* tends to k_3, implying $\phi_1(\xi^{**}, k_1) > -1$. Consequently, if

$$a > -\phi_1(\xi^{**}, k_1) \tag{A.58}$$

the partial derivative in (A.57) is positive and greater than that in (A.54).

Assuming this condition is met, $\phi_2 = 0$ is a monotonically increasing function and the corresponding curve, as shown in Figure 24, intersects the curve representing the function $\phi_1 = 0$ from beneath. Note also that points above $\phi_2 = 0$ correspond to situations where the capital-labour ratio increases, and vice versa.

The arrows in Figure 24 indicate the direction of movement of the variables starting from any point in the admissible set. The fact that the direction of movement seems to show a tendency towards the point $(\bar{\xi}, \bar{k})$ does not represent, however, a satisfactory proof of the convergence of the paths to the stationary-state equilibrium.

To demonstrate the global stability of the system observe that, given (A.58), we have

$$\frac{\partial \phi_1}{\partial \xi_t} + \frac{\partial \phi_2}{\partial k_t} < 0 \tag{A.59}$$

and

$$\frac{\partial \phi_1}{\partial \xi_t} \frac{\partial \phi_2}{\partial k_t} - \frac{\partial \phi_1}{\partial k_t} \frac{\partial \phi_2}{\partial \xi_t} = \frac{\partial \phi_1}{\partial \xi_t} \left[-a - \phi_1 - k_t \frac{\partial \phi_1}{\partial k_t} \right]$$

$$+ \frac{\partial \phi_1}{\partial k_t} k_t \frac{\partial \phi_1}{\partial \xi_t} = \frac{\partial \phi_1}{\partial \xi_t} [-a - \phi_1] \tag{A.60}$$

The condition for (A.60) to be always positive is obviously

$$a > -\phi_1 (\xi_t, k_t) \tag{A.61}$$

This condition is certainly met if, in view of what has already been said,

$$a > 1 \tag{A.61a}$$

which is more restrictive than (A.58).

Lastly, note that we always have:

$$\frac{\partial \phi_1}{\partial k_t} \frac{\partial \phi_2}{\partial \xi_t} \neq 0 \tag{A.62}$$

If (A.61a) — and, *a fortiori*, (A.61) — is satisfied, all the conditions of the Olech theorem are met for the convergence of the natural equilibrium paths to the stationary state.

The meaning of (A.61a) must then be examined more closely. Dividing numerator and denominator of a by $(1 - \sigma k_3 n_3)$ and remembering (A.40), (A.61a) may be rewritten as:

$$a = \frac{1 + \sigma k_1 \dfrac{n_3}{1 - \sigma k_3 n_3}}{\dfrac{n_3}{1 - \sigma k_3 n_3} (k_1 - k_3)} > 1 \tag{A.61b}$$

Observe first that a necessary condition for (A.61a) to hold is that $k_1 > k_3$ — the capital-intensity of the agricultural sector must, in other words, be higher than that of the machine-producing sector. This explains the reason for the assumption made in (A.26), which is the usual stability condition for growth models where the distinction is made between consumer goods and capital goods.[15]

In the context of the Ricardian model the meaning of the condition $k_1 > k_3$ may be clarified with reference to a situation in which, for example, the supply of machines is supposed to be greater than the demand – expressed by (A.32) – corresponding to a given wages fund and a given sectoral distribution of employment. Equilibrium between the demand for and the supply of machines through changes in the employment structure is obtained by increasing the percentage share of sector one (and two) with respect to sector three if $k_1 > k_3$; and vice versa if $k_1 < k_3$. In this latter case, however, the increased percentage share of the third sector, in the subsequent period, would tend to worsen the assumed initial disequilibrium.

Although necessary, $k_1 > k_3$ is not, however, a sufficient condition for (A.61a) to be verified and for the dynamic process described by the model to be stable. Suppose, for instance, that the initial situation is characterized – given (A.36) – by a supply of circulating capital relatively greater than that of fixed capital, so that full employment of both types of capital may be possible only with a relatively high percentage share of employment in the machine-producing sector. This presumably involves the tendency for an inversion of the initial situation with an increase in the stock of machines relatively greater than in the stock of circulating capital. Maintaining full employment of both types of capital in the new situation calls for a change in employment structure towards the agricultural sector. This may, in turn, require a further switch in the direction of adjustment, and so on. This process could clearly turn out to be divergent.

Condition (A.61a) is meant to exclude the possibility that the adjustment process of the employment structure implied by the maintenance of full employment of the available quantities of both types of capital is unstable.

The proof of stability of the natural equilibrium paths – provided they exist and may be unambiguously determined – does not allow a precise definition of their shape; more specifically, it cannot be excluded, in general, that the convergence to the stationary state may be realized along a curve different from what may be called the 'Ricardian path' with a constantly diminishing rate of growth of the economy. That is, even on the assumption that the initial situation is characterized by a stock of both machines and advances to labour less than that of the stationary state, a case might arise of an approach to that situation which passes through values of one or both types of capital higher than the corresponding stationary-state values. Since the time paths of the variables would not be monotonically increasing, they would then exhibit a feature not coinciding with the Ricardian idea of a gradual transition from the progressive to the stationary state.

Numerical tests carried out on the computer seem to exclude this possibility. In particular, they show that to initial conditions in the region ABC in Figure 24 are associated 'Ricardian natural equilibrium paths'.

The natural equilibrium with a uniform capital-labour ratio

Considering now the special case of a uniform capital-labour ratio, we suppose

$$k_1 = k_2 = k_3 = k \qquad (A.26a)$$

and obviously assume that the condition for the model to be 'viable' is respected:

$$1 - \sigma k n_3 > 0 \qquad (A.28a)$$

As can be easily verified in (A.6) and (A.16), absolute prices of commodities are now equal to their corresponding direct labour inputs. Also the form of the profit equation (A.21) is now considerably simplified.[16]

Consequences on the structure of the model

The hypothesis examined here raises special problems for the definition of the position of point natural equilibrium. These problems may be suitably illustrated by reference to the reduced form of the Ricardian three-sector model described above. It was emphasized there that, when the supplies of fixed and circulating capital – (A.36) being met – are given independently of each other, equations (a)-(d) define the position of point natural equilibrium and equations (e) and (f) determine the behaviour of the system over time, i.e. the natural equilibrium path.

With the assumption stated in (A.26a), the demand for machines is strictly proportional to that for advances to labour, and abstracts, as substitution of (A.26a) in (A.32) shows, from the structure of employment. It is therefore impossible in this case to assume independently given quantities of fixed and circulating capital, since this would, in general, be incompatible with the possibility of their joint full employment. Consequently, *only one* type of capital can be taken as independently given.

If *only* the initial quantity of circulating capital is thus assumed to be given, the demand of machines is thereby immediately defined. For the condition of full employment to be fulfilled, the supply of machines must then be supposed to be equal to demand, implying that the initial value of fixed capital is to be considered among the unknowns of the system.

Equations (a)-(d), however, now turn out to contain five variables, namely λ_{1t}, λ_{2t}, r_t, M_t and M_t^s. This means that the position of natural equilibrium cannot be defined on the basis of this subset of equations. The resulting indeterminacy of natural equilibrium may be interpreted as the impossibility of establishing, by means of the system (a)-(d), the employment structure.

Only if the dynamic conditions, and not a single equilibrium position, are considered can this problem be solved. When reference is made to a single equilibrium position, full employment of both types of capital abstracts, as already mentioned, from the employment structure. Yet the latter is crucial in determining the availability of machines and advances to labour in the subsequent period. Machines and corn must, however, continue – on account of (A.26a) – to remain in the given fixed proportion if the possibility of their joint full employment is to be preserved. Obviously, only a particular distribution of employment among sectors can allow such a result to be obtained.

Reference to our reduced-form three-sector model is again useful to show how a consistent solution to this problem can be found. Taking account of the previous argument, equation (c) must be replaced by

$$M_t = g_3(K_t) = \frac{k}{\bar{x}} K_t \qquad (\text{c}')$$

so that (d) becomes

$$M_t^s = \frac{k}{\bar{x}} K_t \qquad (\text{d}')$$

Taking the derivative of (d′) with respect to time,

$$\dot{M}_t^s = \frac{k}{\bar{x}} \dot{K}_t \qquad (\text{d}'')$$

is obtained. If the change in the supply of machines defined by (d″) is to be made consistent with that determined by equation (e), the latter equation, taking account also of (f), must be specified as

$$g_4(\lambda_{1t}, \lambda_{2t}, K_t) = \frac{k}{\bar{x}} \dot{K}_t = \frac{k}{\bar{x}} g_5(\lambda_{1t}, K_t) \qquad (\text{e}')$$

185

The reduced-form three-sector model for the case of a uniform capital–labour ratio turns out, therefore, to be constituted by equations (a), (b), (c'), (d'), (e') and (f). The first five represent a system of equations in five unknowns which, given K_t, defines the point natural equilibrium position of the economy. Equation (f), instead, describes the time path of circulating capital, from which that of all the other variables of the model can be derived.

The point natural equilibrium position

The explicit form of equations (a), (b), (c'), (d') and (e'), which define the position of point natural equilibrium, is as follows:

$$\lambda_{2t} = \frac{1-\alpha}{\alpha} \lambda_{1t} \tag{A.63}$$

$$r_t = \frac{1}{kn_3} \left[1 - \frac{\bar{x}}{f'(N_{1t})} (1+r_t) \right] - \sigma \tag{A.64}$$

$$M_t = \frac{k}{\bar{x}} K_t \tag{A.65}$$

$$M_t = M_t^s \tag{A.66}$$

$$X_{3t} - \sigma \frac{k}{\bar{x}} K_t = \frac{k}{\bar{x}} (X_{1t} - K_t) \tag{A.67}$$

Equation (A.63) coincides with (A.31); equation (A.64) with (A.21) given $k_i = k$; equation (A.65) repeats (c'); equation (A.66) defines the supply of machines in a way compatible with full employment of both types of capital; equation (A.67), lastly, is obtained substituting (A.24) and (A.25a) in (c') and taking account of equations (A.65) and (A.66).

Substituting for X_{1t} and X_{3t} in (A.67),

$$\lambda_{2t} = 1 + kn_3 (1-\sigma) - \left[\lambda_{1t} + kn_3 \frac{f(\lambda_{1t}, K_t)}{K_t} \right] \tag{A.68}$$

is obtained, where $f(\lambda_{1t}, K_t)$ is an increasing function of λ_{1t} for given K_t.

From (A.63) and (A.68) the natural equilibrium solutions for λ_{1t} and λ_{2t} can be found. Denoting the right-hand side of (A.63) and (A.68) as $h_1(\lambda_{1t})$ and $h_2(\lambda_{1t})$ respectively, the solution can be seen in Figure 25.

Bearing in mind that $h_1(\lambda_{1t})$ is an increasing function of λ_{1t}, while the opposite holds for $h_2(\lambda_{1t})$, the condition for the existence of a positive solution is $h_2(0) > 0$, i.e.

$$1 + kn_3 (1-\sigma) - kn_3 \frac{f(0, K_t)}{K_t} > 0 \tag{A.69}$$

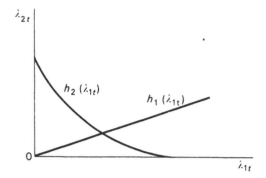

Figure 25

On the assumption already made that $f(0) = 0$, we also have $f(0, K_t) = 0$. Condition (A.69) is therefore always met. It can also be proved that $\lambda_{1t} + \lambda_{2t}$ is always less than one.[17]

On the existence of an economically significant solution for the profit rate given λ_{1t} and K_t, the arguments advanced above with reference to the general case obviously apply.

The stationary-state equilibrium
Letting $r_t = 0$ in (A.64) and solving for $f'(N_{1t})$,

$$f'(N_{1t}) = \frac{\bar{x}}{1 - \sigma k n_3} \tag{A.70}$$

is obtained, which clearly represents a particular case of (A.40) on the assumption that sectoral capital–labour ratios are equal. Here, too, the agricultural labour productivity in the stationary state assumes a value greater than the natural wage, since $(1 - \sigma k_3 n_3)$ is obviously less than one.

The stationary-state values of λ_{1t} and λ_{2t} are, respectively,[18]

$$\bar{\lambda}_1 = \alpha(1 - \sigma k n_3) \tag{A.71}$$
$$\bar{\lambda}_2 = (1 - \alpha)(1 - \sigma k n_3) \tag{A.72}$$

The stationary-state value of circulating capital — which together with $\bar{\lambda}_1$ and $\bar{\lambda}_2$ allows the stationary equilibrium solutions of all the other variables of the model to be deduced — is determined, lastly, by putting the right-hand side of (A.25a) equal to zero. Assuming $f(N_{1t}) = N_{1t}^\alpha$, this value coincides with that defined by (A.44).

The natural equilibrium path
The time path of the system is defined by equation (f) of the reduced-

form model, the explicit form of which is

$$\dot{K}_t = X_{1t} - K_t \tag{A.25a}$$

To examine the solution of this differential equation, especially from the point of view of convergence to the stationary state, X_{1t} must be expressed as a function of the variable K_t.

Since, by equations (A.2), (A.17) and (A.18), we have $N_{1t} = \lambda_{1t}$ $(K_t/\bar{x})$, N_{1t} is an increasing function of both λ_{1t} and K_t. As it can be proved that λ_{1t} is an increasing function of K_t,[19] we can express N_{1t} as a direct function of the sole variable K_t and then write:

$$X_{1t} = X_1(K_t) \tag{A.73}$$

with diminishing returns implying $X_1'(K_t) > 0$ and $X_1''(K_t) < 0$. These properties ensure that the solution of the differential equation (A.25a) gradually converges towards the stationary state. The characteristics of the natural equilibrium path of K_t are illustrated in Figure 26.

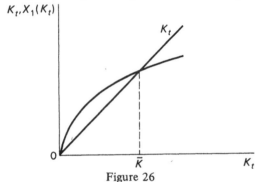

Figure 26

The equilibrium dynamics of the three-sector uniform capital-labour ratio model exhibit analogies both with that of the two-sector (no fixed capital) model and with that of the three-sector different capital–labour ratios model. Equations (A.65) and (A.66) show that the rate of growth of fixed capital is equal to that of circulating capital, which, on account of (A.20a), (A.25) and (A.65), is equal to the general profit rate. From this point of view, the three-sector model with a uniform capital–labour ratio is similar to the two-sector model. When, instead, the fact is considered that the employment structure varies during the process of growth – as the percentage share of agriculture and industry gradually increase at the expense of the share of the machine-producing sector – the case of a uniform capital–labour ratio appears to be close to that of different sectoral proportions of machines to labour.

7 A generalization of the Ricardian two-sector model: problems of traverse

7.1 Preliminary remarks

The aim of the last two chapters was to define the natural equilibrium dynamics of the Ricardian one-sector and two-sector models and to study the disequilibrium paths originating in the failure of one of the initial ('stock') conditions to meet the requirements for the system to start off and move along the natural equilibrium path. Attention will now be addressed to a different type of departure from the equilibrium path – that originating in the change in one of the parameters defining the natural equilibrium growth rate ('flow' conditions) (Hicks (35), ch. 8). As mentioned in Chapter 1, this type of problem – that Hicks ((35), ch. 16) has called 'traverse' – may be studied under the heading of 'disequilibrium dynamics'.

A precondition for the existence of a transition problem is represented by the definition of two (natural) equilibrium paths, each of them characterized by a different set of conditions. The economic system is supposed to develop along one of these paths up to a certain instant of time; at that time, the set of conditions characterizing the other path is 'imposed' (Hicks (35), p. 184). The question can then be raised (Hicks (35)): 'is it possible (or how is it possible) to get into the new equilibrium, which is appropriate to the new conditions?'

The problems of traverse analysed in the present chapter with reference to the two-sector Ricardian model fit into this logical framework. Two different natural equilibrium paths are defined on the basis of different growth rates (flow conditions) and of the same initial (stock) conditions.

It has been seen in Chapter 1 that the definition of the natural equilibrium growth path of the Ricardian model requires that the growth rate of the labour force be treated as an 'endogenous' variable –

the equilibrium condition being represented by the equality between that rate and the accumulation rate. The genesis of traverse problems cannot therefore be attributed to exogenous demographic variations, and the definition of two distinct dynamic equilibrium paths can be effected therefore solely in terms of two distinct values of the accumulation rate.

Different values for the accumulation rate in the Ricardian model may in their turn depend either on a difference in the prevailing technological conditions, or in the parameters characterizing the behaviour of economic agents. It will be seen that plausible transition problems can be posed within the Ricardian framework only on the basis of assumed changes in the behaviour parameters — more specifically in the saving propensity of capitalists. The abandonment of the rigid assumption of total reinvestment of profits, and the consequent introduction of a positive level of consumption by capitalists, obviously represents a generalization of the two-sector model examined in the previous chapter.

The following discussion is in three parts. We first examine various possible ways of generalizing the model to ascertain which are compatible with Ricardo's theoretical framework; second, we analyse the equilibrium dynamics of the 'generalized' model (a problem of 'comparative dynamics' with respect to the 'pure' Ricardian model, where all profits are reinvested); lastly, the traverse problem is dealt with in analytical terms and the resulting transition paths are examined.

7.2 Possible generalizations of the Ricardian model

The Ricardian model examined in the preceding chapters is characterized by a set of assumptions which have so far been accepted in their most rigid version, as indeed is the case in most expositions of Ricardo's theory. In line with the aim of the present chapter, we shall now — without modifying our approach from a 'constructive' to a 'critical' one[1] — consider whether the 'weak', or generalized, version of some of these assumptions is compatible with the structure of Ricardo's thinking.

The first possible type of generalization is that considered by Ricardo himself in his chapter 'On machinery' ((67), ch. 31). It deals with the replacement of circulating by fixed capital and consequent variations in the capital–labour ratio.

An adequate treatment of these problems would require: (i) the explicit consideration of a machine-producing sector; (ii) the formulation of precise assumptions as to the production conditions of machines incorporating the most capital-intensive techniques; and (iii) the definition of a set of rules governing the process of (gradual) substitution of technologically obsolete machines with 'new' machines. None of these requirements is met in the Ricardian model examined in Chapters 5 and 6. Although some steps towards generalization are taken in the appendix to Chapter 6 with the introduction of a machine-producing sector, our interpretative scheme falls short of permitting a systematic treatment of these problems, highly interesting from a dynamic point of view. It should be added that equally inadequate for this study appear different types of approaches, such as that based on the assumption that new machines are exogenously given (Hicks (36), appendix, pp. 168-171) or that – representing a considerable advance on the first – incorporating the assumption that machines are the intermediate product of a vertically integrated process leading, through the use of labour, to the sole production of a consumption good (Hicks (37) and (38)).

A second type of generalization might be conceived in terms of a change in population dynamics. But, as already mentioned, this possibility must be ruled out.

Plausible generalizations of the Ricardian model must then be searched for along different lines – the systematic consideration of 'disembodied' technical progress, or the choice of different (perhaps more realistic) behavioural assumptions for economic agents.

Let us first focus our attention on technical progress, either in the form of a single wave of technological innovations (implying a single upward shift of production functions), or of a constant flow of technical improvements, leading, in each period, to an increase in the productivity of labour. Ricardo seems to have considered only the first of these assumptions, since he believed that technical progress could only postpone in time, but not avoid, the final outcome of the system – the stationary state.[2] In fact a *una tantum* upward shift of the production function, unaccompanied by a change in returns to scale, would not modify the type of growth path of the system, and would therefore be of little interest. Against this, the second assumption, which rules out the gradual reduction of the profit rate, and hence implies the indefinite continuation of growth conditions in the system, entails a substantial alteration in Ricardo's basic assumptions. A fruitful extension of the Ricardian analysis cannot therefore be looked for along these lines.

Greater interest attaches, instead, to generalizations stemming from the relaxation of the rigid assumptions regarding the behaviour of economic agents.

7.3 Positive saving by workers and rentiers

The Ricardian assumptions on the behaviour of the various social classes form the reference point of what is usually called the 'extreme classical saving function' (Hahn and Matthews (31), p. 16), where capitalists' propensity to save is unity and workers and rentiers propensity to save is nil.[3] Let us begin by examining the possibility of generalizing the Ricardian model with reference to the behaviour hypotheses of these latter two social classes. The introduction of a positive level of saving by workers and rentiers can be considered in two contexts. (i) It can be assumed that rentiers and workers abstain from the consumption of all their income, lend the resulting saving to the capitalists and receive in return a rate of interest which coincides with the profit rate. The functional roles assigned to the various social classes by Ricardo are thus retained. (ii) The alternative assumption — modifying these roles and hence making a substantive distinction between functional and personal distribution of income — is that rent and wage earners carry out entrepreneurial activities for that part of their incomes which is saved and invested. The first assumption is examined for workers and the second for rentiers; conclusions in each case can be extended easily to the other.

Loans to capitalists

It must be said at the outset that the hypothesis that workers, with a positive and constant propensity to save, make loans to the capitalists creates logical difficulties in the Ricardian model which seem insuperable.

The first problem concerns the motives for saving during an accumulation process tending towards the stationary state.[4] Workers can be induced to abstain from immediately consuming all of their income only if they have some prospect of a larger future consumption from the interest paid to them on their accumulated saving. Since, as we have pointed out, the interest rate on capital loaned coincides of necessity with the general profit rate, the progressive reduction of the latter must imply that the yield of capital saved also tends to decline to zero. Also supposing that workers accept a gradually diminishing remuneration – which would obviously afford decreasing justification for their saving – a second problem arises in the stationary state; for, even abstracting from the obvious absurdity of a positive level of savings with nil yields, the very definition of the stationary state would be contradicted by the existence of a net investment equal to the amount of saving effected by workers in each period. The assumption of a positive and constant propensity to save by the working class is thus clearly unacceptable within the Ricardian model.

When we consider the alternative (typically neoclassical) assumption of a saving propensity varying with the rate of return and assume that saving ceases when the interest rate reaches a previously determined minimum (which can also be zero), the stationary-state contradictions disappear. The rational justification of the act of saving on the part of the workers – despite first appearances – would, however, still represent an unsolved problem. Indeed, assuming that lenders are conscious of the long-term prospects of the system, there remains the progressive contraction of the income flow generated by the previously accumulated assets, which are essentially non negotiable. (Capitalists cannot be assumed to redeem securities they have issued because this would imply – contrary to the reasons for which they have borrowed resources – handing back to the workers the circulating capital previously lent. This is a problem which would remain even when short-sightedness by lenders to long-term prospects of the system is supposed to overcome the question of the rationality of the act of saving.)

Similar problems would arise with the assumption of positive saving by rentiers, when these are supposed not to turn into capitalists, as regards the use of the proportion of income saved.

For completeness, note that if this type of assumption were none the less introduced in the model it would be necessary to consider (besides the impact on the acceleration of the growth rate) the effects on the structure of the system. These effects – particularly evident in the case of rentiers as they would imply a switch of demand from one sector to another – would be of the same type as those examined in section 7.6 below.

In conclusion, to assume that rentiers and workers loan their savings to capitalists, though leaving substantially unaltered the functional distinction made by Ricardo between classes, encounters insuperable logical difficulties for the Ricardian growth theory and does not supply, therefore, an acceptable basis for generalization.

Direct entrepreneurial activity by rentiers and workers

Entrepreneurial activity by rentiers can be envisaged either, with Malthus ((52) ch. 3), as investment in the agricultural sector only, to improve the land,[5] or more generally as the assumption, on their part, of typically entrepreneurial risks in both sectors of the economy.

In both cases it is no longer possible to distinguish between profits as income received by capitalists and that part of rent directly invested by rentiers, who, for their part, are transformed into capitalists.[6]

The consequent necessity to redefine categories of income can be brought out most effectively when considering problems of the stationary state.

Suppose that a constant fraction of rent, equal to s_r, is saved and directly invested by rentiers. For ease of graphical presentation we refer to the case where a single commodity (corn) is produced in the economy. With reference to equations (2), (4) and (5) of Chapter 5, we may define the amount of investment made in each period as

$$\dot{K}_t = P_t + s_r R_t = s_r f(N_t) + [(1 - s_r) N_t f'(N_t)] - \bar{x} N_t \tag{1}$$

The stationary state, attained when accumulation ceases to occur, is therefore defined by

$$s_r \frac{f(N_t)}{N_t} + (1 - s_r) f'(N_t) = \bar{x} \tag{2}$$

If s_r is equal to zero, obviously we come back to the usual definition of the stationary state where the productivity of labour in the less favourable conditions is equal to the natural wage. In Figure 27 this is reached at point $\bar{N}$, at which profits, in the strict sense of capitalists' income, are nil.

On the contrary, if we suppose that s_r is positive, equation (2) shows that the stationary state is reached at a point intermediate between $\bar{N}$ and N^*, the nearer to N^* the closer to unity the value of rentiers' propensity to save. However, given the original income categories, all stationary-state positions to the right of $\bar{N}$ are contradictory from the economic viewpoint, since they imply a negative income for capitalists (in the strict sense of the word).

This contradiction would disappear only in so far as a new definition of profits (including, in a single and indivisible category, both income of capitalists in the strict sense of the word and that part of rent directly invested by the landowners) is adopted. The *functional* assimilation of these two types of incomes would in this case do away

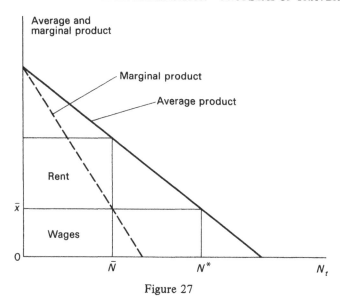

Figure 27

with any justification for a distinction between those who invest. From every point of view rentiers-investors should be regarded as 'capitalists'.

Note that the above conclusions, related for convenience to the one-sector model, are also valid for the two-sector model. The only difference – a purely formal one – consists of the different expression of equation (1), which, in this latter case, should be derived from equations (2), (11) and (13) of Chapter 6.

The assumption that workers directly invest a share of income saved implies economic and analytical considerations entirely similar to those made for rentiers. Equations (1) and (2) become in this case respectively:

$$\dot{K}_t = P_t + s_w W_t = N_t \left[f'(N_t) - \bar{x} \right] + s w \bar{x} N_t \qquad (1a)$$

$$f'(N_t) = (1 - s_w)\bar{x} \qquad (2a)$$

where s_w indicates the workers' propensity to save. Equation (2a) shows clearly that, where s_w is positive, the stationary-state position is found to the right of $\bar{N}$ in Figure 27. In this case, too, the income of capitalists in the strict sense of the word (profits) would therefore be negative. We may then conclude that the attempt to generalize the Ricardian model through the assumption of direct investments by rentiers and workers is not fruitful when an adequate redefinition of

195

income categories is excluded. This redefinition, which from Marx on has led to the functional assimilation of profits and rent, might suggest a different way of considering the assumption of direct investment by rentiers. This approach would involve the total merging of profits and rent into a single income category, part of which is devoted to consumption. But, following this reasoning, it is more appropriate — because more consistent with Ricardo's theoretical framework, where the distinction between profits and rent has a specific relevance — to consider the simpler assumption of non-zero consumption by capitalists. This approach, as we shall see, leads to no contradiction in the Ricardian model and at the same time makes the behaviour assumptions more realistic.

7.4 Positive consumption by capitalists: the role of capitalists in the stationary state

We may then examine the hypothesis that capitalists, with a partial departure from their role of pure *fonctionnaires du capital*, do not allocate all their income to investment but consume a constant portion of it.[7]

This assumption does not create the difficulties mentioned in the previous sections. Contrary to what happens with the assumption of positive savings by workers and rentiers, the definition of the stationary state is not in any way affected, since the reduction of profits to zero automatically involves the simultaneous disappearance of capitalists' consumption.

Incidentally, note that this assumption confers on the capitalist class a more realistic physiognomy reducing the abstractness of their role as depicted in the 'extreme classical savings function' and allowing more general questions on the concept of the stationary state in the Ricardian framework to be raised. In this regard it may be useful to recall explicitly that in the stationary conditions the capitalists are supposed to indefinitely anticipate (at the beginning of each productive cycle) a wages fund which is constant over time, without deriving from it any profit. This assumption can be accepted only to the extent that the capitalist class is assigned a *completely* abstract function which, on this same plane of abstraction, preserves their existence as a social group. However, the assumption becomes logically untenable if capitalists are considered as a concrete category of economic agents which, in the stationary state, receive no income.

In other words, if capitalists are considered as agents impelled by concrete economic motives, it becomes impossible to impute to them a wholly unprofitable stable investment activity. It follows from this, *either* that it is impossible to maintain the definition of stationary state, *or* in so far as the anticipation of the (constant) wages fund is attributed to others (clearly implying a switch to a new institutional organization) that the capitalists would disappear as a social class.

This disappearance could be explained – to borrow Schumpeter's idea of the link between entrepreneurial function and economic growth – by the cessation, implicit in the indefinite perpetuation of the same productive process, of the risk-bearing activity aiming to earn a profit, typical of the Ricardian capitalist-entrepreneur.[8] The disappearance of capitalists' consumption in the stationary state could thus be regarded, in accordance with this interpretation, as a manifestation of the disappearance of capitalists as a social class. In parallel, as we have observed, the anticipation of the (constant) wages fund ought, in that case, to be assigned to 'functionaries' with a role confined to organizing and supervising the productive process. Such 'functionaries' should be included in the category of workers who receive a wage and administer a capital the ownership of which, in this context, seems difficult to attribute.

Alternatively it might be thought that, for reasons advanced by Ricardo ((68), pp. 120-2) and often adopted by authoritative commentators (e.g. Robbins (70), pp. 198-9), the problem of a more realistic presentation of the capitalist class could be solved by assuming that the process of accumulation comes to a halt, not when profits are nil, but before then, when the positive profit rate earned is regarded by entrepreneurs as the *minimum* level beneath which every incentive to invest disappears.

However, to assume the existence of this minimum profit rate, which Robbins (70) calls the 'natural rate of profit', raises insoluble problems and, in the end, contradicts the very definition of the stationary state.[9] For, if we keep unchanged the rigid assumption of capitalists' behaviour whereby profits are completely reinvested until the profit rate is above the pre-defined minimum, a new problem crops up when the profit rate touches its 'natural' level – that of the destination of the capitalists' income flow (constant over time), which for the assumption made is diverted from its previous aim, the broadening of the productive process.

To overcome this difficulty, we should suppose that, where the stationary state corresponds to the 'natural profit rate', capitalists devote their income *entirely* to consumption. In this way, however, we would introduce a behavioural assumption radically different from that characterizing capitalists' *modus agendi* during the progressive phase of the process and, hence, without any logical basis in this context.

On the other hand, discarding the assumption that capitalists in the stationary state consume all their income gives rise to still more serious contradictions and problems. We would have to assume mere profit 'hoarding' in the unconvincing sense that profits are destined neither for consumption nor investment, and thus completely disappear from the national income flow. Even if we are willing to ignore the impact of this type of behaviour in terms of Say's law, this assumption would contradict with the existence of a 'natural profit rate'; for this kind of 'hoarding' of the net income flow generated in each period by capital invested (the wages fund) should of necessity be assimilated to the failure to receive that income, so that the *real* profit rate should be seen as nil.

7.5 The Ricardian model with positive consumption by capitalists

We shall now examine the two-sector Ricardian model on the assumption that capitalists consume a constant proportion of their income (profits). We shall suppose, in addition, that capitalist consumption is devoted exclusively to luxury goods. Their behaviour from this point of view is thus similar to that of the rentiers.

The model incorporating the assumption of a positive saving propensity by capitalists s_π (less than one) is given below in full:

$$X_{1t} = f(N_{1t})$$

Agricultural production function with diminishing returns   (3)

$$R_t = f(N_{1t}) - N_{1t}f'(N_{1t})$$

Rent in terms of corn   (4)

$$P_{1t} = N_{1t}[f'(N_{1t}) - \bar{x}]$$

Agricultural profits in terms of corn   (5)

$$p_{1t} = \frac{1}{f'(N_{1t})}$$

Price of corn   (6)

$$X_{2t} = \beta N_{2t}$$

Industrial production function   (7)

$$p_{2t}P_{2t} = p_{2t}X_{2t} - p_{1t}N_{2t}\bar{x} \qquad \text{Industrial profits in value terms} \tag{8}$$

$$p_{2t} = \frac{1}{\beta} \qquad \text{Price of gold} \tag{9}$$

$$N_{1t} = (1 - \lambda_t)N_t \qquad \text{Employment in agriculture} \tag{10}$$

$$N_{2t} = \lambda_t N_t \qquad \text{Employment in industry} \tag{11}$$

$$W_t = K_t \qquad \text{Wages fund} \tag{12}$$

$$N_t = \frac{W_t}{\bar{x}} \qquad \text{Demand for labour} \tag{13}$$

$$P_t = p_{1t}N_t[f'(N_{1t}) - \bar{x}] \qquad \text{Total profits in value terms} \tag{14}$$

$$p_{2t}X_{2t} = p_{1t}R_t + (1 - s_\pi)P_t \qquad \text{Demand for gold} \tag{15}$$

$$p_{1t}\dot{K}_t = s_\pi P_t \qquad \text{Total investment} \tag{16}$$

Obviously, a different formulation of the demand for luxury goods and for investment characterizes the present 'generalized' model with respect to that analysed in the first sections of Chapter 6, henceforth to be denoted as the 'pure' Ricardian model. This difference implies important consequences for the equilibrium dynamics of the model.

7.6 Natural equilibrium dynamics: structural and distributive aspects

We begin by examining the natural equilibrium dynamics of this Ricardian model by studying the evolution of the employment structure and of the distribution of output. Both present interesting differences from the model analysed in Chapter 6.

In fact, when $s_\pi = 1$, the structure of the system (in terms of employment, value of output and income distribution between rent and profits plus wages) depends solely, as we have seen, on the technology of the agricultural sector, i.e. on the specific characteristics of the production function of corn. In particular, when the elasticity of this function with respect to the labour input is constant,[10] the structure of the system remains unchanged during the process of growth. When, on the contrary, the assumption of positive capitalists' consumption is introduced, this is no longer true and the conclusions reached above appear as a particular case of the general result obtaining in the present context.

To prove this statement, the evolution over time of λ_t, the variable expressing the structural aspects of the system, must be defined.

Recalling that on the one hand corn production is absorbed by labour incomes and by that part of profits devoted to accumulation, and on the other that the value of industrial production always coincides with the number of persons employed in that sector,[11] we may write:

$$Y_{1t} = p_{1t}X_{1t} = p_{1t}W_t + s_\pi P_t = [1-(1-s_\pi)(1-p_{1t}\bar{x})]N_t \quad (17)$$

$$Y_{2t} = p_{2t}X_{2t} = N_{2t} = \lambda_t N_t \quad (18)$$

$$Y_t = Y_{1t} + Y_{2t} = [1 + \lambda_t - (1-s_\pi)(1-p_{1t}\bar{x})]N_t \quad (19)$$

If we substitute equation (15) – showing that the value of industrial production is absorbed by rent and by the proportion of profits consumed $(1-s_\pi)$ – in equation (18), we obtain:

$$\lambda_t N_t = p_{1t}R_t + (1-s_\pi)P_t \quad (20)$$

Since, as was shown in Chapter 6, section 6.5, $p_{1t}R_t = (1-\alpha_t)Y_{1t}$, using (17) and (14), equation (20) becomes:

$$\lambda_t = 1 - \alpha_t[1-(1-s_\pi)(1-p_{1t}\bar{x})] \quad (21)$$

where, as in Chapter 6, α_t indicates the elasticity of the agricultural production function.

The employment structure thus depends here on the technology of the agricultural sector and on the assumptions made about capitalists' behaviour. This circumstance is emphasized by the presence of s_π in equation (21), which coincides with the expression obtained in Chapter 6 when nil capitalists' consumption is assumed. The dependence of λ_t on behavioural assumptions is, however, complex since the parameter expressing the propensity to consume of capitalists multiplies a term, variable over time, representing profit per worker in value terms. This term is, in turn, obviously influenced, through the accumulation rate, by the very assumption about capitalists' behaviour.

The variability of the expression $(1-p_{1t}\bar{x})$, i.e. of the value of profit per person employed, influences the development of the employment structure of the system; for, even if we assume that the elasticity of the agricultural production function is constant $(\alpha_t = \alpha)$ – an assumption which is the basis of the following analysis and which underlies the examination of disequilibrium dynamics in the preceding two chapters – equation (21) emphasizes that λ_t tends to decrease gradually during the accumulation process because of the progressive rise in the price of corn.[12] Equation (20) also shows that, when α is constant, λ_t in the generalized model is greater than the corresponding value in the pure model for all t. This means that the percentage share of industrial employment turns out to be always higher in the present model with respect to the corresponding values in the model examined in Chapter 6.

The stationary-state value of λ_t, reached when profits per worker employed are zero, is equal to

$$\bar{\lambda} = 1 - \alpha \tag{22}$$

The employment structure in the stationary state is not therefore influenced by the behaviour of entrepreneurs and coincides with the corresponding employment structure of the pure model. Intuitive reasoning clearly suggests that it could not be otherwise in a situation where profits are nil and consumption fed by these profits is also nil. In other words, since the divergence between the equilibrium structure of the pure Ricardian model and the structure of this generalized model can be attributed to a switch in capitalists' demand from the agricultural sector – investment – to luxury goods – consumption – obviously this divergence disappears, in the stationary state, with the elimination of profits.

Also, on the assumption that α_t varies over time – though remaining within a range of values compatible with the assumption of diminishing returns – the evolution of λ_t cannot be determined in general, except for the value assumed in the stationary state. This difficulty flows from the fact that p_{1t} is influenced by variations in α_t (even though, presumably, not to any substantial extent) and can therefore show movements of a compensatory nature. The elimination of profits in the stationary state allows us to say, however, that in the end the structure comes to depend solely on technology, as happens when α_t is constant.

The production structure in value terms can now be worked out easily:

$$\frac{Y_{1t}}{Y_t} = \frac{[1 - (1 - s_\pi)(1 - p_{1t}\bar{x})]}{[1 + \lambda_t - (1 - s_\pi)(1 - p_{1t}\bar{x})]}$$

$$= \frac{[1 - (1 - s_\pi)(1 - p_{1t}\bar{x})]}{1 + (1 - \alpha)[1 - (1 - s_\pi)(1 - p_{1t}\bar{x})]} \tag{23}$$

$$\frac{Y_{2t}}{Y_t} = \frac{\lambda_t}{[1 + \lambda_t - (1 - s_\pi)(1 - p_{1t}\bar{x})]}$$

$$= \frac{1 - \alpha[1 - (1 - s_\pi)(1 - p_{1t}\bar{x})]}{1 + (1 - \alpha)[1 - (1 - s_\pi)(1 - p_{1t}\bar{x})]} \tag{24}$$

When these expressions are derived with respect to time, it becomes clear that the percentage share of the value of agricultural production tends to rise. The production structure in value terms, therefore, also varies during the process of growth to the detriment of the industrial sector, as happens for the employment structure λ_t. Equations (23) and (24), in addition, show that, as for λ_t, the stationary-state production structure coincides with the corresponding structure of the pure Ricardian model.[13]

The distributive shares of rent and of profits plus wages, contrary to what happens in the model where $s_\pi = 1$, vary over time — the rent share grows while the other decreases; for, recalling that the proportion of rent in agricultural production is equal to $(1 - \alpha_t)$, and taking into account the fact that now α_t is constant, we can write:

$$\frac{p_{1t}R_t}{Y_t} = (1 - \alpha)\frac{Y_{1t}}{Y_t} \tag{25}$$

The increasing percentage share of agricultural production in total production entails, therefore, a parallel increase of the rent share. The share of wages plus profits is therefore diminishing.

Within the share of wages plus profits, different behaviour over time — a common feature of all the Ricardian models examined — characterizes the two components: wages (whose share increases) and profits (whose share falls). This is clearly shown by the following expressions:

$$\frac{p_{1t}W_t}{Y_t} = \frac{p_{1t}\bar{x}}{[1 + \lambda_t - (1 - s_\pi)(1 - p_{1t}\bar{x})]} \tag{26}$$

$$\frac{P_t}{Y_t} = \frac{1 - p_{1t}\bar{x}}{[1 + \lambda_t - (1 - s_\pi)(1 - p_{1t}\bar{x})]} \tag{27}$$

It may be noted with reference to expressions (25)-(27) that from the viewpoint of distributive shares, too, this model coincides, in the stationary state, with that where the capitalists do not consume any portion of their income.

A difference may be observed between the generalized model and the pure Ricardian one if we compare the behaviour of the percentage share of industrial production with that of rent. While in the latter model these two shares exactly coincide as a direct result of the behaviour assumptions made, in the generalized model the rent share tends to rise and simultaneously the industrial sector's percentage share in total output tends to fall. This is obviously to be attributed to the assumed behaviour of the capitalists whose income now participates, though only in part, in the absorption of the production of luxury goods. The evolution over time of the economic system (in a model where capitalists' consumption is positive) is thus characterized by the increase in the rent share being more than compensated for by the fall in the profit share, independently of the specific value assigned to capitalists' propensity to consume.[14]

To conclude, the introduction of an apparently minor modification in the rigid behaviour assumption of capitalists with respect to the pure Ricardian model produces significant changes in the evolution of the system over time and in the dynamics of distribution of output between social classes.

7.7 Natural equilibrium dynamics: the growth rates

Considerable differences turn out to occur, with respect to the pure Ricardian model, when the growth rates of the main variables are considered. The study of these problems – again carried out in terms of comparative dynamics – completes the analysis of the natural equilibrium dynamics of the generalized model.

Let us focus on capital accumulation. Equation (16) immediately allows the definition of the rate of accumulation to be obtained:

$$G_k = \frac{\dot{K_t}}{K_t} = s_\pi \left[\frac{f'(N_{1t})}{\bar{x}} - 1 \right] \tag{28}$$

This clearly represents a generalization of the definition of the rate of accumulation obtained in the 'pure' Ricardian model. Here, too, the properties underscored in Chapters 5 and 6 are valid: specifically the decline, over time, in the growth rate of capital and its reduction to zero when the marginal productivity of labour in agriculture coincides with the natural wage.

When the accumulation rate defined by equation (28) is compared with that defined by equation (20) in Chapter 6, two results should be emphasized.

(i) For given $f'(N_{1t})$, the accumulation rate in the model with $s_\pi < 1$ is inferior to the corresponding rate in the pure model, the divergence between the two rates being greater, the higher the capitalists' propensity to consume. This fact, however, should not be taken to mean that the growth rate of capital in the generalized model is always (i.e. for all t) lower than the corresponding rate in the pure model. Indeed, the opposite is true; as Figure 28 shows, the former

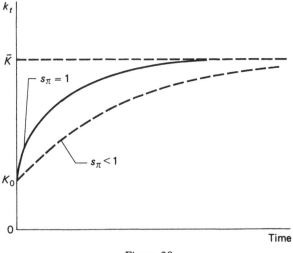

Figure 28

is initially lower (when the effect of diversion of funds from investment to consumption prevails) and later becomes higher than the latter (when the effect of a higher level of the productivity of labour in agriculture associated with the comparatively lower level of employment in this sector becomes predominant).

(ii) The fact that s_π is less than unity does not affect the stationary-state value of capital, which in this model therefore coincides – given equal technology and the natural wage – with the corresponding value in the pure Ricardian model, for in both models the stationary-state value of capital is reached when the marginal product of agricultural labour coincides with the natural wage,[15] and the sectoral structure of employment in the stationary state is the same.[16]

The natural growth path of capital in the model with $s_\pi < 1$ (given the same initial conditions) therefore lies below the corresponding growth path of the pure Ricardian model and takes longer to approximate the stationary-state level. This is shown in Figure 28 (the 'regularity' of the two paths stems directly from the assumptions made concerning the production function of the agricultural sector).

It is clear that the accumulation rate defined by equation (28) no longer coincides with the rate of profit, as was the case in the pure Ricardian model (and in all other models incorporating the 'extreme classical saving function'). The profit rate constitutes only one of the components of the rate of accumulation, the other being the saving propensity of capitalists. Since the latter is *ex hypothesis* less than unity, in the present context the profit rate, during the growth process, is always higher than the rate of accumulation (with the exception of the stationary state, where both these rates are equal to zero).

That the definition of profit rate is the same in both models does not mean, however, that the corresponding time paths coincide; for, as we have seen, the percentage share of agricultural employment in the model with $s_\pi < 1$ is always lower than that – constant given the technological assumptions adopted – for the model without capitalists' consumption. Furthermore, given the natural wage, the growth path of total employment in both models reflects that (already indicated) of total capital. At each point in time, therefore, agricultural employment is less in the generalized model than in the other, while the opposite is true (with diminishing returns) for the marginal product. It follows that during the growth process the path of the rate of profit in the generalized model is always higher than that in the pure Ricardian model. The assumption of diminishing returns gives rise, in other words, to the apparently paradoxical result that during the growth process the rate of return on capital is higher, the greater the capitalists' propensity to consume.[17]

This result has a general importance. It has been stated, for example by Joan Robinson ((74), pp. 42 and 44),[18] that the behavioural assumptions for economic agents, and especially for capitalists, have no influence in determining the value of the profit rate, which, according to this argument, is exclusively defined by technological assumptions and wage dynamics. The points now stressed show that this thesis is not valid in general. It is true instead only for the special situation of constant returns at a given wage rate and for the situation (an obvious extension to the case of technical progress) in which productivity and wages are increasing at the same rate. Note that this conclusion is valid both for the two-sector models – in which capitalists' behaviour influences the employment structure – and for the one-sector models in which behavioural assumptions affect only the dynamics of accumulation. (In fact, in this case too, the diversion of a share of resources from investment to consumption obviously leads to a fall in accumulation; at each point in time the number of persons employed is therefore lower, and, hence – because of the technological assumptions – marginal productivity is higher.)

We now consider the comparative dynamics of the rate of increase of income, both in value and in real terms.[19]

The rate of increase of income in value terms is defined as the logarithmic derivative of equation (19), which expresses total output in value terms. Remembering the definition of λ_t given by equation (21) (where the elasticity of the agricultural production function with respect to labour is constant), and considering that the rate of increase in total employment coincides with that of accumulation, we have:

$$G_y = \frac{\dot{Y}_t}{Y_t} = \frac{(1-\alpha)(1-s_\pi)\bar{x}\dot{p}_{1t}}{[1+\lambda_t-(1-s_\pi)(1-p_{1t}\bar{x})]} + G_k \qquad (29)$$

This expression clearly constitutes a generalization of equation (28) of Chapter 6; the main point here is that the growth rate of total output in value terms is, during the growth process, always higher than the growth rate of capital. The first term of the right-hand side of equation (29) is in fact always positive because of the progressive increase in the price of corn. Also for this aspect the present model differs therefore from the model analysed in Chapter 6, where, with a constant value of α, the two growth rates coincide.

It can be shown that the natural equilibrium path of total income, in terms of value in the model with $s_\pi < 1$, is always below the corresponding path originated by the model where total reinvestment of profits is assumed, and that the stationary-state value is the same for both models (though the time periods necessary to reach the final stage are different in the two cases). As was the case for the rates of accumulation, G_y in the model where $s_\pi < 1$ is, however, not lower for all t than the corresponding rate in the pure Ricardian model — the values of the two rates intersect once in the process of growth, as shown in Figure 29.

The growth rate of income in real terms, calculated as a weighted average of the rates of change of the physical amounts produced in both sectors,[20] with weights equal to the respective percentage shares in total output in terms of value,[21] can be defined as:

$$G_x = G_{x1} \frac{1-(1-s_\pi)(1-p_{1t}\bar{x})}{1+\lambda_t-(1-s_\pi)(1-p_{1t}\bar{x})}$$

$$+ G_{x2} \frac{\lambda_t}{1+\lambda_t-(1-s_\pi)(1-p_{1t}\bar{x})}$$

$$= \frac{1}{1+\lambda_t-(1-s_\pi)(1-p_{1t}\bar{x})} G_k \qquad (30)$$

Recalling equations (26) and (27), it may be said that the growth rate of income in real terms is equal to the growth rate of capital multiplied by the distributive share of profits plus wages. The result

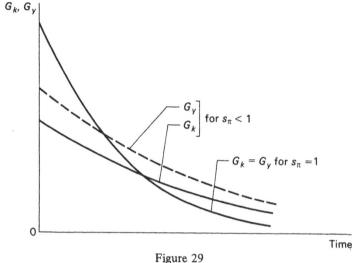

Figure 29

reached with equation (8) of Chapter 5 for the one-sector model and with equation (37) of Chapter 6 for the pure two-sector model is thus confirmed. The ratio between the growth rate of income in real terms and the growth rate of capital, represented by the share of profits plus wages in total income, is not, in other words, affected by a change in the assumption on capitalists' behaviour. This change affects solely the size of the growth rates and that of distributive shares.

Also from this point of view it may then be said that the results of the Ricardian model (characterized by the existence of rent due to the assumption of diminishing returns) represent a generalization of those obtaining in modern growth theory where – with the assumption of constant returns to scale – only profits and wages participate in the division of the social product.

7.8 Disequilibrium dynamics: traverse paths originating in changes in s_π

The consequences of a change in capitalists' behaviour during the growth process are analysed in the rest of this chapter. Assuming that the system moves along the natural equilibrium growth path defined by the assumption of total reinvestment of profits, we suppose that, from a given moment of time, the capitalists devote part of their

207

income to consumption. Since this implies a change in the conditions characterizing the original equilibrium path ('flow conditions'), a traverse problem arises. This consists of the analysis of the existence and of the characteristics of a transition path from the original to the new equilibrium growth path associated with the new set of flow conditions.

It has been pointed out (Spaventa (83), pp. 700ff.) that traverse problems, as distinct from stability problems, have not received adequate attention in modern growth literature, either from the taxonomic or from the methodological point of view. The following analysis touches upon problems of methodology, leaving aside the other type of questions (these clearly go beyond the scope of the present work).

Let us then assume that the system, given the appropriate conditions, initially moves along the equilibrium growth path defined by the pure Ricardian model. Let us also suppose that, from the moment $\bar{t} > 0$, the capitalists' propensity to consume becomes positive and equal to $(1 - s_\pi)$, thus giving rise to an additional demand for luxury goods (gold) and to a corresponding reduction in the demand for agricultural products (corn) for investment purposes. The consequent traverse problem, in spite of some analogies, differs from the sectoral disequilibrium case (examined in Chapter 6), as well as from the macroeconomic disequilibrium case (analysed in Chapter 5), since it is only here that the modification of one of the original conditions for dynamic equilibrium identifies a new equilibrium growth path for the system.

The assumed change in capitalists' behaviour determines, as already noted, a partial switch in demand from one sector to another, and hence − at prices prevailing in the original equilibrium condition − an excess demand for gold and an excess supply of corn. An appropriate change in relative prices is therefore needed to recover equilibrium in both markets. As in Chapter 6, we suppose that the absolute price of gold remains constant and that adjustment is exclusively in terms of changes in the absolute price of corn. The market price of corn p_{1t}, which equalizes demand and supply and is implicitly defined by equation (15), thus turns out to diverge from the equilibrium price of corn p_{1t}^* (the inverse of the marginal labour productivity). More specifically, the former must fall below the latter, if disequilibria in both markets[22] are to be eliminated:

$$p_{1t} < p_{1t}^* \tag{31}$$

The divergence of the market price of corn from the equilibrium one, for reasons set out in the previous chapter,[23] leads to a divergence between the sectoral profit rates, which sets in motion a 'competitive' reaction mechanism on the part of capitalists, who increase the accumulation rate in the most profitable sector (industry) and reduce it in the other (agriculture). This reaction mechanism evidently tends to correct the disequilibrium situation originating in the assumed change in the capitalists' propensity to save. The ensuing types of traverse (disequilibrium) paths depend on the specific assumptions which may be made on the form of the competitive adjustment mechanism. One of the possible assumptions is incorporated in the traverse model presented in the following section.

7.9 The traverse model

The model set out below in full allows the examination of the traverse problem just discussed:

$$X_{1t} = f(N_{1t}) = N_{1t}^{\alpha} \qquad \text{Agricultural production function} \qquad (32)$$

$$R_t = f(N_{1t}) - N_{1t}f'(N_{1t}) \qquad \text{Rent} \qquad (33)$$

$$P_{1t} = N_{1t}\left[f'(N_{1t}) - x_t\right] \qquad \text{Agricultural profits} \qquad (34)$$

$$p_{1t}^* = \frac{1}{f'(N_{1t})} \qquad \text{Natural equilibrium price of corn} \qquad (35)$$

$$X_{2t} = \beta N_{2t} \qquad \text{Industrial production function} \qquad (36)$$

$$p_{2t}P_{2t} = p_{2t}X_{2t} - p_{1t}N_{2t}x_t \qquad \text{Industrial profits} \qquad (37)$$

$$p_{2t} = \frac{1}{\beta} \qquad \text{Price of gold} \qquad (38)$$

$$N_{1t} = (1 - \lambda_t)N_t^D \qquad \text{Employment in agriculture} \qquad (39)$$

$$N_{2t} = \lambda_t N_t^D \qquad \text{Employment in industry} \qquad (40)$$

$$K_t = W_t \qquad \text{Wages fund} \qquad (41)$$

$$N_t^D = \frac{W_t}{x_t} \qquad \text{Demand for labour} \qquad (42)$$

$$\frac{\dot{N}_t^S}{N_t^S} = n_t + \gamma(x_t - \bar{x}) \qquad \text{Labour supply} \qquad (43)$$

$$n_t = s_\pi\left[\frac{f'(N_{1t})}{\bar{x}} - 1\right]$$

Equilibrium component of population growth (44)

$$N_t^D = N_t^S$$

Equilibrium condition in the labour market (45)

$$P_t = p_{1t}P_{1t} + p_{2t}P_{2t}$$

Total profits in terms of value (46)

$$p_{2t}X_{2t} = p_{1t}R_t + (1 - s_\pi)P_t$$

Market price of corn (47)

$$p_{1t}\dot{K}_t = s_\pi P_t$$

Total investment (48)

$$r_{1t} = \frac{1}{p_{1t}^* x_t} - 1$$

Agricultural profit rate (49)

$$r_{2t} = \frac{1}{p_{1t}x_t} - 1$$

Industrial profit rate (50)

$$\frac{\dot{K}_{1t}}{K_{1t}} = \frac{\dot{K}_t}{K_t} - \frac{\dot{\lambda}_t}{1 - \lambda_t}$$

Accumulation rate in the agricultural sector (51)

$$\dot{\lambda}_t = \begin{cases} -\alpha(1 - s_\pi)\bar{x}\dot{p}_{1t}^* & p_{1t} = p_{1t}^* \\ -\delta(r_{1t} - r_{2t}) & p_{1t} \neq p_{1t}^* \end{cases}$$

Change in the sectoral structure (52)

$$s_{\pi t} = \begin{cases} 1 & \text{for } t < \\ \bar{s}_\pi & \text{for } t \geqslant \end{cases}\bar{t} \text{ for } \bar{s}_\pi > 0$$

Capitalists' propensity to save (53)

Note that the model, with equation (53), allows us to examine the traverse problem in the single direction of a move from the equilibrium growth path of the pure Ricardian model ($s_\pi = 1$) to the other equilibrium growth path with positive consumption by capitalists ($s_{\pi t} = \bar{s}_\pi < 1$). It is obvious, however, that the inverse case could be analysed with appropriate modifications in (53).

Note, too, that the model enables the two equilibrium growth paths to be defined separately, provided the two values for the capitalists' propensity to save, indicated by (53), are kept unchanged throughout the whole growth process. This emerges clearly from (44), which determines the equilibrium component of population growth, and from (52), which defines the equilibrium behaviour of the employment structure.

For the analytical formulation of the model we may refer to the disequilibrium model described in Chapter 6, which shows obvious formal analogies with this one. It is thus sufficient to emphasize that the more complex formulation, in equation (52), of the change in the employment sectoral structure depends on the fact that, while in the pure Ricardian model equilibrium is characterized by a constant value of λ_t, in the model with $s_\pi < 1$ the equilibrium value of λ_t varies, as shown by (21) above, during the growth process. The expression in the first 'branch' of (52) is in fact nothing but the derivative of (21) with respect to time.

Observe that the definition of the market price of corn is implicitly given by (47) as the price at which, in accordance with Say's law, the value of the demand for gold is equal to that of the supply of gold. Substituting in this equation the definition of profits in the two sectors given by (34) and (37), the explicit expression of the market price of corn is obtained:

$$p_{1t} = \frac{s_\pi p_{2t} X_{2t}}{R_t + (1 - s_\pi) N_{1t} f'(N_{1t}) - x_t N_t} \tag{47a}$$

The problems of indeterminacy arising when $s_\pi = 0$ (both the numerator and the denominator of (47a) would be zero)[24] can be seen to reflect the obvious absurdity of this type of assumption in the Ricardian context. This explains the limitation imposed by (53) on the value of s_π.

Similar to what was done in Chapter 6 in the study of entrepreneurial responses, the traverse problem is examined here also in terms of a version of the model incorporating the assumption of time lags in the adjustment mechanism. This latter assumption is expressed by:

$$\dot{\lambda}_t = \begin{cases} -\alpha(1 - s_\pi)\bar{x}\dot{p}_{1t}^* & p_{1t} = p_{1t}^* \\ -\delta(r_{1,t-1} - r_{2,t-1}) & p_{1t} \neq p_{1t}^* \end{cases} \tag{52a}$$

7.10 Analysis of traverse paths

The identification of the traverse paths of the main variables in the above model, worked out here in numerical terms because of the extreme difficulty of arriving at analytical solutions, refers to the two versions of the model, that based on equation (52) – indicated here as case one – and that incorporating equation (52a) – case two.

In the calculations, the numerical values of the parameters have been kept unchanged with respect to Chapter 6 ($\alpha = 0.75$, $\beta = 1$, $\gamma = 0.8$ and $\delta = 0.2$). For the capitalists' propensity to save s_π several numerical values have been explored. Since the type of the results is not greatly influenced by changes in s_π (in the admissible range) the following diagrams refer to just one of these values, $s_\pi = 0.6$.

Figures 30–5 show the natural equilibrium paths of the most relevant variables (employment structure, market wage, total employment, profit rates in agriculture, industry and for the economy as a whole) as well as their traverse paths in the two cases considered.

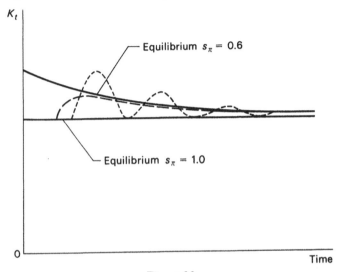

Figure 30

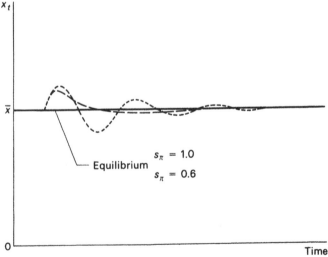

Figure 31

212

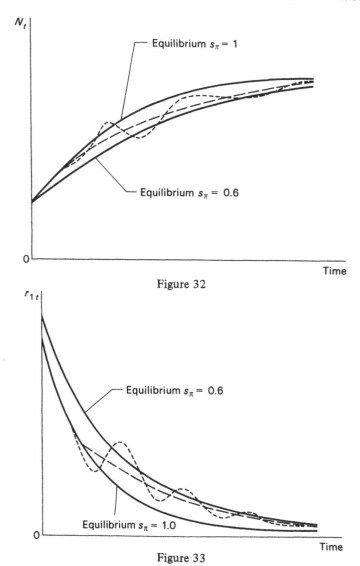

Figure 32

Figure 33

Unbroken lines refer to natural equilibrium paths, while dashed and dotted lines refer respectively to case one and case two of the traverse paths.

A few comments can be made on the results illustrated by the graphs. As regards case one, the first point to be noted is the existence

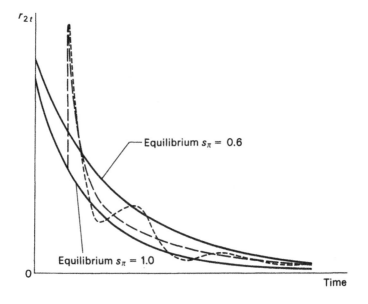

Figure 34

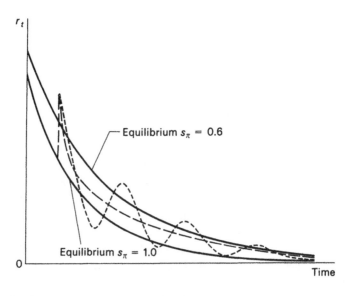

Figure 35

of a traverse between the two predefined equilibrium paths. A second point relates to the difference between two types of transition paths obtained for the variables: (i) paths – such as those for employment structure, total employment and the agricultural profit rate – which exhibit a gradual monotonic convergence to the new equilibrium growth path; and (ii) paths – such as those for wages, industrial and general profit rates – showing instead one oscillation around the new equilibrium path which is then gradually attained. The traverse path of the distributive shares, not reproduced in the graphs, belong to this second group.

When the traverse paths here obtained are compared with the disequilibrium paths resulting from an analogous set of assumptions in Chapter 6, it may be noted that the latter – with the sole exception of the profit rate – belong to group (i). This circumstance may be seen to express the greater complexity of the problems emerging from a change in the behavioural parameters as opposed to a departure from appropriate stock conditions. An economic system characterized by continuous changes in behavioural parameters of economic agents appears, therefore, to be subject to a greater degree of instability. This conclusion might be thought to hold beyond the limits of the present model.

As regards case two, no difference from case one emerges on the problem of existence of traverse paths. As already seen in Chapter 6, the presence of a time lag generates, however, damped oscillations in the disequilibrium paths. The economic explanation for this difference is analogous to that already given in Chapter 6.

The presence of time lags – though obviously considered in the model in a necessarily simplified way as compared with the highly complex forms obtaining in real economic life – is thus seen to re-present the cause of additional complications in the dynamic behaviour of an economy characterized by changes in parameters.

7.11 Conclusions: an overview of the main results of the Ricardian dynamic model

The aim of the second part of this work has been to explore the dynamic implications of the Ricardian concept of natural equilibrium. Appropriate conditions have been accordingly set out in explicit form for the concept of a Ricardian natural equilibrium path to be defined. It has been shown – with reference to some simplified versions of the

Ricardian system – that, when diminishing returns are considered, this path is capable of accounting for the transition of the economy from the progressive to the stationary state. The results obtained in this context constitute a generalization of analogous results which modern *golden age* models, built on the assumption of constant returns, have made us familiar with.

On the basis of this approach, the concept of natural equilibrium becomes a central point of reference for a disequilibrium analysis pivoting on the working of two adjustment mechanisms – the reaction of population to divergences between market and natural wage, and the reaction of capitalists to differences in sectoral rates of profit. The fact that all disequilibrium paths – originating in a divergence of stock conditions from the appropriate values or in a change of flow conditions – tend to converge to the predefined natural path may then be taken to reflect Ricardo's idea that natural equilibrium represents a centre of gravity for the economic system also from a dynamic point of view.

The validity of the method adopted for the study of departures from the equilibrium path – based on behavioural functions in which a reaction term is explicitly taken account of – is also shown by the variety of the results obtainable, even when the origins of disequilibrium phenomena are traced back to extremely simple assumptions (to be taken as mere examples) such as those examined above.

Obviously, the variety of results to which we have just referred is not to be understood in the trivial sense that a very large number of disequilibrium paths can be generated modifying the size of initial disequilibria, the value of behavioural parameters, the intensity of responses, or the specific formulation of adjustment mechanisms. Rather, it is to be understood in the sense that the approach followed lends itself to pointing out the various ways in which the dynamic interdependence between the variables in the model may manifest itself. The emergence of disequilibrium phenomena at any point in the system – whether connected with stock or flow conditions – affects, in other words, the behaviour through time of all the variables. From this point of view our analysis seems to have the methodological implication of suggesting the need for the elaboration of more flexible tools for the interpretation of the real world.

Notes

1 Scope and method of the work

1 See, for instance, Stigler (88), pp. 206–7: 'Measured by the significance of the variables and the manageability of the system, he [Ricardo] fashioned what is probably the most impressive of all models in economic analysis'; and Kaldor (42), pp. 210–11: 'It was through "the laws which regulate distributive shares" that he [Ricardo] was hoping to build what in present-day parlance we would call "a simple macro-economic model".' See also in the same sense Blaug (6), p. 140.

2 See, for instance, Samuelson (77) and Barkai (3). For a critical approach of a more general scope, see also Napoleoni (61).

3 See, for instance, Sraffa (85), Pasinetti (64), Brems (7), Johansen (40), Trezza (92).

4 The difference between the modern theory of growth (in which population is an exogenous variable) and the classical model (in which the rate of change in population is to be taken as endogenously determined) is, according to Solow, to be attributed to 'a genuine historical change in the sensitivity of population growth to economic factors'. For, as Solow adds, '[i]t is not hard to believe that the balance of births and deaths is more open to influence from economic events at low standards of living than at higher' (Solow (82), p. 12).

5 The notion of disequilibrium implicit in the above definition includes both situations in which markets are cleared and situations in which this circumstance does not occur. Considering the absence of a consistent use of that notion in the current literature, we have chosen not to follow those (see, for instance, Hahn and Matthews (31)) who have restricted the use of the term 'disequilibrium dynamics' to the description of situations in which markets are *not* cleared.

6 A similar approach is adopted by Casarosa (14). His analysis – which concentrates on the study of the dynamics of market equilibrium with reference to time intervals in which diminishing returns are assumed away – appears to be of little relevance for the investigation of the crucial issues of the Ricardian system.

7 See in this sense Hicks (35), p. 272.

2 Diminishing returns and the rate of profit in Ricardo's analysis

1 See Robbins (71), p. 173: 'There can be no doubt that the stimulus to much of the abstract analysis came from interest in practical problems: Ricardo's interest in value and distribution was evoked by his interest in the corn laws.' See also Burtt (9), ch. 4, and for a description of the concrete provisions of the corn laws Murphy (60), part II, pp. 463, 469.

2 See Ricardo (68), ch. 31 'On machinery'; Napoleoni (61), pp. 81–5; Grossmann (30), pp. 31ff.

3 See also Caffè (10), pp. 36ff. and Blaug (6), p. 188.

4 On the role of Ricardo's theory in the abolition of the customs duty on corn, see, for example, Coats (17), pp. 29–30; see also Cannan (11), p. 308: 'for the basis of an argument against the Corn Laws, it would have been difficult to invent anything more effective than the Ricardian theory of distribution'.

5 See, for instance, Dobb (20), p. 216.

6 See, for instance, Robinson (75), p. 6: 'What Ricardo was really concerned about was to abolish the corn laws so as to lower the real cost of wage goods and raise the rate of profit. This rise in profits is not at the expense of wages, *for the commodity wage is fixed in any case*' (italics added). See also Hicks (38), pp. 48–9; Pasinetti (64), p. 80 and (66), pp. 8ff.; Napoleoni (61), pp. 81–2; and Vianello (94), pp. xxvi and xxxiv.

7 For the analytical specification of this mechanism, see below, Chapter 5, sections 5.7 and 5.8.

8 See, for instance, Meldolesi (59), pp. 70–1 and Roncaglia (76), pp. 21–2, 54, 74–5.

9 See, for instance, Ricardo (68) ch. 1, section 6.

10 The limitation of the argument to the profits of the 'manufacturers' — with the apparent exclusion of the profits of the 'farmers' — is obviously a slip, as Sraffa's careful annotation (see the editor's notes 1 and 2 in (68), p. 111) may be interpreted to suggest. The general validity of the proposition is in fact quite clear in Ricardo's mind since the time of the *Essay on Profits* ((67), pp. 35–6, italics added): 'A fall in the price of corn . . . will lower the exchangeable value of corn only . . . . If, then, the price of labour falls, which it must do when the price of corn is lowered, the real *profits of all descriptions* must rise.'

11 See Marshall (54), p. 422, note 2: 'the term "corn" was used by them [the English classical economists] as short for agricultural produce in general, somewhat as Petty (*Taxes and Contributions*, ch. 14) speaks

of "the Husbandry of Corn, which we will suppose to contain all necessaries of life, as in the Lord's Prayer we suppose the word Bread doth"'.

12 See Schumpeter (79), p. 591: 'Smith's cost theory he [Ricardo] evidently thought logically unsatisfactory (perhaps *circular*)' (italics added). It may be interesting to recall that Ricardo's choice was regarded by Schumpeter as 'a detour . . . out of the historical line of economists' endeavours' ((79), p. 568). On this point see also Blaug (6), p. 140.

13 See, for instance, Stigler (90), Cassels (15), Blaug (6), p. 140.

14 See Sraffa (85), especially p. xxxviii, and Meek (57), pp. 105–10.

15 Other passages of Sraffa's 'Introduction' ((85), in particular p. xxxii) seem to support this second line of interpretation. See also Napoleoni ((61), ch. 4, in particular p. 62), where the Ricardian problem is explicitly posed in terms of the relation between wages and the rage of profit.

16 See Hahn and Matthews (31), p. 16. On the hypothesis that capitalists save only a constant proportion of their income ('classical saving function') the rate of capital accumulation is proportional to the rate of profit. Some problems related to the operation of the classical saving function in the Ricardian model are examined in Chapter 7.

17 See, for instance, Kaldor and Mirrlees (44).

18 It may also be observed incidentally that in equation (6) the price of machines (p_m) should be expressed in terms of the distributive variables, so that p_2/p_1 would result as a function only of w and r. The form adopted in the text has, however, the advantage of showing more directly the problems stemming from the presence of different capital–labour ratios in the various sectors and hence the crucial simplification obtainable for relative prices when sectoral capital–labour ratios are equal.

19 See the titles of sections 4 and 5 of the chapter 'On value' of the *Principles* ((68), pp. 30 and 38).

20 Blaug ((6), p. 115) does not seem to be far from the truth when he writes: 'What irritated Ricardo was Smith's assumption that the wages of labour can be measured in corn because the price of corn stays constant throughout time.'

21 This can be easily shown on the basis of the analytical definition of rent: $R = f(N_1) - N_1 f'(N_1)$, where N_1 represents agricultural employment and $f(N_1)$ the output of corn (see Chapter 4, section 5.4). Taking the derivative of this expression with respect to N_1 we have $dR/dN_1 = -N_1 f''(N_1)$, which — on account of diminishing returns — is always positive. Intuitive support of this analytical property of the model can be found in Kaldor's well-known diagram illustrating the Ricardian theory of distribution ((42), p. 212).

22 A proof of this proposition can be found, in the context of a rigorous formulation of a two-sector Ricardian model, in Pasinetti (64), pp. 88–9.

23 The difficulties arising for the determination in general of the behaviour of the share of profits in national income are examined in Chapter 4, section 4.6, with reference to Pasinetti's two-sector Ricardian model.

24 See the letter of T. R. Malthus of 5 August 1814 addressed to D. Ricardo, in Sraffa (84), vol. 6, pp. 117-18.

25 For the terminological problems related to the functional relation between w and r and their implications, see Harcourt (32), p. 4.

26 See on this point Pasinetti (66), p. 116, note 40.

27 This is connected with Roncaglia's statement ((76), p. 119) that the distinction between statics and dynamics is 'typically neoclassical' and that Sraffa's theory of value radically departs from the marginal analysis of prices. Sraffa's analysis of the 'prices of production' is certainly quite different from the neoclassical study of 'equilibrium prices', which guarantee the equality between supply and demand. But this does not in the least warrant the attribution to a particular school of thought of concepts, such as those of statics and dynamics, that belong only to the realm of methodology.

28 See the appendix to this chapter.

29 See in this sense Sweezy (91). For a different type of interpretation, see, for instance, Lippi (50), p. 14 and Medio (56), especially p. 382. On the problems of the relation between the Marxian notion of the organic composition of capital and that of the capital–labour ratio, see Robinson (73), ch. 2. We follow here Mrs Robinson's suggestion 'to speak of the organic composition of capital, not as c/v, but as capital per man employed' (p. 7).

30 For a comparative analysis of the properties of these models, see Caravale and Tosato (13), pp. 38-51.

31 See, for example, Napoleoni (62), ch. 2.

32 See Ricardo's letter to Trower, 8 March 1814, in Sraffa (84), vol. 6, p. 104.

33 Equations (11) and (12), though referring to the unit of labour, obviously apply also to the total quantity of labour employed in the economy.

34 See Dobb (21), p. 35: 'Classically, income distribution (e.g. the wage-profit ratio) was a pre-condition of the formation of relative prices. Per contra, in post-Jevonian and Austrian theory income-distribution is derived as part of the general pricing process – as a constituent set of equations in the total equational system of market equilibrium.'

35 This distinction has been introduced by Garegnani in the as yet unpublished paper 'The Marxian transformation problem' (see Eatwell (24)). Both methods are present in Sraffa's analysis (86). While Eatwell emphasizes the role of the first, Steedman, in his relevant contribution (87), implicitly stresses the importance of the second.

36 As regards the properties of non-negative square matrices used in this appendix, see, for instance, Pasinetti (66), pp. 267ff.

37 Ibid., p. 257.

38 See Lancaster (48), pp. 336–8.

39 A different analytical procedure applied to the study of (A.23) shows that (A.26) can also be reached, for the specific case here considered, through a process in which mathematical terms appear which can be interpreted as '*dated* capital–labour ratios'. The definition of these ratios will be given in the following chapter.

3 Sraffa's standard commodity and Ricardo's theory of value and distribution

1 See Chapter 2, section 2.2.

2 This letter is cited by Sraffa precisely in the above-mentioned passage of his 'Introduction'.

3 See in particular Chapter 1, section 1.3, and Chapter 2, section 2.2.

4 'The rate of profits in the Standard system thus appears as a ratio between quantities of commodities irrespective of their prices' (Sraffa (86), p. 22). An expression similar to (4) of the text has been introduced by Pasinetti ((66), pp. 84–5).

5 Taking the linear combination of the equation (6), which is obtained post-multiplying both sides of (6) by x^*, and rearranging terms we have:

$$rpAx^* = p[I - A]x^* - nx^*w$$

Dividing throughout by $p[I - A]x^*$ in line with the choice of *numéraire* (7) – and recalling (2), we have:

$$r\frac{pAx^*}{p[I - A]x^*} = 1 - w^*$$

where w^* is the wage rate in terms of the net standard product. From the definition of R in (1), we can immediately see that the linear relation (5) also holds for the actual system.

6 For the labour theory of value to hold in Sraffa's single production model it is necessary that the technical coefficients per unit of labour employed a_{ij}/n_j be equal in all the j sectors of the economy. This however, would come very close to the definition of a one-commodity model.

7 On this point, see also Pasinetti (66), ch. 5, section 7.

8 See Pasinetti (66), ch. 5, section 12; see also Caravale and Tosato (13), pp. 19–21.

9 In this sense, see also Pasinetti (66), ch. 5, section 6.

10 A detailed discussion of this issue can be found in Caravale and Tosato (13), pp. 8–25.

11 See, for instance, Eatwell (24).

12 See, in this sense, Broome (8).

13 See Chapter 2, section 2.6.

14 See Chapter 2, section 2.9.

15 See on this point Pasinetti (66), ch. 5, section 12.

16 See above, section 3.3.

17 The notion of 'dated quantities' is introduced by Sraffa ((86), ch. 6). A similar concept is used by Dmitriev (19).

18 The problem of the effect of changes in distribution on the prices of commodities is considered by Pasinetti ((66), pp. 82-4). The issue is treated in a slightly different way as compared with equation (17) and the results arrived at, as Pasinetti points out, are not conclusive.

19 This possibility — though with reference to non-dated (current) capital-labour ratios — is underlined by Pasinetti ((66), p. 83, note 16).

20 Sraffa ((86), p. 13, note 1) seems, however, to have posed the problem of the role of the proportions between labour and means of production in the analysis of price movements in terms of current rather than dated quantities.

21 See above, section 3.2.

22 See above, section 3.7 (iii).

23 This conclusion seems to be widely accepted in the literature (see, for instance, Meldolesi (58), pp. 70-1; Roncaglia (76), pp. 74-5; Lippi (50), p. 113). Less clear on this point appears to be the position taken by Eatwell ((24), p. 549) — which might lend itself to a misleading interpretation as to the validity of the standard commodity as *numéraire* in the Ricardian context, notwithstanding the assumed change in technology.

24 The unresolvable problems arising from the point of view of the determination of the rate of profit in a Sraffa-type model in which the standard commodity is the *numéraire* and decreasing returns are allowed for are briefly mentioned in Caravale and Tosato (13), p. 62.

4 Pasinetti's formulation of the Ricardian system

1 The variables taken as given parameters 'are left *as they stand*, that is to say, for these magnitudes we insert the values which are determined by the evolution of the system that has gone up to *t*' (Frisch (25), p. 103) (*t* is clearly the moment of time for which the solution of the model is sought).

2 'In this way is obtained a system which is *static* in the barred letters' (Frisch (25), p. 103). The barred variables are those belonging to the subset with respect to which the system is solved.

3 'This whole process may obviously be carried through at any moment of time .... The "normal" [i.e. 'natural equilibrium'] values ... may therefore be computed as functions of time. They represent the *moving equilibrium* of the various variables' (Frisch (25), p. 103).

4 A wider criticism of the concept of 'moving equilibrium' is put forward by Hicks (35), pp. 22–4.

5 See, in this connection, the often neglected work of Masci (55), of roughly the same period as Frisch's already-mentioned paper. See in particular Masci's ((55), pp. 6–8) definition of economic dynamics: 'So long as we assume . . . initial and terminal equilibrium positions and fixed points of departure and arrival, we remain in the world of statics, since the continuity and the fluidity of the economic movements are locked in a series of static equilibrium positions . . . When it is a question of defining the idea of economic dynamics . . . [it is necessary] to undertake another type of investigation in order to ascertain . . . how the *conditions determining* the equilibrium and the corresponding factors of the economic system vary . . . *continuously* over time following a dynamic line which does not admit of separate equilibrium points . . . . Economic dynamics could thus be defined . . . as the theory of continuous movements over time of the factors and quantities of economic equilibrium.'

6 See above Chapter 2, section 2.9.

7 Pasinetti also considers the condition regarding the non-negativity of production when no worker is employed: $f(0) \geqslant 0$.

8 Say's law has a different implication in Ricardo from what it has in the neoclassical context. See, on this point, Garegnani (27), pp. 599ff, and (29), pp. 338ff. See also Chapter 5, section 5.9.

9 See on this point Barkai (3), Blaug (6), ch. 4, especially pp. 108ff, and Davidson (18).

10 Blaug's opinion ((6), p. 107) on this point does not seem to be accurate. He states, in fact, that the derivatives of relative shares with respect to capital lead to results that are 'extremely messy to interpret', and chooses, therefore, to revert to a one-sector model for the study of the behaviour of these shares. It must be emphasized, instead, that the results obtained in the two-sector model are, as shown in the text, clear as regards the identification of the factors affecting the behaviour of distributive shares and thus their overall interpretation. Turning, as Blaug does, to a one-sector model in order to find clear-cut results may be misleading. For example, while in this latter context the share of wages is steadily increasing, in a two-sector model this result does not obtain in general.

11 From expressions (7) and (9), and taking account of equation (3) and (4), total profits in terms of value are equal to

$$p_1 N[f'(N_1) - \bar{x}] = N[1 - \bar{x}p_1]$$

from which the expression used in the text immediately emerges.

5 A one-sector Ricardian model

1 According to Malthus, an increase of rent (in absolute value and not

necessarily as a percentage share) during the growth process can lead to increased investment in the agricultural sector with a view to making productive improvements; from this point of view, rent can be assimilated to profits. See on this point Barber (2), p. 67.

2 Let $y = f(x_1, x_2, \ldots, x_n)$ be a production function homogeneous of degree μ. The generalized version of Euler's theorem assumes the form $\sum_{i=1}^{n} x_i f_i = \mu y$, where the f_is are the partial derivatives of the function and therefore represent the marginal productivities. See, for example, Chiang (16), p. 367. See also Stigler (88) and Wickstead (95).

3 See Kaldor (42), section 1. The other principle on which the Ricardian theory of distribution is based is obviously represented by the 'surplus principle'.

4 For a fuller justification of this choice, see Caravale (12); see also Akerlof and Stiglitz (1).

5 See, for instance, Lewis (49).

6 See on this point Hicks (36), pp. 148ff.

7 With reference to note 2 above, it should be observed that α represents the degree of homogeneity of the production function and the coefficient of elasticity of output with respect to the labour input. The same type of function is used by Davidson (18).

8 Taking account of equations (3) and (6), equation (12) may be written as follows:

$$\dot{K}_t = \alpha\left(\frac{K_t}{\bar{x}}\right)^{\alpha} - K_t$$

which is a Bernouilli differential equation with solution:

$$K_t = \{K_0^{-(\alpha-1)} e^{(\alpha-1)t} - \alpha\bar{x}^{-\alpha} \cdot [e^{(\alpha-1)t} - 1]\}^{\frac{1}{1-\alpha}}$$

9 This statement may be checked analytically solving the new differential equation in K_t corresponding to (12a) and comparing the results thus obtained with those given in note 8.

10 On this point see Garegnani (29), p. 339. The argument is treated in some detail in section 5.9 below.

11 See, for instance, on this point Stigler (89), pp. 202ff.

12 The different behaviour of employment in the two cases considered depends on the fact that, according to equation (22), the rate of change of population consists of two terms which can assume opposite signs in the case of an initial excess supply of labour.

13 This problem does not arise when both population and the wage rate increase. This turns out to happen only when, the initial situation being one of excess supply of labour, employment starts to increase after the downturn taking place at the beginning of the path.

14 See, in particular, Ricardo (68), ch. 21 'Effects of Accumulation on Profits and Interest'.

15 This type of interpretation assigns a predominant role to the rate of profit as compared with the rate of interest: 'The rate of interest appears in Ricardo only as a phenomenon subordinate to the rate of profits and governed by the latter' (Garegnani (29), p. 339). For an exactly opposite interpretation (which in our opinion is unfounded) of the classical theory of profit, see Blaug ((6), p. 98): 'In the classical period, the theorems about profit [are] in fact theorems about interest rather than profit. If we nevertheless continue to talk about the classical theory of profit, it is only because of customary usage: it would be much better if we spoke of the classical theory of interest.'

6 A two-sector Ricardian model

1 See equation (7) of Chapter 5.

2 To prove this inequality we need only multiply both terms by $(1 + \lambda_t)$. We thus obtain $1 > (1 - \lambda_t^2)$, which is verified for all values of λ_t greater than zero. Note that $\lambda_t = 0$ is not an admissible equilibrium value of λ_t, since it would imply that only corn is produced in the economy; but in this case equation (12) could not be satisfied.

3 As we have mentioned, this property ceases to be true when the capitalists' saving propensity is less than one. See Chapter 7, equation (21).

4 See, for instance, Uzawa (93) and Solow (81).

5 This corresponds to a deflation of money income by means of the Paasche price index with a moving base. See Marris (53), part III.

6 We show later that the only substantial modification consists of a different rule for the determination of the market price of agricultural products.

7 The adjustment mechanism for relative prices could have been formulated also with reference to changes only in the price of gold. It would also be possible in theory to define an adjustment mechanism operating at the same time on the prices of both commodities. It seems, however, difficult in this case to establish plausible criteria for distributing the weight of the adjustment process between the two markets.

8 As discussed in Chapter 2 (section 2.9), this is the key property of what is called the 'corn model'.

9 Note that this conclusion would remain valid even if we were to exclude an initial macroeconomic disequilibrium in the labour market, provided that the assumed sectoral imbalance in employment structure involves a greater than equilibrium percentage weight of industry; for, with a wage rate equal in this case to the natural wage, we would have in (61) a higher labour productivity in agriculture.

10 Considering that, from (22), the value of industrial output is equal to industrial employment and that, from (15), λ_t is defined as the

percentage industrial employment, (59) can be written as $p_{10} = \lambda_0 N_0/R_0$. Taking account of the wages-fund theory ($x_0 = K_0/N_0$), we then obtain $p_{10}x_0 = \lambda_0 K_0/R_0$. Since λ_0 is here greater than the equilibrium value, while K_0 and R_0 coincide with their respective equilibrium values, we have $p_{10}x_0 > p_{10}^*\bar{x}$; with reference to (62), we then have $r_{20} < r_{20}^*$.

11 In the *Principles* Ricardo does not explicitly tackle the problem of the mechanisms which can restore the equality of the sectoral profit rates, but 'carries on his analysis . . . on the assumption that the equalization of the rates of profit has already been permanently achieved' (Pasinetti (64), p. 85).

12 Pasinetti (64) considers also the case of a variety of luxury goods consumed by landowners. While his generalization aims at showing that in this case only the quantities of luxury goods produced are indeterminate (unless the structure of rentiers' demand is specified), the extensions of the Ricardian model considered in this appendix and in the following chapter are addressed mainly to the study of problems in capital accumulation.

13 The notation is that used in the price model of Chapter 2.

14 For the sake of completeness, note that reduction of profits to zero is not, in this model, a sufficient condition for reduction to zero of both components of the accumulation process. From a strictly mathematical point of view, the situation $r_t = 0$ could be consistent with a positive accumulation for one type of capital and a negative accumulation for the other.

15 See, for instance, Uzawa (93).

16 As can be shown rearranging terms, the simplified profit equation would obviously coincide with (16) of Chapter 2 modified so as to take account of a single wage-good.

17 Rewriting (A.68) as

$$\lambda_{2t} = (1 - \sigma k n_3) - k n_3 \frac{X_{1t} - K_t}{K_t} - \lambda_{1t} \tag{A.68a}$$

and considering that, by (A.26a), the growth rate of circulating capital is equal to the profit rate, we have:

$$\lambda_{2t} = [1 - (r_t + \sigma)k n_3] - \lambda_{1t} \tag{A.68b}$$

Given r_t, (A.63) and (A.68b) yield the following solutions for λ_{1t} and λ_{2t}:

$$\lambda_{1t} = \alpha[1 - (r_t + \sigma)k n_3] \tag{A.68c}$$

$$\lambda_{2t} = (1 - \alpha)[1 - (r_t + \sigma)k n_3] \tag{A.68d}$$

We obtain, therefore,

$$\lambda_{1t} + \lambda_{2t} = 1 - (r_t + \sigma)k n_3 \tag{A.68e}$$

whose maximum value, which occurs when $r_t = 0$, is always less than one.

18 See equations (A.68c) and (A.68d) of the previous note.

19 From (A.62) and (A.68):

$$\frac{1}{\alpha}\lambda_{1t} + kn_3 \frac{f\left(\lambda_{1t}\frac{K_t}{\bar{x}}\right)}{K_t} - [1 + kn_3(1 - \sigma)] = \psi(\lambda_{1t}, K_t) = 0 \,(\mathrm{I})$$

is obtained. Taking the derivative of λ_{1t} with respect to K_t

$$\frac{d\lambda_{1t}}{dK_t} = -\frac{\partial\psi/\partial K_t}{\partial\psi/\partial\lambda_{1t}} = -\frac{\dfrac{1}{\alpha} + \dfrac{kn_3}{\bar{x}}f'(N_{1t})}{\dfrac{kn_3}{K_t}\left[\dfrac{f'(N_{1t})}{\bar{x}}\lambda_{1t} - \dfrac{f(N_{1t})}{K_t}\right]} \tag{II}$$

is derived. Since the numerator of (II) is always positive, the derivative is positive only if the denominator of (II) is negative. Dividing both terms in square brackets by $f(N_{1t})/K_t$ we have:

$$\frac{f'(N_{1t})}{f(N_{1t})}\lambda_{1t}\frac{K_t}{\bar{x}} - 1 = \frac{f'(N_{1t})}{f(N_{1t})}N_{1t} - 1 = \alpha - 1 \tag{III}$$

On account of diminishing returns, (III) is negative and the derivative in (II) is thus positive.

7 A generalization of the Ricardian two-sector model: problems of traverse

1 See Chapter 1, section 1.1.

2 See, for example, Ricardo (67), p. 56.

3 It will be observed that modern growth models follow, from this point of view, a Marxian rather than Ricardian approach. Rent is in fact assimilated to profits and not to wages, so that the basic distinction is between labour income and non-labour income. See, e.g., Kaldor (42).

4 The problems discussed in the text do not arise in the case of an economy expanding at a constant positive rate. See Pasinetti (64).

5 According to Ricardo, the short-term effect of agricultural improvements is that of reducing rent, so that landowners have no interest in introducing them. See Ricardo (67), ch. 'On Rent', p. 78. See also Blaug (6), pp. 112ff. Also note that according to Ricardo the drop in rent would be only temporary. The increase in accumulation, in the demand for labour, in wages and in population would lead back, in his opinion, to a situation in which new increases in rent take place.

6 See in this connection the argument relating to equation (5a) in Chapter 5, section 5.3.

7 Note incidentally that an assumption of positive consumption by capitalists (indeed in the 'extreme' form of total consumption of profits) was made by Ricardo in the specific context of the problems tackled in the chapter 'On machinery' (Ricardo (68), p. 388). This is obviously not to be taken as a general assumption underlying his theoretical investigation. It may be thought instead, as Napoleoni ((61), p. 127) suggests, that this assumption was introduced for convenience, i.e. to isolate more clearly the problems arising from a change in the capital–labour ratio.

8 The same conclusions, on the institutional plane, would seem to apply to the hypothesis − analogous to the one discussed in the text − called 'zero growth', the subject of a number of current debates.

9 These problems are generally ignored in current expositions of Ricardo's theory. See, for example, Blaug (6), p. 132.

10 See Chapter 6, section 6.5.

11 See equation (22) of Chapter 6.

12 See Chapter 6, equation (33).

13 See Chapter 6, section 6.6.

14 The derivatives of the distributive shares with respect to time show that the smaller s_π, the more accentuated the difference between the behaviour of the shares of rent and profits: hence the greater, too, the divergence between the rising trend of the rent share and the decreasing trend of industry as a proportion of total income.

15 See equation (28) of this chapter.

16 See equation (22) of this chapter.

17 The idea of an increase in profits as a consequence of an increase in capitalists' consumption (obviously in contexts different from that adopted here) is linked to the names of Keynes (see the parable of the widow's cruse in (46), vol. I, p. 139), Kalecki (45) and Kaldor (42), p. 230 ('capitalists earn what they spend, and workers spend what they earn').

18 See also Kregel (47), p. 16.

19 This expression must be understood in the sense of Chapter 6, section 6.6. The rate of change of income in real terms is thus calculated here by assessing the physical quantities produced in both sectors at the prices ruling in the preceding period.

20 With a procedure similar to that used in section 6.6 of Chapter 6, these rates of change turn out to be:

$$G_{x1} = \frac{1 - \lambda_t}{1 - (1 - s_\pi)(1 - p_{1t}\bar{x})} \left(G_k - \frac{\dot{\lambda}_t}{1 - \lambda_t}\right)$$

$$G_{x2} = \frac{\dot{\lambda}_t}{\lambda_t} + G_k$$

21 See equations (23) and (24) of this chapter.

22 The value of excess demand in the market for industrial products (gold) clearly coincides with the value of excess supply in the market for agricultural products (corn). The change in relative prices which allows the gold market to recover equilibrium therefore restores equilibrium in the corn market as well.

23 See Chapter 6, section 6.11.

24 For $s_\pi = 0$, the denominator of (47a), substituting for the definition of rent given by (33), becomes equal to $[f(N_{1t}) - x_t N_t]$. Since, on this assumption, corn production is completely absorbed by wages $(x_t N_t)$, the denominator is then equal to zero.

Bibliography

1 Akerlof, C. A., and Stiglitz, J. E., 'Capital, wages and structural unemployment', *Economic Journal*, June 1969.
2 Barber, W. J., *A History of Economic Thought*, Harmondsworth, Penguin, 1970.
3 Barkai, H., 'Ricardo on factor prices and income distribution in a growing economy', *Economica*, August 1959.
4 Barone, E., 'Sul trattamento di quistioni dinamiche', *Giornale degli Economisti e Annali di Economia*, 2nd series, November 1894.
5 Baumol, W. J., *Economic Dynamics*, 3rd edn, London, Macmillan, 1970.
6 Blaug, M., *Economic Theory in Retrospect*, 2nd edn, London, Heinemann, 1968.
7 Brems, H., 'An attempt at a rigorous restatement of Ricardo's long-run equilibrium', *Canadian Journal of Economics and Political Science*, February 1960.
8 Broome, J., 'Sraffa's standard commodity', *Australian Economic Papers*, December 1977.
9 Burtt, E. J., *Social Perspectives in the History of Economic Theory*, New York, St Martin's Press, 1972.
10 Caffè, F., *Politica economica — Sistematica e tecniche di analisi*, Turin, Boringhieri, 1966.
11 Cannan, E., *History of the Theories of Production and Distribution in English Political Economy from 1796 to 1848*, 3rd edn, London, Staples Press, 1917, reprinted 1953.
12 Caravale, G., *Fluttuazioni e sviluppo nella dinamica di squilibrio di un sistema economico*, Rome, ISCONA, 1967.
13 Caravale, G., and Tosato, D., 'Saggio di profitto e merce tipo nella teoria di Ricardo', *Rivista di Politica Economica*, January 1978.
14 Casarosa, C., 'A new formulation of the Ricardian system', *Oxford Economic Papers*, March 1978.
15 Cassels, J. M., 'A reinterpretation of Ricardo on value', *Quarterly Journal of Economics*, May 1935.
16 Chiang, A. C., *Fundamental Methods of Mathematical Economics*, New York, McGraw-Hill, 1967.

17 Coats, A. W., 'Editor's Introduction', in *The Classical Economists and Economic Policy*, London, Methuen, 1971.

18 Davidson, P., 'A clarification of the Ricardian rent share', *Canadian Journal of Economics and Political Science*, May 1959.

19 Dmitriev, V. K., *Economic Essays on Value, Competition and Utility*, ed. D. M. Nuti, Cambridge University Press, 1974.

20 Dobb, M., 'The Sraffa system and critique of the neoclassical theory of distribution', in E. K. Hunt and J. G. Schwartz (eds), *A Critique of Economic Theory*, Harmondsworth, Penguin, 1972.

21 Dobb, M., *Theories of Value and Distribution since Adam Smith*, Cambridge University Press, 1973.

22 Domar, E., 'Expansion and employment', *American Economic Review*, March 1947.

23 Dorfman, R., Samuelson, P. A., and Solow, R. M., *Linear Programming and Economic Analysis*, New York, McGraw-Hill, 1958.

24 Eatwell, J., 'Mr. Sraffa's standard commodity and the rate of exploitation', *Quarterly Journal of Economics*, December 1975.

25 Frisch, R., 'On the notion of equilibrium and disequilibrium', *Review of Economic Studies*, 1935-6, pp. 100-6.

26 Gandolfo, G., *Metodi di Dinamica Economica*, Milan, ISEDI, 1973.

27 Garegnani, P., 'Note su consumi, investimenti e domanda effettiva: I', *Economia Internazionale*, November 1964.

28 Garegnani, P., 'On a change in the notion of equilibrium in recent work on value: a comment on Samuelson', in M. Brown, K. Sato and P. Zarembka (eds), *Essays in Modern Capital Theory*, Amsterdam, North-Holland, 1976, pp. 25-45.

29 Garegnani, P., 'Notes on consumption, investment and effective demand: I', *Cambridge Journal of Economics*, December 1978 (abridged version of (27)).

30 Grossmann, H., *Marx, L'Economia Politica Classica e il Problema della Dinamica*, Bari, Laterza, 1971.

31 Hahn, F. H., and Matthews, R. C. O., 'The theory of economic growth – a survey', *Economic Journal*, December 1964.

32 Harcourt, G. C., *Cambridge Controversies in the Theory of Capital*, Cambridge University Press, 1972.

33 Harrod, R. F., *Towards a Dynamic Economics*, London, Macmillan, 1948.

34 Hicks, J. R., 'World recovery after war – a theoretical analysis', *Economic Journal*, June 1947.

35 Hicks, J. R., *Capital and Growth*, London, Oxford University Press, 1965.

36 Hicks, J. R., *A Theory of Economic History*, London, Oxford University Press, 1969.

37 Hicks, J. R., 'A neo-Austrian growth theory', *Economic Journal*, June 1970.

38 Hicks, J. R., *Capital and Time*, London, Oxford University Press, 1973.

39 Hicks, J. R., and Hollander, S., 'Mr. Ricardo and the moderns', *Quarterly Journal of Economics*, August 1977.

40 Johansen, L., 'A classical model of economic growth', in C. H. Feinstein

(ed.), *Socialism, Capitalism and Economic Growth – Essays Presented to Maurice Dobb*, Cambridge University Press, 1967, pp. 13–29.

41 Kahn, R. F., 'Exercises in the analysis of growth', *Oxford Economic Papers*, June 1959.

42 Kaldor, N., 'Alternative theories of distribution', *Review of Economic Studies*, vol. 23, 1956, pp. 83–100, reprinted in N. Kaldor, *Essays on Value and Distribution*, London, Duckworth, 1960.

43 Kaldor, N., 'Capital accumulation and economic growth', in F. A. Lutz and D. C. Hague (eds), *The Theory of Capital*, London, Macmillan, 1961, pp. 177–222.

44 Kaldor, N., and Mirrlees, J. A., 'A new model of economic growth', *Review of Economic Studies*, vol. 29, 1961–2, pp. 174–90.

45 Kalecki, M., 'A theory of profits', *Economic Journal*, June–September 1942.

46 Keynes, J. M., *Treatise on Money*, London, Macmillan, 1930.

47 Kregel, J. A., *Rate of Profit, Distribution and Growth: Two Views*, London, Macmillan, 1972.

48 Lancaster, K., *Mathematical Economics*, London, Macmillan, 1968.

49 Lewis, W. A., 'Economic development with unlimited supplies of labour', *Manchester School of Economic and Social Studies*, May 1954.

50 Lippi, M., *Marx – Il valore come costo sociale reale*, Milan, Etas Libri, 1976.

51 McCulloch, J. R., *Principles of Political Economy*, 4th edn, Edinburgh, Alan and Charles Black, London, Longman, Brown, Green & Longmans, 1849.

52 Malthus, R. T., *Principles of Political Economy*, New York, Kelley, 1951.

53 Marris, R., *Economic Arithmetic*, London, Macmillan, 1958.

54 Marshall, A., *Principles of Economics*, 8th edn, London, Macmillan, 1966.

55 Masci, G., 'Sul concetto di dinamica economica', *Atti dell'Istituto Nazionale delle Assicurazioni*, Città di Castello, 1936, vol. 8.

56 Medio, A., 'Neoclassicals, neo-Ricardians and Marx', in J. Schwartz (ed), *The Subtle Anatomy of Capitalism*, Santa Monica, Calif., Goodyear, 1977.

57 Meek, R. L., *Studies in the Labour Theory of Value*, 2nd edn, London, Lawrence & Wishart, 1973.

58 Meldolesi, L., 'La derivazione ricardiana di *Produzione di merci a mezzo di merci* di Piero Sraffa', in P. Sylos-Labini (ed), *Prezzi Relativi e Distribuzione del Reddito*, Turin, Boringhieri, 1973, pp. 47–74.

59 Mill, J. S., *Principles of Political Economy*, Parker, London, 1848.

60 Murphy, B., *A History of the British Economy 1740–1970*, London, Longman, 1973.

61 Napoleoni, C., *Smith, Ricardo, Marx*, Oxford, Blackwell, 1975.

62 Napoleoni, C., *Valore*, Milan, ISEDI, 1976.

63 von Neumann, J., 'A model of general economic equilibrium', *Review of Economic Studies*, vol. 13, 1945–6, pp. 1–9.

64 Pasinetti, L. L., 'A mathematical formulation of the Ricardian system', *Review of Economic Studies*, February 1960.

65 Pasinetti, L. L., 'Rate of profit and income distribution in relation to the rate of economic growth', *Review of Economic Studies*, October 1962.

66 Pasinetti, L. L., *Lectures on the Theory of Production*, London, Macmillan, 1977.

67 Ricardo, D., *An Essay on the Influence of a Low Price of Corn on the Profits of Stock*, in (84), vol. 4, pp. 1–41.

68 Ricardo, D., *On the Principles of Political Economy and Taxation*, in (84), vol. 1.

69 Ricardo, D., *Absolute Value and Exchangeable Value*, in (84), vol. 4, pp. 357–412.

70 Robbins, L., 'On a certain ambiguity in the conception of stationary equilibrium', *Economic Journal*, June, 1930.

71 Robbins, L., *The Theory of Economic Policy in English Classical Political Economy*, London, Macmillan, 1952.

72 Robinson, J., *The Accumulation of Capital*, London, Macmillan, 1956.

73 Robinson, J., *An Essay on Marxian Economics*, 2nd edn, London, Macmillan, 1966.

74 Robinson, J., *Economic Heresies*, London, Macmillan, 1971.

75 Robinson, J., *Reflections on the Theory of International Trade*, Manchester University Press, 1974.

76 Roncaglia, A., *Sraffa and the Theory of Prices*, New York, Wiley, 1978.

77 Samuelson, P. A., 'A modern treatment of the Ricardian economy', *Quarterly Journal of Political Economy*, February and May 1959.

78 Schefold, B., 'Mr. Sraffa on Joint Production', mimeo, Basel, 1974.

79 Schumpeter, J. A., *History of Economic Analysis*, London, Allen & Unwin, 1961.

80 Smith, A., *An Inquiry into the Nature and Causes of the Wealth of Nations*, ed. R. A. Seligman, London, Dent, 1954.

81 Solow, R. M., 'Note on Uzawa's two-sector model of economic growth', *Review of Economic Studies*, October 1961.

82 Solow, R. M., *Growth Theory – An Exposition*, Oxford, Clarendon Press, 1970.

83 Spaventa, L., 'Significato e portata della critica alla teoria marginalistica della distribuzione', *Giornale degli Economisti e Annali di Economia*, September–October 1970.

84 Sraffa, P. (with the collaboration of M. H. Dobb) (ed.), *The Works and Correspondence of David Ricardo*, Cambridge University Press, 1951–73.

85 Sraffa, P., 'Introduction', in (84).

86 Sraffa, P., *Production of Commodities by means of Commodities*, Cambridge University Press, 1960.

87 Steedman, I., *Marx after Sraffa*, London, New Left Books, 1977.

88 Stigler, G. J., *Production and Distribution Theories*, New York, Macmillan, 1943.

89 Stigler, G. J., 'The Ricardian theory of value and distribution', *Journal of Political Economy*, June 1952.

BIBLIOGRAPHY

90 Stigler, G. J., 'Ricardo and the 93% labour theory of value', *American Economic Review,* June 1958.
91 Sweezy, P., *The Theory of Capitalistic Development,* New York, Monthly Review Press, 1942.
92 Trezza, B., 'Sull'esistenza di fenomeni ciclici e sulla stabilità globale del processo di sviluppo del sistema ricardiano', *Giornale degli Economisti e Annali di Economia,* May–June 1969.
93 Uzawa, H., 'On a two-sector model of economic growth: I and II', *Review of Economic Studies,* October 1961 and June 1963.
94 Vianello, F., 'Introduzione', in *Ricardo,* Milan, ISEDI, 1976.
95 Wicksteed, P. H., *Co-ordination of the Laws of Distribution,* London, London School of Economics Reprint No. 12, 1932.

Author index

Subject index

accumulation of capital, *see* rate of growth of capital

agricultural production function: case of constant elasticity of output with respect to labour, 114f, 148–51; and diminishing returns, 96, 107, 136

'balanced industry' in Sraffa, definition and criticism, 76–9

'bargaining power' hypothesis, 126–8

basic commodities, 33, 39

capital: circulating and fixed, 12 depreciation of, 23, 44, 81f; as joint product, 80–2; mobility of, *see* competition; organic composition of, *see* capital intensity

capital intensity: different in the various sectors, 25f, 173; uniform, 26, 184

comparative statistics, 6

competition, and sectoral disequilibria, 155–8

corn laws, 12d

corn model, 4, 39, 41f, 45

disequilibrium: dynamics, 11 119–23, 129–34, 156–66, 217 n5; path, 10f; sources of, 116f, 151–3, 207–9; traverse paths, *see* 'traverse'

equilibrium: dynamics, 11; market, 99–102, 107–14, 136–48, 198–207; moving *vs* dynamic, 95; moving *vs* stationary, 94; natural equilibrium path, 8, 10f, 178–84, 187f; point natural, 94f, 99–102, 173–8, 186f; *see also* full employment

Euler's theorem, 110, 224 n2

full employment, as condition of equilibrium growth 9, 111–14; *see also* Say's law

general Ricardian price model, 31, 46–50

golden age: bastard, 9, 112; definition (general) 112, (in Ricardian theory) 10, 113

income distribution: as absolute shares, 27–30; 'aggregative' *vs* 'simultaneous' approach within classical theory, 45, 70; as relative shares, 18, 27–30, 102–5, 142f, 202; classical *vs* neoclassical theory, 45, 220 n34; problem of independence from price determination, 70–2; *see also* 'profit equation'; 'wage equation'

invariable standard of value: requisites for, 15f, 55–63; role in Ricardo, 5, 54f; and Sraffa's standard commodity, 63f

For Product Safety Concerns and Information please contact our EU representative GPSR@taylorandfrancis.com Taylor & Francis Verlag GmbH, Kaufingerstraße 24, 80331 München, Germany

Printed and bound by CPI Group (UK) Ltd, Croydon, CR0 4YY
08/05/2025
01864457-0003